Memphis Country Club

Memphis Country Club

A CENTENNIAL HISTORY

PERRE MAGNESS

Hillsboro Press
PROVIDENCE PUBLISHING CORPORATION
FRANKLIN, TENNESSEE

Tennessee Heritage Library

Copyright 2005 by Memphis Country Club

All rights reserved. Written permission must be secured from the publisher to use or reproduce any part of this book, except for brief quotations in critical reviews or articles.

Printed in the United States of America

09   08   07   06   05   1   2   3   4   5

Library of Congress Control Number: 2005920779

ISBN: 1-57736-326-4

Cover photos by Murray Riss

Cover design by Hope Seth

Hillsboro Press
an imprint of
Providence Publishing Corporation
238 Seaboard Lane • Franklin, Tennessee 37067
www.providence-publishing.com
800-321-5692

Contents

THE CENTENNIAL COMMITTEE	vii
PRESIDENT'S LETTER	ix
PROLOGUE—THE TURN OF THE CENTURY	xi

Chapter I	The Beginning of the Memphis Country Club	1
Chapter II	The Second Clubhouse	17
Chapter III	Golf	27
Chapter IV	The Teens and Twenties	47
Chapter V	The Richmond McKinney Era	67
Chapter VI	Cotton Carnival	81
Chapter VII	The 1940s	89
Chapter VIII	The 1950s	109
Chapter IX	The 1960s	129
Chapter X	The 1970s	145
Chapter XI	The 1980s	163
Chapter XII	Into the Twenty-first Century	177

APPENDIX A: OFFICERS OF THE MEMPHIS COUNTRY CLUB	203
APPENDIX B: GOLF TOURNAMENT WINNERS	213
APPENDIX C: TENNIS TOURNAMENT WINNERS	223
APPENDIX D: GIN RUMMY TOURNAMENT WINNERS	231
BIBLIOGRAPHY	232
INDEX	233
ABOUT THE AUTHOR AND THE PHOTOGRAPHER	238

The Centennial Committee

I have been honored to be chairman of the Memphis Country Club centennial history. Our committee had fun researching the information to place in the book and cannot say how interesting it has been to work with Mrs. Perre Magness. On behalf of the entire committee, I would like to thank all the members that have taken their time and effort to give us stories and photos, and to share their past with us. They have helped make this book something that all members will be proud to display in their homes or offices.

Sincerely,
T. Scott Fisher
Chairman

Members of the Centennial Committee

Mrs. Ellen Clark	Mrs. Cathie Kirk
Dr. George Coors	Mr. Richard Leatherman
Mrs. Diana Crump	Mr. Neely Mallory Jr.
Mr. Patrick Demere	Mr. Lewis McKee
Mr. Roger Fakes	Mrs. Dottie Pennepacker
Mr. Trow Gillespie	Mr. Billy Webster
Mr. Jan Gwin	Mrs. Nancy Welsh
Mrs. Carla Gwin	Michael Babb, Club Manager

Mr. Cary Whitehead, Honorary Committee Member

Dear Members and Families,

The Memphis Country Club: A Centennial History is the result of more than three years of research and labor by our membership, board, staff, and many other friends of our Club. The photographs you see were gathered from the Club archives, as well as from the personal collections of members, the archives of the *Memphis Commercial Appeal* and *Press Scimitar* newspapers, and an untold number of scrapbooks.

The book itself was written by Memphis author and historian, Mrs. Perre Magness. I want to thank Perre for her tireless patience exhibited during the production of this work. I also want to issue a special thank you to the Centennial Committee, which was so ably led by its chairman, Mr. Thomas Scott Fisher. Lastly, thanks to my predecessor, Mr. W. Cary Whitehead, who was responsible for initiating the entire project.

The Memphis Country Club has both changed and stayed the same over the last one hundred years. Facilities, members, social life, and sporting activities, like everything else in our world, have changed over time. On the other hand, the spirit of the Club—its camaraderie and family atmosphere—has remained strong and steadfast over the past century. During that time, our membership has provided much of the city's business, charitable, educational, and political leadership. The Club's facilities and its members have provided a focal point for much of the city and region's social life throughout its history. It is undoubtedly a history of which the membership should be very proud.

It is the Board of Directors' sincere hope that this book will invoke fond remembrances, jar a few memories of those who have been here a good long while, and educate those too young to remember.

Sincerely,
J. Stillman McFadden
President, 2002–2004
March 18, 2005

PROLOGUE
The Turn of the Century

The twentieth century rode in with the automobile. And the automobile made possible the Memphis Country Club. At first, the strange machine was regarded as a mere plaything of the rich, an inconvenience which taxed the time and abilities of the neighborhood bicycle shop just to keep it running. It gained a bit of credibility when, in the summer of 1899, William McKinley became the first president of the United States to ride in one, when he took a brief ride in a Stanley Steamer at his home in Canton, Ohio.

But before long, people were discovering the convenience—not to mention the excitement—of going where you wanted when you wanted without the trouble of hitching up the horses or waiting for a tram. In 1900, there were only about 8,000 automobiles in the whole country. Ten years later, nearly 200,000 were rolling out of factories yearly.

The Automobile Club of America held the first automobile show in Madison Square Garden in New York City in November 1900. Still, automobiles were considered useless toys by most people in the United States, who depended upon some eighteen million horses and mules to provide transportation. One editor wrote, "It is well named the 'devil wagon.'"

General Samuel T. Carnes brought the first automobile to Memphis. He demonstrated it in the Confederate Reunion parade in 1901, where it delighted horse lovers by having a breakdown in the midst of the festivities.

The *Literary Digest* pronounced, "The ordinary horseless carriage is at present a luxury for the wealthy, and although its price will probably fall in the future, it will never, of course, come into as common use as the bicycle."

Nevertheless, Memphis's turn-of-the-century mayor, J. J. Williams, was sufficiently impressed to announce that he was considering the purchase of a Locomobile for a police patrol wagon. Memphis had about one hundred seventy-five miles of streets in 1900, and only twelve miles were paved, hard surfaced with stone, brick, or wooden blocks. The rest of the roads were gravel or dirt, dusty in summer and muddy in winter. Five years later, still only twenty-two miles were paved.

By 1902, automobiles were more than a curiosity, they were a worry. The *Commercial Appeal* reported, "The rapid gait of the automobile is apt to cause many runaways and much damage to life and property . . . We can readily imagine the day when the farmers and country people will repel this danger just as did their forefathers the perils of the wilderness."

The peril kept growing. By 1903, there were about forty automobiles in Memphis, and the *Commercial Appeal* spoke of streets "crowded with fast moving machines." Rather than fight the trend, the newspaper joined it, and began devoting a whole page in the Sunday newspaper to the care and upkeep of automobiles.

Soon, automobiles became a fact of life. They enabled families to enjoy drives into the country, and then they wanted a destination. After 1905, the new country club at Buntyn's Station was the ideal place to go.

THE TURN OF THE CENTURY

The Spanish-American War was over with a peace treaty signed in 1899. This marked the entrance of the United States onto the world stage as a colonial power with global interests. More American soldiers had fallen to the yellow fever in Cuba than to enemy bullets. A commission, headed by Dr. Walter Reed, established that the mosquito was the carrier of the disease. A member of the commission was the nurse Lena Angevine Warner of Memphis.

President William McKinley was reelected in November 1900, with Governor Theodore Roosevelt of New York as vice president. On

September 6, 1901, a young anarchist shot the president at the Pan-American Exposition in Buffalo, New York.

The forty-three-year-old vice president was suddenly president, to the horror of the Republican leadership, who had given him the vice-presidential nomination partly to keep him out of the way in what they considered a harmless position.

The temperance movement turned less than temperate when Carry Nation and her anti-liquor followers vandalized saloons and took as their symbol a hatchet.

Among the books popular in the early years of the century were Theodore Dreiser's *Sister Carrie*, Frank Norris's *McTeague*, Alice Hegan Rice's *Mrs. Wiggs of the Cabbage Patch*, Kate Douglas Wiggins's *Rebecca of Sunnybrook Farm*, Jack London's *The Call of the Wild*, Henry James's *The Wings of the Dove*, and Edith Wharton's *The House of Mirth*.

Popular songs included "I'm Only a Bird in a Gilded Cage," "My Wild Irish Rose," "In the Good Old Summertime," and "Bill Bailey Won't You Please Come Home." Richard Wagner's *Parsifal* premiered at the Metropolitan Opera in 1904 and was called "profanity, a sacrilege, and a gigantic outrage."

Fashion favored the mature woman, with heavy corsets throwing the breast forward and the hips back, producing a fashionable S shape. Cascades of lace were everywhere, and high boned collars were stylish. The hair was piled high on the head, and hats were trimmed with plumes.

For formal occasions, men still wore top hats and frock coats, but the lounge suit with a homburg hat was gaining popularity. Trousers were narrow, and young men increasingly wore them with permanent turnups and a sharp crease in front.

Casey Jones left Memphis on the morning of April 30, 1900, and crashed the *Cannonball Express* in Canton, Mississippi. In 1903, Wilbur and Orville Wright achieved the first powered flight in a heavier-than-air machine at Kitty Hawk, North Carolina.

In 1903, the first postseason World Series of baseball was played. The first Olympic Games to be held in the United States were part of the St. Louis Exposition of 1904. Another first for the St. Louis Exposition: a British tea merchant was distressed when high temperatures kept people from sampling his cups of hot tea, so he poured some over crushed ice, and iced tea was born.

In 1905, it cost $150 to attend Harvard. A standard Oldsmobile Runabout cost $650, and you could buy a house for $2,000. Eastman Kodak introduced the Brownie Box Camera in 1900; it cost $1 and a six shot roll of film cost 10¢ to 15¢. Also in 1905, former president Grover Cleveland was quoted in the *Ladies Home Journal:* "Sensible and responsible women do not want to vote. The relative positions to be assumed by man and woman in the working of our civilization were assigned long ago by a higher intelligence than ours."

MEMPHIS

What did Memphis look like at the turn of the century? Downtown extended for twelve blocks along the river and three blocks back. Cotton was still king. On Front Street, cotton bales were piled on the street in season, and cotton sampling tables spilled over into the sidewalks and streets.

Memphis at the turn of the century.

Hardwood was beginning to challenge cotton as an economic factor. By 1900, the lumber industry was cutting its way through miles of untouched Delta forests. There were fourteen sawmills and six planing mills on the banks of the Mississippi and the Wolf Rivers.

The construction on Court Square of the first skyscraper south of St. Louis in 1895 marked a new era in building. Now called the D. T. Porter Building, it was steel framed and had a circulating hot water heating system. People paid a dime to ride the elevator to the roof garden; some were so terrified by the experience they insisted on walking down the eleven flights of steps.

The red sandstone Romanesque Cossitt Library building was constructed in 1893, and it and the two-towered Custom House, built in 1876 and enlarged in 1903, dominated the river bluff and impressed passengers arriving by steamboat. Over on Adams Avenue, the classical Shelby County Courthouse, with its seated figures of Justice, Wisdom, Liberty, Authority, Peace, and Prosperity, was built in 1904–05. It was said, "This court house is surpassed in symmetry of design and convenience of arrangement by no other county building in the United States." Other landmarks were the rebuilt Gayoso Hotel and the Grand Opera House.

The fashionable residential streets were Adams, Jefferson, Poplar, Waldran, Union, Linden, and Vance. In 1903, Brinkley Snowden and T. O. Vinton moved east to develop Annesdale Park, at present-day Lamar and Central Avenues. It was said that a prospective buyer would get a lot only "if his position in society is such that his presence in Annesdale Park will add to its social importance." Buyers were promised that they would live in "the most fashionable and the most exclusive section of the city."

What we would notice most about Memphis a century ago would be the dirt. Streets were in horrible condition. The cobblestone paving virtually stopped at Poplar and Beale. Second Street was an avenue of mud and slime. Drays hauling cotton to warehouses frequently dropped into the holes created by rotting blocks of wooden Nicholson paving. If a horse or a mule broke its leg in one of the sinkholes, the carcass might be left to rot. Garbage was still being dumped over the river bluff on Front Street.

But the new Waring sewer system was a marvel. The discovery of artesian wells in 1887 meant a constant source of pure water. As more streets were paved, many miles of granolith sidewalks were laid to replace walks of board, cinder, and old brick. Concrete bridges replaced wooden bridges. The recently formed Park Commission established parks at either end of the newly designed Parkway system, Overton Park on the east and Riverside Park on the southwest.

Economist Robert Sigafoos writes that Memphis had been badly hurt by the yellow fever epidemics of the 1870s and the surrender of the city charter until 1891. In an effort to heal the emotional scars, the period from 1880 to 1914 was a period of intense boosterism and an effort to put Memphis in the mainstream of economic life. The Businessmen's Club was formed in 1899 and coined the slogan "Before the dawn of Christianity, the boast of Man was 'I am a Roman.' Today the Same Man would say 'I am a Memphian!'"

The expansion of streetcars meant the building of new suburbs. Then, in 1899, the city expanded its boundaries by annexing its suburbs, including the towns of Idlewild, Lenox, and Madison Heights. It added twelve miles of territory and changed the axis of development from north/south toward the east. The *Commercial Appeal* crowed, "You can hear the town growing early in the morning before the streetcars are running."

The annexation boosted the population from 64,495 in 1890 to 102,320 in 1900. Memphis had been behind Atlanta, Nashville, Richmond, New Orleans, and St. Louis; now only the last two cities were larger. When the 1900 census results came in giving the city's population as over 100,000, the newspaper called it "Memphis's Greatest Day." The new century opened in a mood of progress and optimism.

Memphis was no longer a town; it was now a city. Its leaders knew that it needed what other cities had. Memphis needed a country club.

CLUBS AND COUNTRY CLUBS

James M. Mayo, in a book called *The American Country Club*, cites four factors in the development of country clubs. Men's city clubs had long existed and set the rules and rituals of club life. Summer resorts played a key role in defining how elite families separated recreational life from everyday life in the city. The growth of sports provided incentives for club activity, and increasing suburbanization enabled these influences to cohere into a new form.

The development of city clubs for gentlemen depended upon the growth of the national economy and the establishment of a wealthy urban class, who congregated in certain neighborhoods, rather than living near the place of work as artisans and shopkeepers did. An increasing separation of home and work marked the upper class.

The oldest social clubs in the United States were patterned on British models. The oldest was the South River Club in Annapolis, founded in 1700, followed by the Fish House Club (1732) in Schuylkill, Pennsylvania, and the Wednesday Evening Club (1777) in Boston. The clubs enabled men to share interests in literature, politics, and news in an informal setting, and soon formed an identity of prestige.

The nineteenth century saw clubs formed in most cities. By the late nineteenth and early twentieth centuries, women were forming clubs of their own.

During the expansive years of the nineteenth century, anyone who could afford it left the city during the hot summers. Spas like Saratoga Springs in New York and White Sulphur Springs in West Virginia were popular. In seaside resorts like Newport, Rhode Island, and Nahant, Massachusetts, rich families built "cottages," which resembled their city mansions more than rustic retreats. An attempt at rusticity marked the grand camps of the Adirondacks, where hunting and fishing were popular.

All these resorts had some orientation toward the out of doors. People swam, danced, sailed, bowled, took walks, played croquet, and played cards. Wide porches and green lawns were places for guests to meet and visit. Clubs formed in the summer resorts, uniting people of the same social standing from different cities. Some clubs had specialized sporting interests: racing, sailing, horses, or fox hunting, sports that were beyond the financial reach of most folks.

In 1879, a Boston lawyer recruited one hundred fifty members of the Somerset and University Clubs in the city. They built a clubhouse on two hundred acres near Winchester, Massachusetts, with a tennis court, an area to play baseball, billiard rooms, card parlors, and a dining room. But the primary focus was fox hunting. The Myopia Hunt Club was the first American "country club."

The idea developed slowly in the 1880s and blossomed in the 1890s. By 1901, there were more then one thousand country clubs, in all the forty-eight states. The increasing popularity of sports contributed to the growth. Clubs provided facilities for bowling, shuffleboard, billiards, card rooms, archery, croquet, skeet shooting, and boating. In the north, some featured curling, figure skating, ice hockey, and tobogganing. In the south, equestrian sports, like coaching, driving, and polo, dominated. Cricket and croquet were played, and lawn tennis grew increasingly popular.

There might be competition among members for their favorite sport, but the clubhouse proved a unifying factor. The first clubhouses were country homes or farmhouses, then purpose-built buildings developed. The absence of the libraries and reading rooms of the city clubs signaled what members wanted the new clubs to be about: leisure and sport and the outdoor life. Members integrated sports and social life by organizing tournaments, races, and regattas, which provided competition, food, and drink, as well as fashion and merriment.

Getting to the country club often required a railroad or streetcar stop. In Los Angeles, those getting off at the trolley stop raised a flag that could be seen from the clubhouse to signal for the wagonette. Other clubs had large bells which signaled when the shuttle would leave. Eventually, the telephone replaced flags and bells.

Between 1900 and 1920, the automobile became a central feature of the country club life. Many clubs drew up elaborate rules for motorists and had separate drives for automobiles.

By far the most popular sport was golf. The first golf club in the United States was St. Andrew's Golf Club in Yonkers, New York. The enthusiasm spread like wild fire. From one course in 1885, the sport grew to more than one thousand courses by 1900. Most of these were built by private clubs, whose numerous members made building courses affordable.

Club members transferred their interest from horses to golf. Many clubs adopted uniforms for their golfing members. Most wore red coats like fox hunters.

The purpose of the country clubs was to provide a leisure space for its members apart from the business of everyday life. The communal space provided by the clubs confirmed social status and values. The number of people in the upper class was growing. The elite setting of the country club became a part of the national dream of the good life.

The Beginning of the Memphis Country Club

The idea for a Memphis country club began with six men sipping drinks after playing a round of golf at the North Memphis Driving Park. The course they had played was a makeshift affair of nine holes laid out over the flat area contained within the oval of the race track.

The six included Harry Price Johnson, William Cumming Johnson, Harrod C. Newland, Frank Clark Milton, Laurence Lamb, and Philips P. Williams. Harry Price Johnson was a real estate man with the firm Johnson and Haley. William Cumming

The invitation to the organizational meeting, 1905.

Johnson was the son of one of Memphis's premier philanthropists and founder of the Tennessee Fiber Company which manufactured products from cottonseed hulls. Frank Clark Milton was a stockbroker. Laurence Lamb was also with Johnson and Haley, and Philips P. Williams was president of the P. P. Williams Company of Vicksburg.

They lamented the fact that the only golf course in town was such a poor one and that there was no place in town where "men and women of good social standing could go for outdoor recreation." They began to plan for a modern eighteen-hole golf course and clubhouse. They decided to form a secret committee to propose a list of prospective members for a country club.

On January 17, 1905, the *Commercial Appeal* reported, "The organization of a golf and country club is an assured fact. A meeting was held in the dining room of the Tennessee Club several days ago by a number of men interested, and matters concerning the immediate organization of the club and the selection of a site were discussed. H. P. Johnson presided at the meeting."

More than a third of the money thought necessary was subscribed, and committees were appointed: Finance with P. P. Van Vleet, F. P. Williams, and A. S. Caldwell; Location with W. C. Johnson, R. C. Milton, and Laurence Lamb; and Organization with W. Poston Maury, A. S. Caldwell, and Percy Galbreath.

The Location Committee had already been at work, and reported on an ideal site, a tract of seventy-two acres that could be obtained for $17,000. The Finance Committee already had over $6,000 in hand and was charged to raise the rest, including money for a projected $20,000 clubhouse, with sleeping rooms, dining room, kitchen, billiard hall, and possibly a bowling alley. A nine-hole golf course was proposed. Clay pigeon traps, a tennis court, and provisions for other outdoor sports were planned.

An invitation went out to prospective members, signed by Harrod C. Newland as acting secretary, and dated March 17, 1905: "Your presence is urgently requested at a meeting to be held at the Memphis Merchants Exchange, Saturday night, March 18, at eight o'clock, to perfect a permanent organization of the Memphis Golf and Country Club. If it is impossible for you to attend, please sign the enclosed postal card that your name may be included in the list of those who make application for the Charter."

According to Samuel Evan Ragland's history of the club:

> It was easy to find the property and prices were reasonable, but money back in that day was not as plentiful and cheap as it is now. Many men of substance, character and ability were interviewed for advice and aid, and then a secret committee of a few men of the highest social standing and probity were selected to prepare a list containing 450 names of men who would be invited to become members. The memberships were sold at $100 each. Nearly everyone whose name was on the list accepted the invitation and paid the price. The few who declined were replaced by others of equal standing so that $45,000 stood to the credit of the club in the bank by the time it was needed.

A charter was filed on March 31, 1905. The general purposes of the club were:

> The establishment and maintenance of a club for social enjoyment, and not for profit, with reading and club rooms in connection therewith; the promotion of social feeling and intercourse generally among the members; the establishment of a gymnastic and gymnasium club, golf, tennis, polo, baseball, cricket and gun clubs and other exhibitions for entertainment and exercise; and all other clubs for the promotion of athletic sports or entertainment, so far as the same is authorized under the legislation of the State of Tennessee, known as the act of 1875 . . .

On April 13, 1905, the newspaper reported that the newly organized Memphis Country Club had taken options on 101 acres of land just north of Buntyn's Station.

> . . . comprising what are known as the old Martin place, the Redmond tract, the Skinner tract, and the Fontaine tract . . . It is the purpose of the club to make here one of the finest country clubs in the entire South. Golf links, tennis courts, bowling alleys, and other games will be prepared, the principal attention being bestowed upon the golf links, however.

The clubrooms will be provided with a well-selected library, and every provision will be taken to prevent allowing bad weather to interfere too seriously with the pleasures of the members . . . The Memphis Country Club is a thing of very recent existence. In fact, it is not regularly organized now, although there are 350 members pledged to the organization, which is to be effected at a meeting which will be called for the purpose next week. It is probable that after effecting a permanent organization the membership of the club will be increased to 450.

The Memphis Country Club still has the early ballot books for 1905–14, heavy leather-bound books from S. C. Toof and Company, embossed in gold "Balloting Book of The Memphis Country Club." A member had to be vouched for by three members, then everyone interested in his candidacy for membership signed a ledger page headed by the candidate's name.

If a candidate received too many foul ballots, his name was rejected. At one board meeting, the president stated that a certain gentleman had been put up for election and that on two occasions "he had been foul balloted . . . the president was instructed to notify his vouchers that it was decided that the last ballot was a foul ballot and that they would have the privilege of putting his name up again."

On April 25, the *Commercial Appeal* reported that, after "a spirited contest," officers and a permanent board of directors of ten members were elected.

Peter Percy Van Vleet (1849–1915) was chosen as the first president. Born in Michigan of Dutch ancestry, he attended Kalamazoo College. After college he began a career as a drug clerk. In 1871 he set out to travel, and when he arrived in Memphis he was impressed with the opportunities of the town. It was said that he arrived on the steamer *Belle Lee*, "He came ashore as the boat docked on a moonlight evening and was so charmed by his first impression of the place that he concluded to remain." He was employed by the G. W. Jones Company for fourteen years, becoming a partner. Later he organized a wholesale drug firm that bore his name, then merged other companies into the Van Vleet Mansfield Drug Company, of which he was president.

He was a director of the Bank of Commerce and was active with both the Baptist Hospital and the Memphis Medical Hospital. He was a world traveler and an active sportsman and clubman, being a member of the Tennessee Club, the Chickasaw Club, the Wapanoca Club, the Hatchie Coon Club, the Bear River Duck Club, the Mud Lake Duck Club, and the Tarpon Club of Tarpon, Texas.

The Van Vleet family had a cottage at the Solid Comfort Club on Lake Erie, a summer colony for many Memphians, later called the Humberstone Club. When the family moved to Canada for the summer, they took with them two Japanese servants from their home on Poplar.

It was said of him, "His social qualities were such as made for popularity among all who knew him. The sterling traits of his character were many, and by reason of his upright life and his admirable qualities his acquaintances were fast converted into warm friends. He was rich in the possession of all those things which men most admire in the individual and the business man and through the steps of an orderly progression he came to a point of leadership in America."

Samuel T. Carnes was elected vice president, with Percy Galbreath as secretary and E. B. McHenry as treasurer. Other board members were H. P. Johnson, Laurence Lamb, W. C. Johnson, F. C. Milton, P. P. Williams, H. C. Newland, and J. P. Edrington.

About eighty of the members were present at the meeting, "notwithstanding the inclemency of the weather and considerable enthusiasm was manifested by all."

The $45,000 raised in the initial subscription was enough to enable the new officers to purchase the Martin place, as the home built by Geraldus Buntyn was then called. It was six miles east of Memphis along the railroad track. Some surrounding lots that had been part of Buntyn's farm were also purchased, making a tract of over 110 acres.

Geraldus Buntyn was one of the early settlers in Shelby County. He arrived in the 1830s and began buying land east of the town of Memphis, including what is today Audubon Park. Buntyn was prominent in politics and business and a pillar of the Baptist church, donating land for the First Baptist Church downtown, a church in Whitehaven, and Eudora Baptist Church at Perkins and Poplar.

Buntyn and his family first lived in downtown Memphis on Adams, then he built a large, comfortable home with wide verandas and tall columns six miles east of Memphis. In the 1850s, when the Memphis and Charleston Railroad was built, the home was a landmark along the tracks. There was a railroad stop nearby, and the area was called Buntyn's Station.

P. P. Van Vleet, first president of the Memphis Country Club.

During the Civil War, the Union Army occupied Memphis after a naval engagement on June 6, 1862, in which the remains of the Confederate river navy were destroyed. As an occupied city, Memphis suffered little physical damage, although the Confederate lines were just south of the city.

The history of the 119th Infantry of Illinois Volunteers, Company G, records that they were assigned to the area the next year, marching from Huntington, Tennessee, over bad roads in terrible weather. "Our headquarters were established at Buntyn's Station; about six miles out from Memphis. This was about March 10, 1863. At this point, and at one or two others along the road, we guarded the approach to Memphis. This we did effectually, and much to our enjoyment, until May 30, 1863, we were ordered into Memphis, and assigned to the Fourth Brigade."

The regiment remained on duty in and around Memphis, guarding the roads and doing provost duty until January 1864,

The first clubhouse.

when it was transferred down the river to Vicksburg. The regimental historian wrote, "If I except the daily drills, squad, company and battalion, this was the 'good time' of our recollection."

The gracious Buntyn House overlooked the Union Army camp and survived the war intact. Geraldus Buntyn, however, died, aged sixty-five, in July 1865 "of anxieties, like countless old men of the South, begotten by the war between the States," according to a book published in 1874 by Elmwood Cemetery. His estate totaled 1,405 acres, and he had already given each of his children sizable gifts of land around his home.

One Buntyn family house still stands, at 487 Goodwyn. In 1864, his son, Dr. Geraldus Oscar Buntyn, built a brick home west of his father's, facing what is today the golf course. After the elder Buntyn's wife Ann Eliza died in 1866, some of the home place was divided into lots of three to five acres and was on its way to becoming a suburban neighborhood.

The railroad stop called Buntyn's Station meant the area was convenient to downtown, and a number of dairy and truck farms developed in the area because produce could be shipped easily to market. The area now called Chickasaw Gardens was once known as "Buttermilk Town" because of the number of dairies.

At the turn of the century, the Buntyn's Station community had churches, a school, stores, doctors, and a post office. Messick School opened as a twelve-grade county school in 1908. Children from a seven-mile area came to school in horse-drawn wagonettes.

Colonel G. C. White of Holly Springs bought the Buntyn House in 1868. In 1857, his daughter Rosa had married John Donelson Martin, a descendent of the founder of Nashville and a nephew of Rachel and Andrew Jackson. Brigadier General Martin was killed at Corinth, Mississippi, at the beginning of the Civil War in 1862, leaving Rosa with two little boys. Rosa then married John Martin's brother, Andrew Jackson Donelson Martin. They inherited the house at Buntyn from her father.

The grand old house saw its share of tragedies. During the yellow fever epidemics of the 1870s, several families moved from town to the supposedly more salubrious air of Buntyn's Station. The Martins rented their house to banker Addison Hayes and his wife Peggy. Her brother, Jefferson Davis Jr., son of the former Confederate president, came with them from Memphis to escape the fever.

Then the dreaded disease came to Buntyn's Station, and young Davis died in a second-floor bedroom on October 16, 1878. The *Memphis Appeal* reported that thirteen people attended his funeral, the largest attendance at the cemetery during the height of the epidemic.

Another tragedy struck the Martins at Buntyn. Rosa's son John D. Martin II closed his house in Memphis on Lauderdale and moved to his mother's house at Buntyn in the summers. He commuted to Memphis to continue his law practice. On a beautiful summer evening, June 21, 1890, John Martin decided to break in a new horse to the buggy. He was an excellent horseman, but there was an accident, and he was thrown out of the buggy. The newspaper described him crying out, "Oh my God, my God, I am killed."

He was paralyzed and lived only a few days, dying at the same age, about thirty-two, that his father had been killed in battle. A Bar Association memorial recounted "At the hour of sunset, John Donelson Martin, in the vigor of his manhood, the fullness of hope and plenitude of promise, had by a horrible casualty, been mortally hurt and had been the first to proclaim his own doom."

Fifteen years later, when the founders of the country club looked for a location for their golf course, they found the old Buntyn farm and house to be a suitable location. Mr. and Mrs. Martin sold the property to them on June 1, 1905. The spacious house, with four tall columns and a triangular pediment over the entrance and wide porches on both sides, became the clubhouse.

Adjacent property was acquired in April and May 1905: from Napoleon Hill and his wife Mary, and Noland Fontaine and his wife Jennie, 7.82 acres for $3,128, where holes 9 and 18 are now located; from J. W. Skinner and his wife Bunnie, and Adolph Kupfer and his wife Flora, 47.56 acres for $9,512, all or part of holes 5, 6, 7, 8, 11, 12, 13, 15, 16, and 17; from Charles Jones and his wife, 8 acres for $3,000, parts of holes 5 and 13. In March 1906, P. P. Van Vleet sold 1.34 acres to the club for $1,000, where the golf pro shop and indoor tennis building are now located.

At first, nine rough holes for golf were laid out in the fields to the north of the house. According to *The History of Tennessee Golf*, the first nine holes were laid out by James Foulis Jr.

Mrs. William Park Metcalf arrives at the club in her buggy.

Samuel Ragland, writing about the early days of the Memphis Country Club, said of the proposed golf course:

> Back toward the north, shorn of its erstwhile pristine beauty, its bare face, shimmering in the heat of the sunlight, lay the future golf course. Fretted and tortured by long use of the plow, bereft of its soil by erosion, it presented a picture of desolation that reflected the result of farming practice quite generally employed at that time.
>
> The first nine holes laid out looked more like a battlefield than a golf course, and indeed, the struggle involved in play was more like fighting than sport. The fairways were rough, the greens uneven and almost bare of sod. Each putting green was fortified on the approach side with a deep ditch with earthen embankment thrown up on the side next to the green, grim reminder of the breastworks employed during the war between the states!

Even if the golf course left something to be desired, members took up the sport with vigor. Before long, the society editor of the *Commercial Appeal* lamented that "the social education of the modern girl has been woefully neglected if she has not even a speaking acquaintance with golf."

The wide verandas and spacious rooms of the Buntyn-Martin home were perfect places for the members of the country club to enjoy a cool drink and a warm dinner. A $40,000 addition was built, and the clubhouse was called "one of the handsomest in the South."

The *Commercial Appeal* reported in 1905, "Backed by plenty of capital and men who are socially competent to make the club a success, the work of improving the property will begin without delay. The object of the organization is to establish and maintain a country clubhouse with all modern improvements for the pleasure and diversion of the members, their families and friends."

A special picture section published in the newspaper on September 16, 1906, described the club effusively:

> Memphis has many beautiful places in which one loves to tarry, many spots where the noise and the din of the city is hushed in the wildwood lullaby. But none surpass in beauty the home of the country club at Buntyn. There one loves to rest in the shadow of the great old trees. Overhead the mockers carol, underfoot the crickets chirp, while all around the wildwood sounds echo and re-echo, sounding to a gypsy heart like vacation bells to the schoolboy.

The article, by Susie M. Harrington, went on to describe the grounds: "the wonderfully beautiful foliage forming a symposium of colors that delight the eye and at the same time bespeak the rest that comes with the autumn days." Golden and wood-brown auriculas bloomed around the broad plazas and bordered walks that led to the tennis courts. "As far as the eye can see the beauty of the landscape is unmarred by even the slightest note of discord."

The interior was described just as fulsomely, as "tone poems in pastel shades. Restful, indeed, are they to body and mind, after a turn on the links or the courts."

The furniture was described as Mission Style:

> while enjoying its stately beauty one can but call to mind that city by the Western seas, and the old adobe missions that long ago sent matin chimes across the Western hills . . . Truly it is an ideal home wherein to commune with nature, to rest if you are weary and restore the blessing of good health if it has been lost. Every nook and corner of the place that lends a chance for carrying out the mission style has been graced with an arch. Even the dining room where the Shaw banquet was given and the main hallway and lounging rooms are suggestive of the period when the good Father Junipero Serra showered blessings on his little flock in far away California.

Ceiling beams, chandeliers, and open chimney places carried out the theme.

Lady golfers.

On the first floor there were living rooms, a dining room, an office, a men's café, and a men's locker room. Upstairs there were seven commodious apartments with fourteen sleeping rooms, a small ladies' locker room, and a private suite for the manager and his wife. Only the latest accoutrements were used for the convenience of golfers: steel and wire lockers, shower baths, and the regulation tub in both the ladies' and men's apartments.

"Maids and men servants are in attendance, while a perfectly trained corps of waiters have charge of the café. Over all Mr. Bamberger and his charming wife have a watchful eye, and better managers would be hard to find."

A yearbook from 1906–07 gives the rules of the club. Standing Committees included the House Committee, the Greens Committee, the Entertainment Committee, the Finance Committee, and the Games Committee. All members had to be twenty-one years or older. Application for membership had to be accompanied by a written recommendation signed by at least three members, stating the name of the proposed member and residence and business addresses; his occupation; how long he had resided in Shelby County; how long he had been personally known to each of the endorsers; and "Such information touching his qualification as may be within the knowledge of the indorsers [sic]." A copy of the application was to be attached to a page of the ballot book, and the candidate was balloted upon for not less than twenty-one days. A candidate had to receive at least fifty votes. Three black balls were enough to disqualify the candidate. Votes were to be cast "without personal prejudice or bias of a personal kind whatever, but purely upon the question of social qualification and fitness for membership in the Club."

Annual dues were set at $48 a year for resident members, and $15 for nonresidents. "No member shall be allowed to become indebted to the Club for more than $25 on house account in any one month."

> Ladies of a member's family and living in his house shall be admitted to the Club House and grounds at all times . . . and may invite to the Club House and grounds as their guests any ladies, but such guests shall not be entitled to play any outdoor games during the afternoon, and may only be entitled to play any such games during the morning hours of the day, upon payment of such charges by the inviting member . . .

Children under fifteen were only admitted when accompanied by one or both parents or an adult member of the club. Boys under twenty-one were denied the privileges of the club unless accompanied by their parents or guardian and were not allowed in the Tap Room under any circumstances.

> No member shall be permitted to lie or sleep on any sofa or lounge in the Club House.

> No gambling for money shall be allowed within the precincts of the Club and no card playing except on the first floor. Dice shaking is permissible only in the Tap Room, and shaking for money or markers is strictly prohibited.

> A charge of 50 cents shall be made for each meal served to servants, coachmen or chauffeurs.

Soon the Memphis Country Club was the center of social activities. In 1906, Mrs. B. J. Goodbar planned a party for the Saturday night after Thanksgiving. The menu included caviar canapés, cream of tomato soup, celery, olives and radishes, turkey with cranberry jelly, hot rolls, brandied sweet potatoes, green peas, an aspic jelly mayonnaise, and pink moose [sic] ice cream with pecans. Some prices were listed in an account book: caviar at $4, tomatoes at $3, the turkey at $12, and the ice cream at $3.

One of the most popular bands that played at country club parties was that of W. C. Handy. Born in Florence, Alabama, he struggled to get a musical education. When the boy bought a guitar, his father, a preacher, made him trade it in for a dictionary and said he'd rather see his son in a hearse than see his son a musician.

But Handy would not be deterred. He became a band and voice teacher at Alabama Agricultural and Mechanical College, then in the Mississippi Delta, where he also began playing for subscription dances. In 1903, at the age of thirty, he came to Memphis as the director of the Knights of Pythias Band.

He discovered that the white audience at dances were more enthusiastic about "Negro" music than they were about standard dance tunes. He began to write down what became known as the blues.

Handy's band played at the Alaskan Roof Garden atop the Falls Building overlooking the Mississippi River. Soon they were regulars at Memphis Country Club parties. According to historian Paul Coppock, one of the favorite songs at the country club parties was "Jogo Blues." Later Handy revised it and named it "The St. Louis Blues." Handy used more than seventy bandsmen, in combos from four up, so that "Handy's Band" could appear at several parties on the same night, with or without Handy.

In the 1909 mayoral race, the candidates hired bands to play for lunchtime crowds on street corners. Handy was hired by Edward Hull Crump. Handy wrote "Mr. Crump don't 'low no easy riders here. We don't care what Mr. Crump don't 'low, we gonna barrelhouse any how." By Crump's 1912 reelection campaign, the song was known as "The Memphis Blues."

Handy moved to New York after 1917. Soon his songs were on phonograph records and player piano rolls. He wrote hymns, a waltz, and other songs, but his fame rests upon his blues. He lived in Memphis for fifteen years, and it was the first place his great original music was heard.

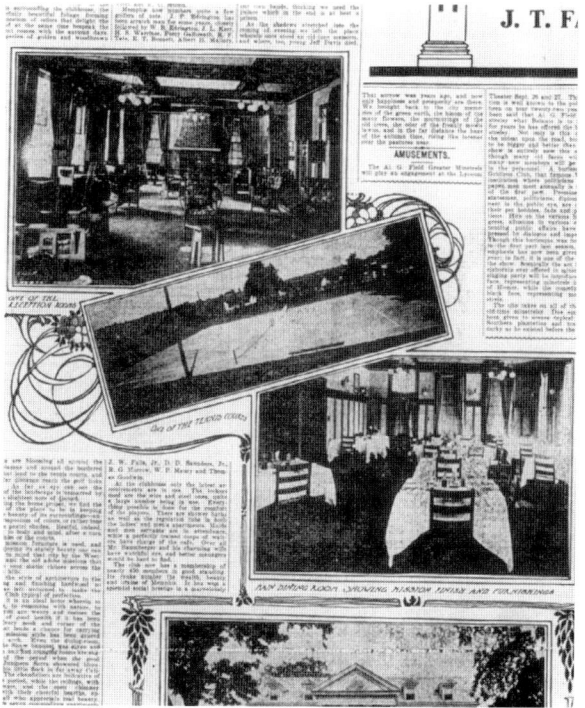

Pictures of the new club in the Commercial Appeal, *September 16, 1906.*

The Beginning of the Memphis Country Club

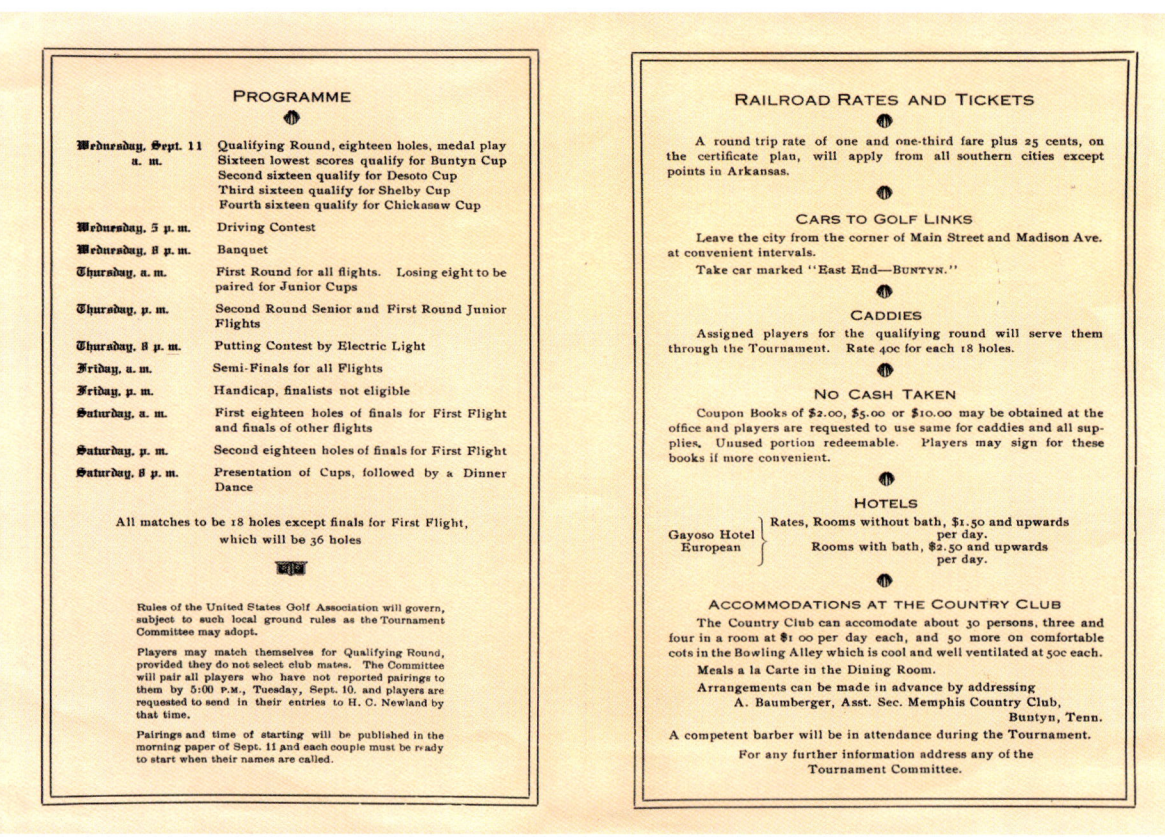

"Programme" from 1907 golf tournament.

THE FIRST GOLF TOURNAMENT

Golf was still the focus of the club. *The History of Tennessee Golf* says, "There was no host more gracious than Memphis Country Club in the early years of Tennessee golf." The first golf tournament to be played at the new Memphis Country Club was held in September 1906. Golfers from around the South came to play on the new links.

The *Commercial Appeal* reported on September 15:

> The second day of the golf tournament at the Memphis Country Club yesterday developed a number of surprises that had their beginning when John L. Kerr finished first over R. F. Tate in the morning glory event, and did not discontinue until Dr. Saunders of Memphis fell a victim at the last hole of an eighteen station round to H. H. Lurton of Nashville just as dusk was falling over the links . . . The observant local public had pinned its faith on the chances of J. P. Edrington and Albert H. Mallory in yesterday's semi-finals. These hopes were shattered by W. W. Ward of Birmingham, who in the morning distanced John Edrington and in the afternoon defeated Mallory.

J. L. Kerr of Memphis won the Buntyn Cup, the most important prize, by defeating W. W. Ward of Birmingham. H. H. Lurton of Nashville beat G. C. Oliver of Birmingham for the DeSoto Cup. Oliver broke the course record on the second day, scoring 34 for nine holes. The Reverend Dr. Duncan of Birmingham won the Consolation Cup, defeating E. C. Cochran of Memphis. A large and enthusiastic gallery followed the players.

The newspaper pictured "Prominent Memphians Who Have Taken to the Game": Judge Heiskell, S. H. Phillips, and J. H. Mallory. Other local players who distinguished themselves were H. C. Newland, H. L. Warriner, Percy Galbreath, W. P. Halliday, and R. G. Morrow. Fortunately, in the first tournament on its own course, the Memphis team won the Club Team Match Cup.

That evening,

> Cups, large and small in size and elaborate in design, were presented to the successful ones shortly after sunset in the house of the country club. S. H. Phillips acted as master of ceremonies, and in a happy style summoned each winner to the center with well chosen words. Each responded in a manner denoting that pleasant experiences had been encountered, the reply of Rev. Dr. Duncan being noteworthy for a rare bit of a golfing joke that was applauded by the large crowd of men and women who congregated.

In other words, a good time was had by all.

When Samuel T. Carnes became the second president in 1906, Mr. R. F. Tate was chosen chairman of the Greens Committee. In 1907, they saw that nine holes were not enough to accommodate the growing number of golfers. Mr. Tate and Mr. J. L. Kerr laid out nine more holes. Willis Clyde Sherwood became the golf instructor and course manager.

The "Programme" for a 1907 golf tournament listed several events over several days

DeSoto Cup Trophy for runner-up, R. G. Morrow.

George C. Oliver and J. P. Edrington at the 1907 golf tournament.

and set the pattern for future years. On Wednesday, September 11, the morning was devoted to qualifying rounds, a driving contest at 5:00 P.M., and a banquet that night. On Thursday, there was a putting contest by electric light at 5:00 P.M. Friday saw the semi-finals and the handicap rounds. Saturday saw the final rounds, followed by the presentation of the cups, and a dinner dance.

The program also gave directions for out-of-towners. A round-trip rate of one and one third fare plus 25¢ applied to all southern cities except points in Arkansas. Then golfers were instructed to take the streetcar marked "East End—Buntyn," which left the corner of Main and Madison at convenient intervals.

Costs for visitors were listed: caddies were assigned at a rate of forty cents for each eighteen holes, and coupon books were available to cover caddies and supplies. Meals were available in the dining room, and "A competent barber will be in attendance during the Tournament." The country club could accommodate about thirty persons, three or four in a room, at $1.00 a day each, and fifty more on comfortable cots in the Bowling Alley "which is cool and well ventilated" at 50¢ each. The Gayoso Hotel charged $1.50 "and upwards" a day for rooms without baths, and $2.50 "and upwards" for rooms with baths.

In September 1910, representatives of many southern golf and country clubs came again for the annual tournament. The *Commercial Appeal* reported that there was every evidence that eighty of the best golfers in the region would be present, but it put its money on a local man, J. P. Edrington, who had introduced golf to Memphis. Edrington, "generally regarded as the best golfer in the South and former champion, will have an opportunity to show his true 1910 style in the coming event . . . He has been going nicely over the local course." But, even with "clear skies overhead and a fast course underfoot" on his home course, Edrington lost to George C. Oliver of Birmingham.

The course hummed with golfers and the clubhouse bustled with guests. Then the unthinkable happened. Let Samuel Ragland tell the story.

At about two o'clock, on November 16, 1910, the young golf pro, W. C. Sherwood, and Dr. C. H. Gardner, a visitor from Providence, Rhode Island, had just made long drives from what is now the number three tee. "They were walking up the long fairway toward the north, when, urged by a strong impulse, 'Sherry' turned and looked toward the club house. He saw smoke. Gardner suggested that someone was burning leaves. The smoke was now billowing high above the house and 'Sherry' was running toward it as fast as his legs would carry him."

The newspaper reported that the fire originated in the boiler room with an overheated furnace. The three-story frame building burned like tinder, aided by a strong breeze. Club members, employees, and neighbors from the Buntyn's Station area dragged furnishings and draperies out of the building, then the wind changed and the pile of salvaged goods went up in smoke. The building was destroyed.

The *Commercial Appeal* reported that the fire started at 2:30 P.M. and by 3:00, nothing remained but ashes. It had burned so quickly that it was unsafe to try to save anything. Several handsome trophies won by the club and its members were lost.

F. T. Woolverton, the bookkeeper at the club, sustained injuries while trying to rescue his personal belongings from the second floor. He was burned about the hands. The manager of the club, E. C. Ellison, who lived with his wife in the adjoining apartment, lost everything except the clothes he was wearing.

Lucille Terrell Knowlton Fisher grew up in a house on Southern Avenue, adjoining the club, with her five siblings. Her father, Dr. Samuel Durr Terrell, was an early member of the club and served as doctor for the staff and guests. The Terrell children felt that the golf course was an extension of their backyard and often played there. She remembered running from her nearby schoolhouse to watch as the fire raged.

Even as the club was burning, General Samuel T. Carnes, then president, was planning to rebuild. But first there were immediate needs. Two vacant cottages at the north end of the grounds were leased for temporary quarters. One served as a café and ladies' locker room and the other as men's locker room.

The disaster did not delay the golf tournament that had been scheduled to start Thanksgiving Day. Chick Evans, a great amateur from Chicago, wired Sherwood that he and other crack Windy City amateurs were interested in winter golf in the South and would come. Otto Hackworth of St. Louis was one of a trio of brothers among the professionals. Alex Smith, open champion, wired from New Rochelle, New York, that he was eager to come to Memphis, "Will be in Memphis with bells on. Don't think I'll foozle at the nineteenth hole."

Visiting golfers were put up in downtown hotels instead of in the clubhouse. Despite the tragedy of the fire, the golf tournament was accounted a success. Milton Dorgan of Atlanta, vice president of the United States Golf Association, said that the course could be made one of the finest in the country.

Ragland gave the old building's eulogy: "Like a brilliant sunset that fades into the darkness of night, the glamorous old mansion passed from the blazing apex of her glory into the shades of eternity, leaving behind only a ghostly chimney to mark the resting place of her ashes."

The Second Clubhouse

Even as the old Buntyn place was burning, a new building was planned. "Of course, we'll rebuild!" the club president, Samuel Carnes, was quoted as saying, as he and others discussed the future of the club while watching the fire.

Samuel Tate Carnes became president of the club in 1906 and served until 1916. He was one of the most interesting characters in Memphis history. He is often called "Memphis's great innovator." He has a strong claim to the title: he introduced the telephone, the electric light, and the automobile to the city.

Born in Hardeman County in 1851, Carnes came to Memphis when he was sixteen and began his career as a runner for the Savings Bank. Undaunted by an early business failure, Carnes tried again. His next idea produced guffaws from his friends—he opened the first telephone company in Memphis.

Only a year after Alexander Graham Bell's great invention, Memphis became one of the first cities to have the telephone when the first call in town was made on October 18, 1877. Carnes opened the first exchange in 1879 with twenty-five customers. Saying to someone, "Call me on the telephone" was a sure sign of status. Carnes lined up 224 subscribers, then in 1883 he sold out to the Cumberland Telephone and Telegraph of Nashville, which was later absorbed by Southern Bell.

In 1883 Carnes bought a big house at Linden and Wellington, with fifteen-foot ceilings, a billiard room, and a ballroom, and turned his attention to another new invention, the electric light. He acquired the Memphis rights to patents and opened the Brush Electric Light Company in 1883, arranging a demonstration for February 7, 1884.

There was a small generator near the waterfront on the Promenade north of Jefferson. Each home had a set of batteries that could operate twenty lights for four hours, then they had to be recharged by a line to the generator, and restarted with a crank. Court Square was illuminated, to the awe of spectators.

Sam Carnes, second president.

As if phones and electric lights were not enough, General Carnes drove the first automobile in Memphis, an electric car he purchased in 1894.

He was president of the Memphis chapter of the Red Cross for many years. His title of general came from his office in the Chickasaw Guards, a drill company formed in 1874, whose clubrooms atop the Exchange Building had a ballroom where many parties were held. In 1917, Carnes was called out of retirement to settle some difficulties in the police department and was briefly named chief of police. He died on January 26, 1932, aged eighty-one.

THE NEW CLUBHOUSE

As soon as the fire was out, President Carnes called a general meeting of the members and a Building Committee was appointed. The architect chosen to design the new clubhouse was a charter member of the country club, Charles Oscar Pfeil (1881–1927). He had been educated at the University of Illinois and, with his partner

Increasingly, automobiles brought members to the club.

George Awsumb, was responsible for building Ellis Auditorium in the 1920s, remodeling the Gayoso Hotel, and designing South Side High School, Humes Junior High, and several large homes, including his own two-story stucco house at 333 Goodwyn, adjacent to the club.

Pfeil was also an important figure in Tennessee golf. He brought several important tournaments to the country club. He served as president of the Western Golf Association from 1923 to 1925. He died suddenly at the age of forty-six in 1927, just one month before he was to be nominated as the president of the United States Golf Association.

At the same time the new clubhouse was being built, plans to improve the golf course were under way. An audit of the club's finances on April 30, 1911, lists $1,467 for "new course." A man just starting out in his American career who was to become the most eminent golf course architect of his day was chosen to design it—Donald Ross.

Even while the plans were being drawn, another calamity loomed. A proposed county road threatened the golf course. To accommodate eighteen holes, the easement for Midland Avenue had to be abandoned. Neighbors agreed to give up the easement if golfers would stop playing in their front yards. A hedge was put in around the course.

The Second Clubhouse

The rose arbor.

It was said that the new clubhouse would cost $55,000. It was 220 feet long and 110 feet wide. It had a vaguely Spanish design with a low-pitched, red-tiled roof and concrete walls. There were four stories, including the basement. The first floor was entirely given to men's and ladies' locker rooms and baths, with two hundred lockers in the men's room and one hundred for women, making it the most spacious ladies' room in the country.

The second floor had a seventy foot by thirty foot living room, a sixty foot by thirty foot ballroom, with a mezzanine for the orchestra, a sixty foot by thirty foot dining room, a private dining room, parlor, and club office. The top floor was devoted to sleeping quarters. The east end held bachelor quarters with seven bedrooms with baths between the rooms. On the west end were similar rooms for married people and the manager's suite.

The front had a porte cochere, where automobiles, increasing in number, could deposit guests. On the walkway to the front door there were arches covered with flowering vines.

Once again, there were deep verandas on one side of the front and across the back with views to the golf course. They were furnished with comfortable wicker chairs. Urns overflowed with flowers.

The new clubhouse was elaborately decorated for its debut on November 4, 1911. The *Commercial Appeal* reported:

Society was out en masse yesterday afternoon and evening at the informal opening of the new Country Club. The walls in the large hall were completely hidden by autumn leaves. The windows and doorways were outlined with delicate smilax, while fragrant American Beauty roses added a touch of brilliant color. In the living rooms and library, the only flowers used in ornamentation were long stemmed American Beauty roses skillfully arranged. The decorations in the dining room were especially beautiful. The walls were hung with canvas, covered with autumn leaves, and the leaves in brilliant colors and smilax were used on the tables, where chrysanthemums and American Beauty roses formed the central decoration.

Three hundred twenty guests turned out to enjoy tea, which was served from three until six o'clock, and dinner, served from seven until nine. From eight until eleven, there was informal dancing.

A large committee of members and their wives planned the event. In addition, there

The porch of the second clubhouse.

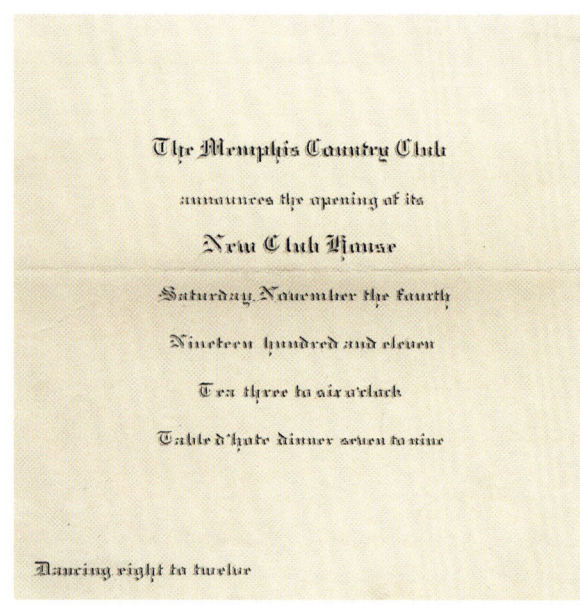

The invitation to the opening of the new clubhouse.

were several private parties. Mr. and Mrs. Frank G. Jones entertained ten friends, Mr. and Mrs. C. C. Selden entertained fourteen, and Mr. and Mrs. George I. Drew had fifteen guests.

The audit report of Homer K. Jones, public accountant and auditor, delivered on April 30, 1911, listed the fire loss as $17,671.99. Other expenses included stable and feed, $938.55; transplanting trees, $30; bridge luncheon, $5.40; and greens expense, $3,495.09. Income included membership dues of $27,000 and the golf ball account of $1,025.70.

The Memphis Country Club was now a part of community life. Judge J. P. Young wrote in his 1912 history of Memphis, "The Country Club has a beautiful country home at Buntyn, a suburb of Memphis. There the men and women who are fortunate enough to be members enjoy the comfortable clubhouse and grounds. In the house, books, magazines, games, conversation and other social diversions are enjoyed, while the spacious grounds afford out-of-door games. The golf links especially are good."

The fine new clubhouse was featured in *The Saturday Evening Post* in 1913 in an advertisement for Firestone Tires. A touring car with two golfers was pictured in front of the handsome building.

This is the clubhouse that Pulitzer Prize-winning author, Peter Taylor, used as the background of several of his novels and stories. In "The Old Forest," he makes the distinction between the sort of girls proper young gentlemen would take to the Memphis Country Club, and those "demimondaines [who] took the lighthearted view they did about not going to the MCC, because it was the last place most of us would have wished to take them . . . To have brought one of those girls to the Club would have required, at any rate, a boy who was a much bolder and freer spirit than I was at twenty-three."

The swimming pool became a popular place in the 1920s. In the story "Daphne's Lover" in the collection *In the Miro District*, Taylor writes about the proper kind of girls and boys:

> We had been watching the Sunday-night movie in the main lounge at the country club. When the movie was over, a group of us wandered out onto the wide veranda that used to go round three sides of the old clubhouse. (The old clubhouse was a pleasant, unpretentious building, not at all like the trite Georgian

The Firestone Company used the new clubhouse in its advertising.

Marker (Goblet) Trophy.

place they have put up since the War.) Frank was there with Mary Edenton. Janet Turner and two other girls were there without escorts. We were on the part of the veranda that overlooked the swimming pool. Frank and Mary had strolled over to the edge of the porch and stood by the banister looking out over the dark water of the pool.

TENNIS AND GOLF

The tennis courts became a focal point in the teens. The first mention of tennis in America came in 1659, when Governor Peter Stuyvesant of New Netherlands issued a proclamation forbidding the playing of the game on certain days. Lawn tennis appeared in 1874, when a New Yorker named Mary Ewing Outerbridge discovered the game in Bermuda and came home to lay out a court on Staten Island. It was such a genteel game that ladies could play in their long skirts, since they were not expected to run about. The United States Lawn Tennis Association was organized in 1881 by the leaders of several eastern clubs.

Tennis came to Memphis around 1890. The first tennis court in town was a grass court at the Randolph mansion at the corner of Beale and Lauderdale. The Randolph children grew up playing tennis, and soon their friends and neighbors joined in. Around 1893, the Memphis Tennis Club was organized, with courts laid out at Madison and Manassas, just north of the Werts and Rhea School (forerunner of the Memphis University School). Ladies began to play there, wearing skirts only a little shorter than street wear. Some of the first ladies to take up the game were Mrs. Brinkley Snowden and Mrs. S. M. Neely.

The game was slow in those days, and endurance mattered. The rackets were longer and heavier and so loosely strung that placing the ball as it is done today was virtually impossible. Anyone who could hit a ball backhanded was considered a marvel. The tennis club moved to Jefferson Avenue behind the ballpark in 1906 and built a clubhouse and clay courts.

By 1912, the Memphis Country Club had taken up tennis. The first local tournament between the country club and the tennis club was held in 1914. Nat Emerson won the singles, and Leroy Cooper and H. M. Sanders won doubles.

Ladies were playing golf as well as tennis. In 1911, the *Commercial Appeal* published a picture of several avid golfers, including W. D. Mallory, S. T. Carnes, F. G. Jones, and Mrs. Jones, clad in a long pale skirt, a stiff blouse, and an elaborate hat that would have been more at home at church or a tea than on the golf course.

Mrs. Jones was one of the organizers of the Women's Southern Golf Association in 1911 and was elected the first president. Nina Jones won their tournaments in 1912 and 1914.

An important event, the Western Open Golf Tournament, was held at the club in October 1913. The newspaper reported that "At least 48 of the experts who will participate in the championship will attack Col. Bogey in the best ball match today." Two Boston golfers won the best ball preliminary.

The course was reported to be in excellent condition. Along with golfers from Oklahoma City, Atlanta, Peoria, Nashville, Topeka, Indianapolis, Des Moines, Chicago, and Milwaukee, local players competed: the club pro Willis Clyde Sherwood, Dave Patrick, F. D. Gardner, George Bingley, M. J. Condon, J. P. Edrington, J. C. Cunningham, W. A. Hood, S. M. Williamson, and L. L. Heiskell. Condon won the medal as low amateur.

Southern Golf Association Tournament Trophy, 1914.

The Memphis Country Club had begun as a golf club, and the interest in golf was ever increasing. The crucial decision to hire Donald Ross as course architect assured the club a place in golf history.

III

Golf

Scotland claims to be the home of the game of golf, although some writers would trace it back to a Roman game called *paganica*. Most devotees say that golf developed from Scottish shepherds, who used their crooks to hit stones in the open fields. Soon a leather ball stuffed with feathers replaced the stones, and a bent stick replaced the shepherd's crook.

There is evidence that golf was already popular in St. Andrews, Scotland, when the venerable university was founded in 1413.

By 1457, the sport had begun to interfere with the archery practice required of soldiers. An edict of the Scots Parliament of King James II ruled "that Futeball and Golfe be utterly cryed downe and not be used."

The parliament tried again to forbid golf in 1471 under James III. Twenty years later, James IV again ordained that neither golf nor other unprofitable sport be played, as it interfered with more important duties. But according to the Royal Financial Account, the king violated his own rule when he played golf with the Earl of Bothwell in 1503.

Golf was obviously winning over the lawmakers. If they couldn't stop it entirely, they tried to limit the times it could be played. In 1592, the Edinburgh Town Council prohibited playing on Sundays. The next year, a similar act specified that playing was forbidden "during divine services," and imposed a 45 shilling fine for violations. Ministers, however, were among those fined for breaking the rules.

When the invention of gunpowder made the bow obsolete as weapon of war, statutes prohibiting golf were useless. In 1603, James VI appointed William Mayne as royal club maker, and in 1618 James Melvill as ball maker. In the seventeenth century there were acts permitting golf instead of banning it. In 1618 the king authorized the playing of golf on Sundays, with the stipulation that divine services be attended first.

The first golfing society, the Honorable Company of Edinburgh Golfers was organized in 1744, and the first tournament held at the links near Leith. The St. Andrews Society of Golfers was founded in 1754, and the title of the Royal and Ancient Club was conferred by William IV in 1834.

Golf spread from Scotland. It was first played near London in 1608, but not until 1761 was there an English golf club. The first reference to golf in America was a complaint issued by the sheriff of Fort Orange (now Albany), New York, against three men for playing "kolven" on a Sunday.

The first true golf club in the United States was probably the Foxbury Golf Club in Foxbury, Pennsylvania, founded in 1887, as the result of one John Mickle Fox's trip to Scotland, where he learned the game. The founding of the St. Andrew's Club in Yonkers, New York, with three holes in a cow pasture, in 1887, marked the point when golf became firmly rooted in the United States, and soon there were clubs in Boston and Philadelphia. By 1894, there were one hundred courses in the country, including a course just for women in Morristown, New Jersey.

Golf was a game for the well-to-do. The players often wore odd costumes, including scarlet coats patterned on those worn by fox hunters, and were frequently subjects of ridicule. But despite the laughter, the sport was spreading.

Equipment improved. Before 1848, balls were known as "featheries," small spheroids of leather stuffed with approximately one top hat full of feathers. They were tedious to make, requiring three pieces sewn together, and the feathers inserted through a small pinhole. Sometimes they burst on impact, and the feathers would fly.

In 1845, the Reverend Dr. Robert Adams Patterson made the first "guttie" from a substance used as protective packing for items shipped from India to England. Gutta percha (a resin or gum from certain Malayan trees of the sapodilla family), resembled rubber and made balls easier to make, more durable, and cheaper. Gutties carried a longer distance, were more accurate, and responded more favorably to wind, although golf professionals detested them at first, and since they were hard as bricks, they must have packed a wallop for the players' shoulders. Coburn Haskell, a Cleveland golfer, invented the liquid center ball in 1899.

There were no golf bags—players carried their clubs by hand until the 1880s—and there was no specific number of clubs in a set. Clubs had wooden shafts, and all but two—the steel-headed niblick and the cleek—had wooden heads. The niblick was the trouble club, used to extract the ball from cartwheel ruts, horse tracks, potholes, and bunkers. Courses consisted of from five to eighteen holes. Teeing grounds were unknown; the start of a new hole was designated by a number of club lengths from the last hole played.

As the number of courses grew, so did the number of professionals. Their duties varied; some were greenskeepers or custodians, some were instructors. Some were only a step above a caddy, and many performed that duty, too.

During the 1880s and 1890s, golf spread like wild fire. The first amateur invitational championship was played at Newport, Rhode Island, in 1894, the same year the Amateur Golf Association was formed on December 22, 1894, at a meeting of five golf clubs from New York, Massachusetts, Rhode Island, and Chicago. Later the name was changed to American Golf Association, then to the United States Golf Association. Its purpose was "To promote the interest of the game of golf, to conduct the Amateur and Open championships, and to establish a code of rules for the game of golf." By 1920, the USGA had 477 clubs as members.

During the 1920s, no sport expanded faster than golf. Some of its popularity was related to social status rather than to fun or healthful properties. Along with growth of suburbia came the proliferation of golf courses and country clubs. The game was expensive, with membership fees, clubs, balls, and stylish plus fours to wear. By the late twenties, golfers were spending more than $200 million a year on the sport. The number of golf courses in United States mushroomed to 5,700 by 1931. There were some 4,450 private clubs, over 500 municipal courses, and 700 privately owned public fee courses. It was estimated that there were 9,000 courses throughout the world, of which 2,000 were in the British Empire.

Along with the rise of golf, miniature golf became popular. The "Tom Thumb Course" was invented by Garnet Carter of Chattanooga, Tennessee, and required only a putter.

GOLF COMES TO MEMPHIS

Golf arrived in Memphis in 1896. John Price Edrington, an insurance and investment man, learned the game on a trip to Denver in the spring of that year. He brought back a set of three clubs and began to teach his friends. By fall, some of the town "bloods" had bought their own clubs. They began by playing on a three hole course with tomato cans for holes.

Then they laid out a nine hole course on a common area near the bluff where

Peabody Avenue began, adjacent to Edrington's house. The second green was where St. John's Methodist Church stands today, and the third near present-day Bruce School. Edrington and his cousin, W. P. Halliday, repaired clubs and made balls in his garage.

An early golf magazine, writing about golf in the South in 1898, described the early course as:

> situated about two and a half miles from the center of the city (close and convenient) upon the beautiful Peabody Heights . . . There is no club-house at present, but do not imagine for a moment that that is allowed to detract from the social aspect of the game . . . It so happens that some half dozen of the members reside within a few yards of the first tee, and their houses are usually pressed into service, and here a good fellow can always find a welcome, a glass of water and a wee "drap" of something in it.

On May 23, 1897, the *Commercial Appeal* thought it necessary to run a full-page explanation of the game, complete with pictures. The object, said the newspaper, was "to hit the ball with a crooked stick." In 1898, the first golf professional, "Professor" W. B. Hoare, arrived to give lessons. The newspaper called him "one of the golf champions in the United States."

Also in 1898, Frank Graham Jones offered the infield of his new North Memphis Driving Park for a golf course. Jones, a native of Iowa, came to Memphis as manager of the street railway company, consolidated the various lines into a company that managed seventy-five cars on over one hundred miles of track, then sold the company for $2.5 million to a New York group. He was involved with Samuel Carnes in the Consolidated Gas and Electric Company, and with C.K.G. Billings in the North Memphis Driving Park.

Gentlemen golfers at the Memphis Driving Park: John Kerr, Jack Edrington, unidentified player, the pro, Poston Maury, and Frank Allen.

Players at the club in 1912.

The racetrack was located between Dunlap and Manassas Streets and included the site of today's Manassas High School. It had a mile-long track for trotting races. From 1902 to 1904, the Memphis Gold Cup was offered by the United States Trotting Association as the world championship prize for gentlemen drivers. The golf course was built in the center of the oval racetrack, and Jones turned over the clubhouse to the golfers when races were not being held.

On May 8, 1899, the *Commercial Appeal* reported: "The ancient Scottish game which has been so popular with the fashionable set in the east and north has finally taken hold in Memphis, and is increasing among women as well as men." Frank Graham Jones's wife Nina was one of the best of the lady golfers.

Golfers were derided as sissies at first. But when President Taft took up the game, it gained popularity. Some of the English cotton buyers in Memphis were among the first to embrace the game.

There were about fifty members of the Memphis Golf Club playing at the racetrack.

Caddies in 1912.

They included R. G. Morrow, D. S. Weaver, W. P. Halliday, Percy Galbreath, W. D. Mallory, Gilbert Raine, Tom Goodwyn, Poston Maury, F. M. Crump, Hugh Wynne, T. L. Treadwell, and S. M. Williamson. Edrington was elected president. This provided the nucleus for the idea of a country club in 1905.

At the same time the country club was being organized, other courses were planned. A public course was planned for the new Overton Park in 1904. It was designed by W. C. Sherwood, who became the Memphis Country Club golf professional, and who also designed an eighteen-hole course built at Riverside Park in 1913. By 1927, there were six courses in Memphis: Overton Park, Memphis Country Club, Riverside Park, Colonial Country Club, Ridgeway Country Club, and Chickasaw Country Club. Clarence Saunders planned a private course for his estate on Central Avenue across from the country club course.

Golf was a lifetime sport. In 1935, the newspaper reported that the three oldest regular golfers, J. P. Edrington, D. S. Weaver, and Martin Condon, still played together weekly at the Memphis Country Club. Condon was seventy-seven and could shoot his age.

DONALD ROSS

Donald Ross has been called "America's all-time favorite golf architect." Writer Michael Konik says, "It's not an overstatement to say that Ross's vision and craftsmanship transformed the American game. Or that his presence is still felt today, though he died in 1948."

He was born in 1872, in Dornoch, on the east coast of the Scottish highlands. His father, Murdo, was a stonemason. As a teenager, Donald became a carpenter's apprentice, but he was an accomplished golfer, and he attracted the attention of the club secretary at Dornoch, who took him on and groomed him as a greenskeeper. He was sent to St. Andrews to learn from a golf legend, Tom Morris, golf's most highly regarded pro, who had won the British Open three of its first four years. Donald worked in the clubmaker's shop and learned course layout. He spent a year at another course at Carnoustie. In 1893, he returned to Dornoch as professional and greenskeeper. His future seemed assured.

A Harvard professor, Robert Willson, played at Dornoch and was impressed with Ross. He told him that golf was catching on in the United States and urged him to go there. Ross was making one hundred pounds a year in Scotland, and was tempted by the idea of a salary of sixty dollars a month, plus fifty cents an hour for lessons. Against his mother's advice, he gave up his secure position and emigrated to the United States in 1899, where he became pro and greenskeeper at the Oakley Country Club in Watertown, Massachusetts. One of his earliest duties was to redesign the Oakley course.

In 1900, James Tufts of the American Soda Fountain Company hired Ross to build a course at a large tract of land he had bought in the sand hills of Pinehurst,

A caddy's handmade distance book.

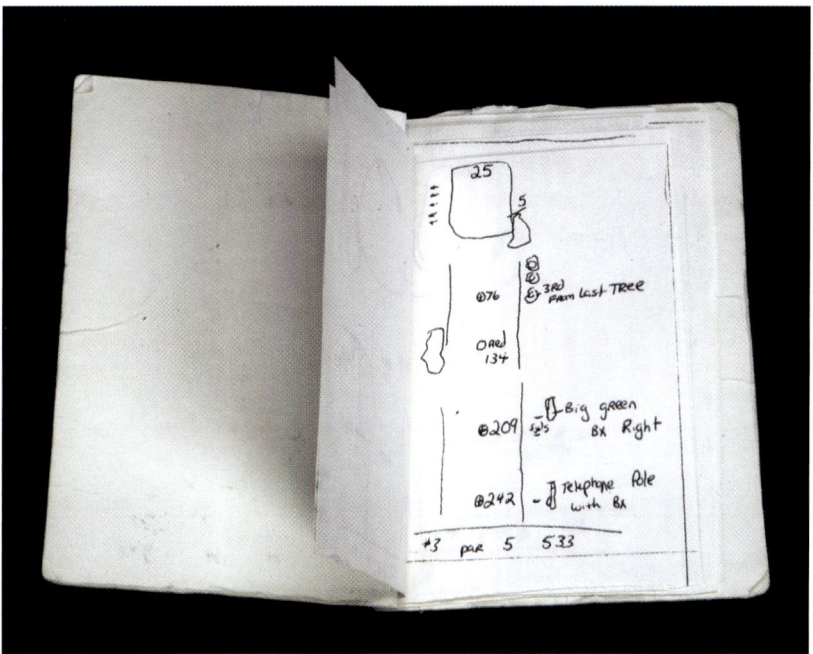

Donald Ross.

North Carolina, where he wanted to establish a winter resort away from the harsh New England weather. Ross became the director of golf at Pinehurst, and this set the pattern for his life: New England in the summers, North Carolina in the winters.

During his first decade in the United States, Ross won several tournaments and designed and redesigned several courses. Soon the demands of golf course architecture absorbed all of his time. Donald J. Ross Associates was established in 1916, and soon he employed some thirty building crews and twenty-five hundred men, designing and constructing more than 380 courses. His courses became the favorite sites for professional and amateur tournaments. From 1919 to 1930, the National Open Tournament was played on no fewer than seven Ross designs.

By the time of his death from a heart attack in 1948, he had designed courses in thirty states, Canada, Nova Scotia, and Cuba. His simple but effective methods of solving problems are still used by courses across America.

Each of his courses was original and designed specifically for the terrain on which it was built. Unlike the work of many of his peers, Ross courses do not repeat each other. In each case, he wanted to return to the clubhouse in two loops if possible, and to take advantage of existing plateaus and hills. He designed and built sensible bunkers that were not penal in nature, and if possible, avoided use of water hazards. He believed that playing golf should be a pleasure, not a penance, and his courses were playable by every level of player.

In a book of his commentaries called *Golf Has Never Failed Me*, Ross said, "The ideal course is one that presents a test of golf for the everyday golfer and the first-class player. A properly designed golf course can take care of every class of player. My aim is to bring out of the player the best golf that is in him."

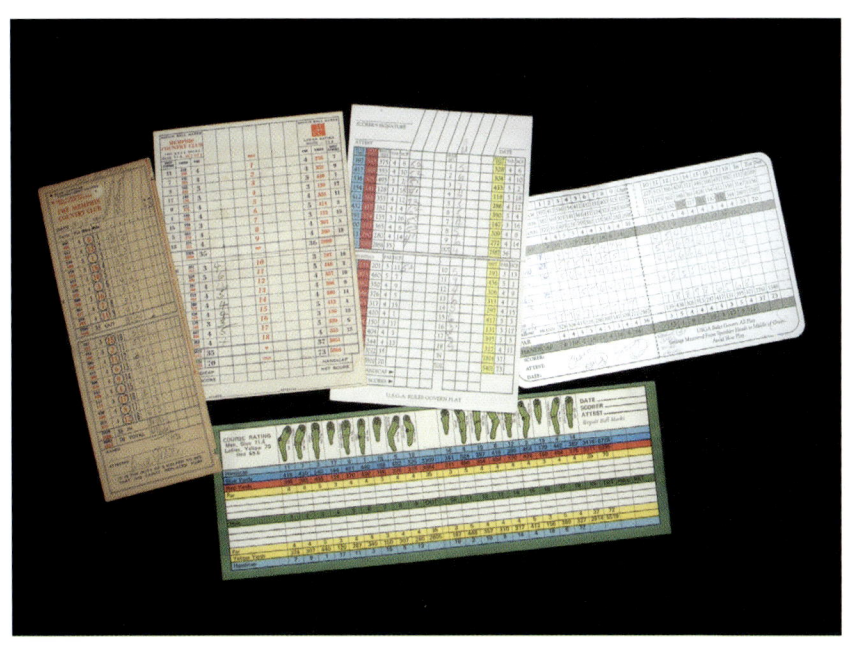

An assortment of score cards.

D. S. Weaver, J. W. S. Rhea, and A. H. Mallory at a tournament in September 1910.

An aerial photo of the course in 1937.

Ross's courses were meant to flow without interruption; he treated changes in elevation subtly, with gradual rather than sudden rises. His courses lack drastic directional changes, gently turning the player in different directions rather than using the endless back-and-forth pattern favored by many designers. This also permitted him to use the prevailing winds to aid or hinder. Ross believed in the adjustable tee. All of his courses have two or more tees for each hole.

He believed that the most dramatic shot in a game was a well-struck long iron. Many of his courses favor long par fours, many of which are designed to be played into the prevailing wind. His greens reward well-played shots. If a player landed a less than competent shot on the green, he would have trouble keeping it there or two putt for par. The inverted saucer green is a Ross trademark.

Donald Ross wrote of his standards, "Make each hole present a different problem. So arrange it so that every stroke must be made with a full concentration and attention necessary to good golf. Build each hole in such a manner that it wastes none of the ground at my disposal, and takes advantage of every possibility I can see."

His designs are always practical. In the early days, the dirt had to be moved by horse or ox cart rather then by earthmoving machines. His workers would remove tree stumps and boulders, pile them up, and cover them with dirt, adding mounds to the terrain.

Golf

Because of his background as a greenskeeper, he was always attentive to proper drainage. Fairways, greens, tees, and bunkers were positioned to utilize natural slopes to carry water away. Where the land was flat, Ross dug drainage ditches and then built contoured slopes to drain the water.

ROSS AND THE MEMPHIS COUNTRY CLUB

Ross was at the beginning of his career when the members of the Memphis Country Club hired him in 1910 to redesign the golf course. It was a wise decision. He went on to design courses around the country, including nine other courses in Tennessee, but the Memphis Country Club course was one of his first courses, and remains one of the least changed from his original plans.

While many of Ross's designs have been modified over the years, the MCC course has remained essentially unchanged from Ross's original design largely because it is landlocked. The course occupies some 110 acres. Modern courses cover from 160 to 200 acres. The MCC course is tight and narrow, and shows the genius of Ross's original plan. Thirteen of the greens are original 1910 greens: numbers 1, 4, 5, 6, 7, 10, 11, 12, 13, 14, 15, 16, and 17. This is unheard of in golfdom, where greens on many courses are reconfigured every few years.

Well-known Memphis sportsman Nash Buckingham wrote about the country club golf course for *American Golfer*:

> Several years ago Donald Ross took the makeshift old course with its straitlaced figure and yawning traps in hand and turned it into a real, worthwhile problem. Rather than an easy, placid proposition to the casual eye, accustomed to picturesque or ferocious scenery, but all in all not to be tampered with or like matrimony—

Children at golf camp on the green in 2003.

Children at golf camp in 2003.

"entered into lightly or unadvisedly." Once off the line nothing but the kindly hand of 'Old Luck' or a friendly miracle is going to save a lost stroke.

In 1910, the easement for Midland Avenue had to be abandoned to make room for nine more holes. The neighbors agreed to give up the easement if golfers would stop playing in their front yards. A hedge was put in around the golf course, but it was porous, and some residents of Central and Greer would sneak onto the course to play. Those players were said to have a "hedgerow membership." The course was fenced in 1973.

Photographs show that there were few trees in the beginning, and the course showed its recent use as farmland. Although tall trees are now the glory of the course, planting them encountered initial resistance from golfers.

According to Samuel Ragland's history of the club, during the 1920s:

After much prodding, the board consented to the planting of a few young trees over the course. It was claimed that they had no proper place on a golf course because they had a maddening habit of getting in the way. Nevertheless, about five hundred were planted in out-of-the-way places where no golf ball had any preemptive right . . .

Two or three were placed on the back and on the sunny side of each tee. Several rows were planted back from the fairways. Clumps were set quite out of the way of proper play. In midsummer, when the fierce rays of the sun are bearing down on the weary, perspiring golfer, the cooling shade of these trees is like the vision of an oasis in the sands of a desert.

The story goes that some golfers encouraged the planting of trees and tall hedges at the northeast corner of the course, so that

Golf

48th U.S.G.A. AM...

STARTING TIMES FOR...
MEMPH...

FIRST QUARTER

Time	No.	1st ROUND				
7:30	1	Davis W. Smith, Jr., Gastonia, N. C.	Jacobson 7&5	Kocsis 4&3	Kocsis 1 up	Kocsis 6-5 Michigan
	2	Robert J. Jacobson, Deal, N. J.				
7:35	3	Glenn Oatman, Kansas City, Mo.	Kocsis 5&4			
	4	Charles Kocsis, Royal Oak, Mich.				
	5	Wm. C. Campbell, Huntington, W. Va. Bye	Campbell	Stone 2 up		
7:41	6	Hal M. Stone, Jr., Bloomington, Ill.	Stone 1 up			
	7	J. Pete Barnes, Atlanta, Ga.				
7:46	8	H. H. Pritchett, Tuscaloosa, Ala.	Pritchett 2 up	Pritchett 2 up	Simonsen 4&3	
	9	Robert D. Mitchell, Dallas, Texas				
	10	John Griscom, Nashville, Tenn. Bye	Griscom			
	11	Willie Barber, Woodland Hill, Calif.	Simonsen 7&6	Simonsen 7&6		
	12	Adrian Simonsen, Minneapolis, Minn.				
	13	Gilbert Stubbs, Corsicana, Texas Bye	Stubbs			Stranahan
7:57	14	H. S. Chamberlain, Lookout Mt., Tenn.	Dudley 2&1	Stranahan 1 up		
	15	Charles B. Dudley, Greenville, S. C.				
8:03	16	Frank Strafaci, Flushing, N. Y.	Stranahan 4&3		Stranahan 3-2	Stranahan 3-1 Ohio
	17	Frank R. Stranahan, Toledo, Ohio				
	18	Robert Lowry, Jr., Huntsville, Ala. Bye	Lowry	Stembler 3&2		
8:08	19	William Y. Stembler, Miami, Fla.	Stembler 1 up			
	20	Frank S. Souchak, Oakmont, Pa.				
8:14	21	Richard L. Smart, Pine Bluff, Ark.	Smart 2 up	Smart 4&3	Smart 1 up	
	22	Roland R. MacKenzie, Baltimore, Md.				
	23	Richard D. Chapman, Pinehurst, N. C. Bye	Chapman			
8:19	24	John W. Coyle, Springfield, Ill.	Coyle 6&4	Robinson 4&2		
7:52	25	Max Felix, Los Angeles, Calif.				
8:25	26	Jack W. Robinson, Santa Ana, Cal.	Robinson 1 up			
	27	Guy Owen, Cut Bank, Mont.				
	28	Gene Williams, Tuscaloosa, Ala. Bye	Williams	Ford 6&5	Cestone 2-1	
8:30	29	Douglas M. Ford, Larchmont, N. Y.	Ford 4&3			
	30	Gordon C. Clay, Atlanta, Ga.				
	31	Michael Cestone, West Orange, N. J. Bye	Cestone	Cestone 1 up		Billows 3-2 New York
8:36	32	James G. Jackson, Kirkwood, Mo.	Jackson 6&4			
	33	Marcel J. Bellande, Gulfport, Miss.				
8:41	34	John E. Lehman, Chicago, Ill.	Lehman 3&1	McCreary 1 up	Billows 4-3	
	35	Russell DeCarteret, Miami, Fla.				
	36	Richard McCreary, Houston, Texas Bye	McCreary			
8:47	37	Don Schumacher, Dallas, Texas	Schumacher 4&2	Billows 2&1		
	38	Edwin R. Butler, W. Palm Beach, Fla.				
8:52	39	Ray Billows, Poughkeepsie, N. Y.	Billows 6&5			Billows 5-4
	40	Stanley S. Taylor, Jr., Honolulu, Hawaii				
	41	Frank W. Godwin, Jr., Miami, Fla. Bye	Godwin	Wright 6&5	Wright 4-3	
8:58	42	Claude L. Wright, Englewood, Colo.	Wright 5&3			
	43	James A. Wittenberg, Memphis, Tenn.				
	44	E. J. Rogers, Sr., Oklahoma City, Okla. Bye	Rogers	Rogers 1 up		Barrett 1 up Tennessee
9:03	45	C. McVicker, Cincinnati, Ohio	Sweeny 4&3			
	46	Robert J. Sweeny, Jr., Westbury, N. Y.				
	47	Wesley G. Brown, Chattanooga, Tenn. Bye	Brown	Barrett 4&3	Barrett 4-3	
9:09	48	William K. Barrett, Jr., Memphis, Tenn.	Barrett 6&5			
	49	Arnold D. Palmer, Latrobe, Pa.				
	50	Mal Galletta, Douglaston, N. Y. Bye	Galletta	Galletta 1 up		
9:14	51	Sam Urzetta, East Rochester, N. Y.	Houdry 1 up			
	52	Jacques Houdry, Ardmore, Pa.				

Scorecard from the U.S.G.A. Championship held at Memphis Country Club in 1948.

UR CHAMPIONSHIP
AY, AUGUST 30, 1948
TRY CLUB

SECOND QUARTER

Time	No.	1st ROUND				
9:20	53	John A. Zoller, Columbus, Ohio	Boros 2+1	Boros 1 up	Boros 5-3	Boros
	54	Julius Boros, Bridgeport, Conn.	Leonard 1 up			5-3
9:25	55	Daryl F. Schoonover, Topeka, Kans.	Becka	Connelly 1 up		Connecticut
	56	Thomas J. Leonard, Jr., Nashua, N. H.				
	57	Charles J. Becka, Jr., Homewood, Ill.	Connelly 3+2			
		Bye				
9:31	58	William R. Jones, Wichita, Kans.	Sanders 2+1	Wagner 2+1	Sloan 2-1	
	59	Harold J. Connelly, St. Louis, Mo.				
9:36	60	W. E. Sanders, Kansas City, Mo.	Wagner			
	61	H. A. McGrath, Jr., Winchester, Mass.				
	62	John E. Wagner, Glencoe, Ill.	Sloan 1 up	Sloan 3+2		Boros
		Bye				4-3
9:42	63	William H. Zimmerman, Augusta, Ga.	Martz			
	64	Herbert A. Sloan, Kansas City, Mo.				
	65	Lloyd A. Martz, Royal Oak, Mich.	Dana 2+1	Coe 7+6	Coe 3-2	
		Bye				
9:47	66	Larry Dana, Jr., Bradford, Pa.	Coe 1 up			Coe 6-4
	67	James E. Funston, Detroit, Mich.				Oklahoma
9:53	68	Junius J. Hebert, Baton Rouge, La.	Welch	Key 4+2		
	69	Charles R. Coe, Oklahoma City, Okla.				
	70	Harry Welch, Salisbury, N. C.	Key 4+3		Hardwicke 3-2	
		Bye				
9:58	71	Jack B. Key, Jr., Columbus, Ga.	Hardwicke 4+2	Hardwicke 2+1		
	72	Ralph T. Strafaci, Hempstead, N. Y.	Andrews			
10:04	73	B. B. Lotspeich, Miami, Fla.	Mayer	Brownell 2+1		
	74	Clarke Hardwicke, Los Angeles, Cal.				
	75	Arthur H. Andrews, Jr., St. Charles, Ill.	Brownell			
		Bye				
10:09	76	A. Richard Mayer, Mamaroneck, N. Y.	Sanok 5-3	Brink 5+4	Armstrong 5-4	Armstrong 2-1
	77	Jack Purdum, Webster Groves, Mo.				Hawaii
10:15	78	Ronald Williams, Mt. Clemens, Mich.	Brink 1 up			
	79	Robert W. Brownell, Norbeck, Md.				
	80	Chester Sanok, Englewood, N. J.	Dickinson	Armstrong 5+4		
		Bye				
10:20	81	Russell A. Allen, Jr., Kansas City, Mo.	Armstrong 3+2			
	82	Harold Brink, Belmont, Mich.				
	83	Gardner E. Dickinson, Jr., Baton Rouge	Bishop 2+1	Spomer 1 up	Buzick 3-2	Armstrong 3-2
		Bye				
10:26	84	Arthur Armstrong, Honolulu, Hawaii	Spomer 3+2			
	85	Albert E. Campbell, Seattle, Wash.				
10:31	86	Stanley E. Bishop, Islington, Mass.	Buzick	Buzick 1 up		
	87	E. K. Gravely, Rocky Mount, N. C.				
10:37	88	Don R. Spomer, Lincoln, Neb.	McHale 1 up			
	89	Ben Smith, Grosse Pointe Woods, Mich.				
	90	John W. Buzick, Jr., Jonesboro, Ark.	Semple 1 up	Fowler 6+4	Fowler 2-1	Levinson 3-2
		Bye				Maine
10:42	91	J. C. Hamilton, Jr., Oklahoma City	Fowler			
	92	James B. McHale, Jr., Bethlehem, Pa.				
10:48	93	Tom Whiteway, Cleveland, Ohio	McNair 8+7	McNair 1 up		
	94	Harton S. Semple, Sewickley, Pa.				
	95	Keith Fowler, Bartlesville, Okla.	Jones		Levinson 2-1	
		Bye				
10:53	96	W. R. Dowtin, Charlotte, N. C.	Levinson 4+2	Levinson 4 up		
	97	James M. McNair, Aiken, S. C.	Kay			
	98	Thomas Jones, Jr., Canfield, Ohio				
		Bye				
10:59	99	J. O. Levinson, Kennebunk Beach, Me.	Rosburg 1 up	Cash 4+2		
	100	Edward A. Johnston, Towson, Md.	Cash 7+6			
	101	Oliver Kay, Toledo, Ohio				
		Bye				
11:04	102	R. E. Weston, Jr., Spokane, Wash.				
	103	Robert R. Rosburg, Stanford Univ., Calif.				
1:10	104	Walter Cash, Springfield, Mo.				
	105	Del Ryder, Grand Island, Neb.				

James D. Robinson Trophy.

Sunday morning golfers would not be visible to those attending neighboring St. John's Episcopal Church.

Although the big trees which shade the course look ancient, they are relatively recent additions. Many of the tall oaks were planted in the 1950s. Current greens superintendent Rodney Lingle says that a golf course provides ideal growing conditions for native trees because of the frequent watering and fertilizing.

At first the course was mowed with horse-drawn mowers. The horses were stabled in the old Buntyn carriage barn in the middle of the course. Gasoline-powered riding mowers proved to be hard on the course contours; now the greens are cut with walking mowers.

Irrigation began in 1935. A new well and sprinkling system was installed in 1936, saving the course from summer droughts. The watering system allowed for eight months of rye greens from October through May, and four months of Bermuda greens in June, July, August, and September.

One of the more significant changes in golf occurred in the 1950s, when many clubs introduced watering systems for the fairways. Fairways had been hard and fast, and by midsummer the turf was usually brown and burned out. Only the greens and tees were eternally green. Watered fairways changed the nature of golf. It became more important to move the ball in the air rather than on the ground, as balls did not roll as far on lush fairways. At the Memphis Country Club, fairways were still watered manually, but a system of automatic watering was installed on greens and tees in 1963. The process was not without difficulty. The company originally hired to do the work went out of business; lawsuits followed, and the work was completed by another company. New, fully automated sprinklers were added to the whole course in the 1980s.

Agronomists developed new strains of grass, and greens could be cut lower, making putting more difficult and more important in scoring. The MCC course was closed from June to August 1999, when the fairways were converted from common Bermuda to zoysia, and the greens were converted from 328 Bermuda to champion Bermuda.

Balls and clubs have steadily improved. Electric carts came into use in the 1950s and 1960s. They put many of the caddies out of work and were hard on the course. Asphalt cart paths were added to the course in 1979, and concrete was laid in 1999 and 2000.

In 1932, club president Dr. Richmond McKinney said, "We have a golf course that is most deceptive in appearance. To the casual golfer it appears as though it should be easy to play, but the only easy thing about it, and this is a feature which appeals to most golfers, is that it is not tiresome to the players, since it has an undulating surface, and no breathtaking hills to climb, but its thorough trappings and abundance of rough requires that all shots be played straight."

In 1989, John LaFoy was hired to renovate the tees and bunkers. LaFoy is a noted golf course architect, and also an authority on Donald Ross courses. He was educated at Clemson University and served in the U.S. Marine Corps in Vietnam, retiring with the rank of major. He began his career as a golf course architect with George W. Cobb, in Greenville, South Carolina, and spent five years at Augusta National Golf Club. He opened his own practice in 1982.

He has renovated or redesigned parts or all of thirteen Ross courses, and renovated courses of other "old masters" like Robert Trent Jones, Albert Tillinghast, and others. His own designs have won prizes: the Quarry Oaks Golf Club in Ashland, Nebraska, won the Golf Digest Best New Public Course of 1997, and the Glenmore Country Club in Charlottesville, Virginia, was named a top ten course by *Golf Course Magazine*. He served as president of the American Society of Golf Course Architects in 1999.

At the Memphis Country Club course, he reshaped the bunkers in the style of Ross, and re-leveled the tees, leaving the bunkers in the original locations. He added "chocolate drop" mounding on holes 9, 11, and 18.

Lady golfers and caddies at the Driving Park: Walter Lamb, Ruth Heyer of Mobile, Estelle Lamb Allen, and Evelyn Tate.

James Hamner was greens superintendent for forty years. He and Hugh Francis Sr., Greens Committee chairman, worked together for many years to groom and improve the course.

Rodney Lingle became superintendent in 1979. Lingle earned a B.S. in Agronomy with a speciality in Golf Course Management from Mississippi State University in 1973. He was superintendent of the golf course at the Hattiesburg, Mississippi, Country Club before coming to the Memphis Country Club.

He is proud of using the golf course maintenance crew for improvements instead of contracting the work outside. In 1982, they designed and installed the first completely automatic irrigation system. In 1988, they rebuilt all the bunkers, and in 1998, they reconstructed all the cart paths in concrete.

Big storms have damaged the trees on the course. In 1994, a February ice storm struck. On July 22, 2003, "straight line winds" took down about fifty trees but, according to Lingle, would have been much worse were it not for the constant care given to the trees.

The course plays at 6,700 yards from the championship tees, with a par of 70. It has been called "the hardest easy course in America."

The Golfer's Garland ~ 1793

Of rural diversions too long has the Chace,
All the honors usurped, and assumed the chief place;
But truth bids the Muse from henceforward proclaim,
That Goff, first of sports, shall stand foremost in frame.
O'er the Heath, see our heroes in uniform clad,
In parties well match'd, how they gracefully spread;
While with long strokes and short strokes they tend to the goal,
And with putt well directed plump into the hole.

At Goff we contend without rancour or spleen,
And bloodless the laurels we reap on the green;
From vig'rous exertions our raptures arise,
And to crown our delights no poor fugitive dies.
From exercise keen, from strength active and bold,
We'll traverse the green, and forget we grow old;
Blue devils, diseases, dull sorrow and care,
Knock'd down by our balls as they whiz thro' the air.
Health, happiness, harmony, friendship, and fame,
Are the fruits and rewards of our favorite game;
A sport so distinguish'd the fair must approve,
Then to Goff give the day, and the ev'ning to love.

Our first standing toast we'll to Goffing assign,
No other amusement's so truly divine;
It has charms for the aged, as well as the young,
Then as first of field sports let its praises be sung.

The next we shall drink to our friends far and near,
And the memory of those who no longer appear;
Who have play'd their last round, and pass'ed over that bourne
From which the best Goffer can never return.

"The Goff. Heori-Comical Poem in Three Cantos."
Quoted in Nevin Gibson's, The Pictorial Encyclopedia of Golf.

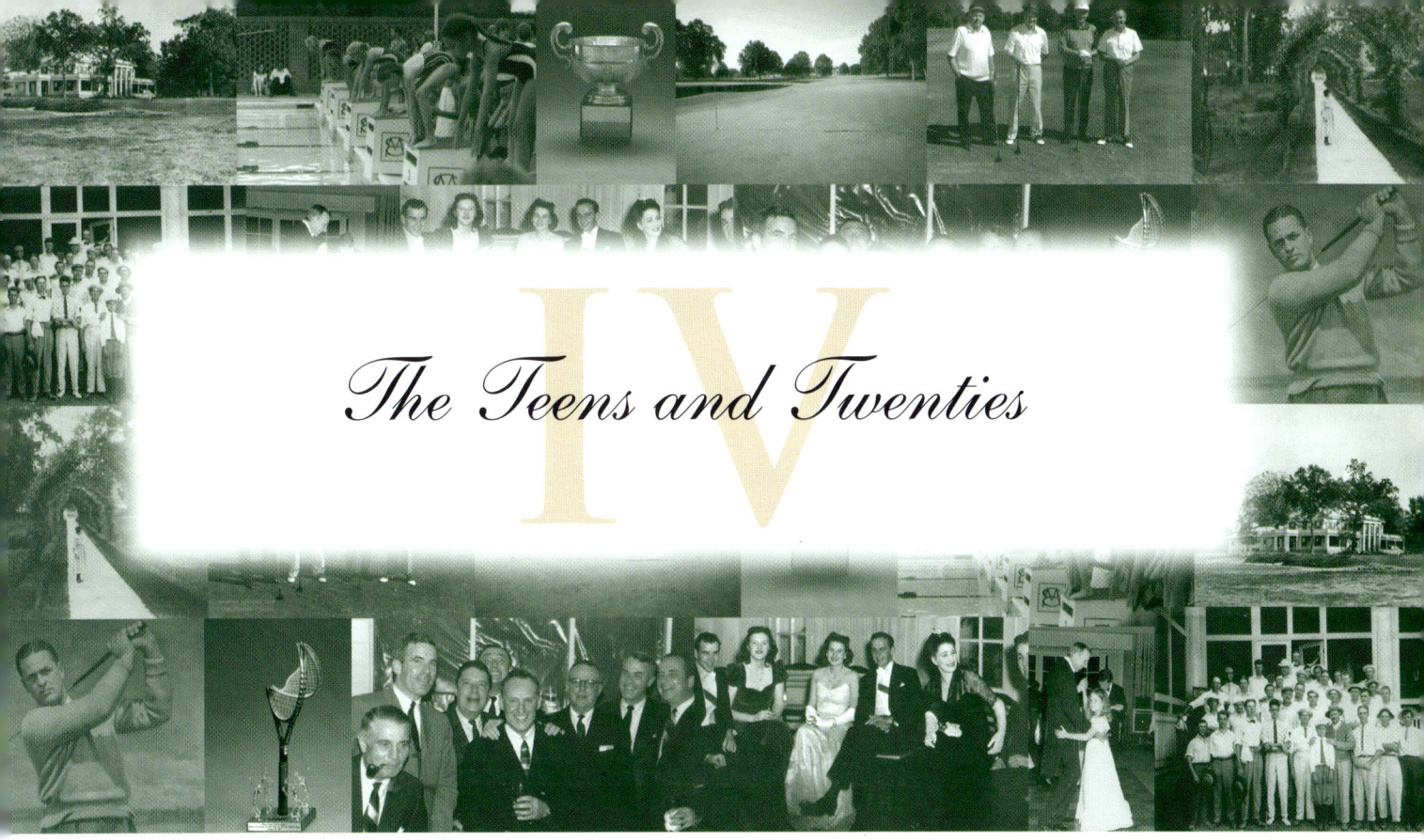

IV

The Teens and Twenties

While Memphians enjoyed their new country club, war was ravaging Europe. Americans watched nervously. In 1915, German U-boats sank the British steamship *Lusitania*, and many Americans were drowned. Woodrow Wilson was reelected, campaigning on the slogan "He kept us out of war," but most people thought it was just a matter of time before the United States became involved.

Closer to home, the revolutionary and bandit Pancho Villa was causing trouble on the Mexican border, and General John J. Pershing was ordered to capture him.

In 1916, the submachine gun was invented by Brigadier General John T. Thompson and known as the Tommy gun. By 1917, it was clear that the United States would not be able to stay out of the war. A special session of Congress in April passed war resolutions and diplomatic relations with Germany were severed. Troops were recalled from the Mexican border and prepared for service in Europe. The Selective Service Act was passed. In June, the first U.S. troops arrived in France. Soon the names of the Marne, Belleau Wood, the Meuse, and the Argonne were in daily headlines.

World War I ended with the signing of the armistice at the eleventh hour of the eleventh day of the eleventh month in 1918. Parades and celebrations welcomed the peace.

During the war years, Martin J. Condon served as the third president of the country club. He had the unusual distinction of serving as president of both the Nashville Golf and Country Club, forerunner of the Belle Meade Country Club, and the Memphis Country Club.

Born in Rogersville, Tennessee, in 1857, Condon was educated at Georgetown University in Washington, D.C. He was elected mayor of Knoxville at the age of twenty-five, before moving to Nashville in 1888 where he bought an interest in Bruton Brothers & Deadrick and changed the name to Bruton & Condon Snuff Company. In 1900, he was elected president of the organizing group which secured a charter for the Nashville Golf and Country Club, which then moved to Belle Meade in 1914 and changed its name in 1921. In the early 1900s, Condon was elected president of the American Snuff Company and lived in New York for a number of years, until company headquarters moved to Memphis in 1912.

The company, with offices in the Exchange Building at Second and Madison, concentrated on manufacturing snuff from 1912 to 1952, when it acquired a producer of chewing tobacco. In the 1950s and 1960s, the company expanded to include insecticides and popcorn. In 1966, the name of the company was changed to Conwood, a contraction of the names of its two chief executives, Martin Condon III and James E. Harwood Jr., both later presidents of the country club.

The elder Condon was an outstanding golfer. Although he never won a state championship, he was called "the Father of Tennessee Golf," and the Tennessee State Amateur trophy bears his name. He was runner-up in the Tennessee State Championship when he was sixty-nine years old and was also United States

Martin J. Condon, president 1916–1919.

Senior Golf Champion. He died in Memphis in 1940.

Condon's term as president lasted from 1916 to 1919. The yearly dues for regular resident members were raised from $60 to $80, lady members from $10 to $25, and junior members from $10 to $25 a year. The president stated that, in view of the dues raises, some necessary improvements should be made as soon as possible.

Each member was to have the privilege of inviting six guests to the Saturday evening dinner dances, provided that the assistant secretary of the club was given their names by six P.M. the previous day. It was stressed that members were to be responsible for the conduct of guests while in the club.

MARGUERITE GAUT

In 1916, the Women's Tennessee Golf Association was organized, and the first tournament was played at the Memphis Country Club. Marguerite Gaut of Memphis was the winner and went on to become one of Tennessee's famous golfers.

She was born Marguerite Thrasher in Knoxville in 1888, and married David C. Gaut in 1910. That year she started playing golf on the advice of her doctor, who told her to get outdoors. David Gaut was also a talented golfer and the couple played golf together twice a week during the season for more than fifty-four years.

The Gauts moved to Memphis in 1912 and joined the Memphis Country Club. Dave Gaut was credit manager at Bry's Department Store, worked at Union Planters Bank and Brodnax, then spent thirty-three years with the Mutual Benefit Life Insurance Company.

Marguerite Gaut won her first tournament, the Women's Southern title, in 1913. She credited the Scottish pro at the Memphis Country Club, Bill Brown, with telling her, "You can recover from any shot except a missed putt." She said her putting was responsible for her many wins. She beat Babe Didrickson Zaharias in a 1936 tournament in Texas by sinking a twenty-foot putt on the nineteenth hole.

In 1918 she received a medal for organizing a tournament with a record number of entries to benefit war work in World War I, and in 1948 she was given an award for her

Marguerite Gaut.

service to the Red Cross during the Second World War.

In 1922 she held four championships at once: city, state, western, and southern. In 1937 she was responsible for bringing the United States Women's Golf Association Tournament to Memphis and the Memphis Country Club. It was the first USWGA tournament held in the South. The MCC board presented her with an engraved diamond and sapphire wristwatch.

The *Nashville Banner* called Mrs. Gaut "the South's most energetic worker in the interest of golf." Trophy cases at her home on Union were bulging with trophies. Her titles included the Women's Southern Amateur six times, the Women's Western Amateur in 1922, and eleven Memphis city titles.

She was president of the Women's Southern Golf Association in 1930. She became the southern representative on the boards of the Women's Western Golf Association and the Tennessee Golf Association. In 1961, the Southern Women's Golf Association named a tournament in her honor, the Marguerite Gaut Senior Women's Golf Invitational Tournament.

She died at age seventy-nine, on December 11, 1967, the day after her fifty-seventh wedding anniversary. Her husband died nine days later. She became the first woman inducted into the Tennessee Sports Hall of Fame in 1967. In 2003, she was inducted into the Tennessee Golf Hall of Fame.

COUNTRY CLUB LIFE

Social events flourished at the Memphis Country Club. At the meeting of the Board of

The sapphire and diamond watch presented to Marguerite Gaut by the Memphis Country Club.

Directors on May 14, 1919, it was proposed that the club entertain with a dance in November in honor of debutantes, and a committee was appointed to make plans.

That year Mr. and Mrs. James Rogers Smith invited two hundred guests to a party honoring their daughter Eleanor. The newspaper reported that Mrs. Smith wore "a model of black satin trimmed in lace, with a corsage bouquet of pink roses." Her daughter wore "a frock of pink Pompadour taffeta with silver trimmings and edged with pansies, with which she wore a corsage bouquet of pink and lavender sweetpeas." The guests enjoyed dancing in the ballroom, where "palms were used abundantly to make the scene a more attractive one. Midway of the evening a buffet was served to those who had the pleasure of enjoying Mrs. Smith's hospitality."

At the annual meeting in May 1920, the president reported that the club operated at a profit of twelve thousand dollars. But costs were going up, and dues were increased to one hundred dollars a year. The president reported that he had communicated with all members about the dues raise, and no objection had been made except by two members.

Then came a change in the United States Constitution threatening the conviviality of country clubs. On December 18, 1917, the Eighteenth Amendment to the Constitution outlawed the manufacture, sale, or transportation of alcoholic liquors. It was ratified in January 1919. Prohibition became the law of the land. Bootleggers flourished.

When the Board of Directors of the country club met on January 23, 1920, one of the items up for discussion was "the matter of enforcement of the National Prohibition Law," which had gone into effect on January 16. The president was instructed to "take such steps necessary to enforce the law, and to notify members in writing that it was the duty of the Board to enforce the law so far as the Club was concerned, and they were requested not to bring or consume liquor on the Club grounds."

The Western Amateur Golf Championship, "by far the most important golf tournament ever held in the South," was held at the club from July 12 through July 17, 1920. The country club president reported that C. O. Pfeil, chairman of the golf committee, secured the tournament for the club by "making certain promises as to Tennessee still being 'Wet' and got by with it."

A youthful golfer from Atlanta was the focus of attention at that tournament. On July 13, eighteen-year-old Bobby Jones fired a record-setting 69, better than any round ever played on the course, finishing ahead of some 150 competitors in the first half of the qualifying round.

Robert Tyre Jones was only eighteen when he first played in Memphis, but he went on to become one of the best-known golfers, and according to the *New Yorker* magazine, "golf's chivalric ideal . . . handsome, gracious, literate—and, never forsaking his amateur status, he played golf like a dream."

Born in Atlanta in 1902, Jones was a clean-cut American hero, with degrees in engineering and law. In a career lasting only ten years, he won thirteen of the twenty-one major championships he entered. He kept his amateur status but won three British Opens and four U.S. Opens in his ten-year career. In 1930 he won what was known as the Grand Slam: the British Amateur Championship, the British Open, the U.S. Open, and the

The Teens and Twenties

Bobby Jones.

U.S. Amateur Championship. After that feat, he retired from tournament golf. He was only twenty-eight. The *New York Times* marked the event with verse: "With dignity he quits the memorable scene/ On which he nothing common did, or mean."

He became a lawyer, was a founder of Augusta National Golf Club, and made several instructional golf films. His health deteriorated, and he spent his last years in a wheelchair, dying in 1971.

The *Commercial Appeal* called Jones's game at the Memphis Country Club "the greatest round of golf ever shot in Memphis" and described it in loving detail.

The dogleg eighth, 388 yards long, usually a bugbear to visiting golfers, came mighty close to tossing the youthful Georgian off his record-breaking stride. As it was, it broke his string of consecutive par or better holes. He hooked into the rough, overshot the green with his second and was too strong coming out. However, he retained his putting touch and holed out in five, one above par.

But just by way of showing that little things like that don't distress him, Bob promptly proceeded to take a three on the 312 yard ninth, one under par. His drive was easily 250 yards down the middle of the slot. His niblick second dropped dead three inches from the pin. A blind man could have holed that putt.

His second round was equally brilliant. "After spinning out a Babe Ruth tee wallop, Bob spanked his iron second with too much enthusiasm, and it hopped over the green. He chipped up close and was down in a par four . . . His drive was strong and straight off the seventeenth tee . . . His run-up approach left him with a ten footer, and he conquered it with his longest putt of the day . . . The 363 yard eighteenth was simply played, his second was on the green and he was down in two putts."

But even the spectacular round did not win the tournament for Jones. Chick Evans of Chicago defeated Jones and went on to defeat Clarence Wolff of St. Louis in the final round to win his fifth Western Open title.

Memphians had another chance to see Jones play. After the tournament was over, "the Atlanta marvel" played an exhibition match on Sunday afternoon. Jones and Charlie Pfeil of Memphis played Jimmy Ward of Kansas City, paired with local star Jack Edrington.

THE ROARING TWENTIES

Thomas Jefferson Turley brought the country club into the twenties, serving as president from 1919 until 1926. A graduate of Virginia Military Institute and the University of Virginia, he was the son of United States Senator Thomas Battle Turley, and grandson of Thomas Jefferson Turley, a leading lawyer in the early days of Shelby County.

The first T. J. Turley died in 1854 in a freak accident. He was attending court at Raleigh when he leaned on his cane, it broke, and the sharp end pierced his side. The second T J. Turley was president of the Turley Bullington Company and lived in the Buntyn neighborhood.

Americans greeted the end of the war with glee and launched into a spree of spending and gaiety. It was the Jazz Age, when all America seemed to go on a binge. Times were flush, Americans flaunted Prohibition, danced the Charleston, and followed the activities of Babe Ruth, Charles Lindbergh, Al Jolson, Al Capone, and Rudolph Valentino. The election of 1920 turned into a referendum on Woodrow Wilson's efforts to take the country into the League of Nations. Americans, tired of international involvement, elected the Republican candidate, Warren G. Harding.

During the hot summer of 1920, the Tennessee legislature met in Nashville to vote on the Nineteenth Amendment, which would give women the right to vote. Tennessee was the thirty-sixth and final state to ratify the amendment; passage in Tennessee made it the law of the land. Suffragettes and Antis from across the country swarmed the state capital for a hard-fought fight. The

Suffs sported yellow ribbons and roses, and the Antis wore red.

Although former governor Malcolm Patterson, an MCC member, had said earlier, "Let the women pray and the men vote," many of the most fervent supporters of the Suffrage Amendment were Memphians, and the Shelby County delegation to the legislature voted unanimously for the amendment. Several of the active supporters were country club members, including Edward H. Crump, Guston Fitzhugh, Frank Rice, and C. P. J. Mooney.

Fashion followed the new freedom. Women's skirts crept higher and higher, and the more daring Flappers rolled their stockings lower and lower. In reaction to the busts and bustles of earlier days, the silhouette was straight and narrow. Well-endowed women strapped their bosoms down to achieve the little boy look. Hair was bobbed and hats fitted the head closely.

An article in *The American Golfer* in 1920 urged women to wear knickerbockers like men wore. Called "The Curse of the Skirt," the article claimed that "If knickerbockers do replace skirts on the links, mixed foursomes may become more harmonious. At least the husband will lose one alibi for not playing with his wife. He can no longer complain that the fluttering and flapping of her skirt on a windy day interferes with his putting."

Perhaps women took their new freedoms too seriously. In May 1921, it was reported that Mrs. S. H. Phillips and Mrs. J. H. Hodges were throwing dice for money on the country club's living room floor! President Turley himself had observed the proceedings for fifteen or twenty minutes, as had other members. The board agreed that this was a gross violation of the rules of the club. Mr. Phillips and Major Hodges were each fined twenty-five dollars for the conduct of their wives.

Thomas J. Turley, president 1919–1926.

Ladies were in disrepute for another infraction. The board was of the unanimous opinion that smoking by ladies should not be allowed in any part of the club except the ladies' locker room and the private dining room.

In downtown Memphis, the civic auditorium opened in 1924 with March King John Philip Sousa and his band playing the opening concert. The Gothic towers of Southwestern College, now Rhodes College, were going up on North Parkway. The new $5 million Peabody Hotel opened its doors on September 1, 1925, and the city boasted a new "skyscraper," the Columbian Mutual Tower on Main at Court Square.

These were the obvious signs of Memphis's progress. When the Federal Census

Bureau estimated the population of Memphis at 172,000 in 1924, Mayor Rowlett Paine and the city fathers were indignant, claiming a population of 200,000. The city was growing, they insisted, and the buildings downtown showed it.

Memphis was called "the Buckle of the Bible Belt," but it also was known as "the Murder Capital of America." Under the sanctimonious outer layer was a raunchy side, with saloons and houses of ill-fame on Beale Street and in such colorfully named neighborhoods as Shirt Tail Bend, Happy Valley, Whiskey Hollow, and Hell's Half Acre.

The country club board meetings' minutes tactfully avoid mention of liquor and drinking during the twenties. Prohibition was the law of the land, but when the front doors of the saloons along Beale Street closed, the proprietors just opened the back doors and operated as "blind pigs." Bootlegging was enormously profitable and was about the only truly racially integrated occupation in Memphis. As the president of the United States, Calvin Coolidge, said, "The business of America is business."

At the Memphis Country Club, the board was called upon to settle disputes between members. In September 1922, Mr. G. W. Mewborn registered a complaint against Mr. Brown for "ungentlemanly conduct in the caddy house." Mr. Wortham Agee supported Mr. Brown, while Mr. Landis Rowe substantiated statements made by Mr. Mewborn. The gentlemen steamed, but the board decided that no action was necessary.

Improvements in 1922 included the purchase of a $285 dishwasher and the installation of a laundry at a cost of $1,260. But a motion to build a dancing pavilion on the grounds was defeated. Although the club operated with a profit of some $7,500 that year, the auditors found a discrepancy in the accounts, and the bookkeeper resigned.

In 1923, an engineer reported on the water system of the club. The deep well that supplied

The water tower was a feature at the second clubhouse.

water was deemed insufficient for the current usage. A new steel water tank and tower was built, where the Health Club aerobics room is today. The foundation for the water tank was found while excavating for the aerobics room. The club was finally connected to the city water system in 1926.

A committee reported that the furniture, carpets, and decorations in the large living room and large dining room "make a very bad appearance and are very much out of date. . . . to fix the club up along modern lines with the proper decorations" would cost between ten thousand and thirteen thousand dollars. There was much discussion about the running expenses, the proposed improvements, and retiring the bonded indebtedness. The Entertainment Committee was once again charged with taking measures to stop the "objectionable habits" of visitors at club dances.

During the 1920s, Clarence Saunders, a member of the Memphis Country Club decided to build his own golf course, just across the street from the club course. Saunders launched the first Piggly Wiggly store in Memphis in 1916. His store allowed shoppers to help themselves to products, rather than depending upon clerks to get the groceries, and it revolutionized grocery shopping. By 1923, there were twenty-six hundred self-service stores nationwide. Saunders lost control of his company but rebounded to try other innovative methods of merchandizing before his death in 1953.

At one point Saunders owned a professional football team, called the Sole Owner Tigers, named after his next chain of stores called "Clarence Saunders Sole Owner of My Name." The story goes that he arrived late to a game and demanded that the officials start the play over. When they refused, he said, "I own the field, I own the team, now start over." They did.

Shields McIlwaine, in his book *Memphis Down in Dixie*, says that Saunders was poor at golf but expansive in betting.

Club Team Competition Trophy, 1924.

> Memphis has not had so popular a golfer as this man. Club members argued over whose turn it was to play with him and sometimes had to match coins for the decision . . . Clarence Saunders was the gilded dub: he would bet anything—$100 a game or $100 a hole . . .

> Local gossip has it that the Memphis Country Club by protesting—albeit futilely—against these gold-rush foursomes caused the grocery king to add a private course to the super estate on which, in the fullness of his glory, he began to erect a salmon-colored granite and marble pile, now known as the Pink Palace.

Saunders lost his first fortune in 1924; the unfinished mansion became a city museum, and the proposed golf course became the subdivision Chickasaw Gardens.

A dispute arose over Saunders's membership in the country club. As part of the bankruptcy proceedings, his club membership certificate had been turned over to the bankruptcy trustee and offered for sale. A legal opinion said that Saunders did not have membership privileges.

Saunders insisted that he did. He was furious. He wrote to President Turley:

> Certainly I have been "hounded" sufficiently by that same crowd to make this last attempted outrage unnecessary. Some "sneak" telephoned Mr. Chas. W. Thompson (the bankruptcy trustee) and represented himself as Mr. Churchill, the Secretary of the Club, and demanded that he, Mr. Chas. W. Thompson, remit immediately for what the "sneak" claimed over the phone to be a past due bill that the "sneak" claimed to be owing the Club . . . Despicable is a mild word to use for one who would do such a dishonest thing as to thus represent himself as Mr. Churchill . . . what I am saying in this letter is to fit only those who have attempted to invade my social life in the "sneaking" manner that is so manifest . . . why even discuss such a preposterous proposition when I own now the self-same Certificate of Membership . . . not only do I own this membership Certificate now, but I have never ceased to own it, and I have physical possession of the certificate.

Legal opinion was against Saunders but said that if he bought the certificate back from the trustee, he would have to be reelected to membership. Then Saunders was spotted playing golf at the club with Mr. Miles and Mr. Fitzhugh. The treasurer was instructed not to deposit Saunders's dues checks until the matter was settled. Saunders remained a member of the country club.

From the beginning of the club, new members had been elected by a vote of the whole membership. A candidate's name was entered into a large leather ledger, and members signed their names indicating approval. When a candidate got fifty signatures, he was elected. Now it was reported that few country clubs in the country used this system, and that, due to the growth of Memphis, it was increasingly impractical. "The majority of the applicants are practically unknown to the members of the Club . . . there is no way for the Board of Directors to keep an undesirable man from being elected and there is also no way to ascertain whether or not the black ball privilege is being properly used."

A secret Membership Committee was proposed. If the committee, after examining the candidate, recommended him, the name would be posted in a prominent place in the clubhouse for twenty-one days, then the Board of Directors would consider any objections that members gave to his election. Two negative votes from the board would keep a candidate from being elected. "It being understood that the Board in voting on applicants shall consider only the social fitness and character, and not personal prejudice or bias." After two years of wrangling, the board decided to go back to the old system, with the exception that four blackballs were needed now for a proposed member to be rejected.

In 1925, the club entertained two golf tournaments, the City of Memphis championship and the State of Tennessee championship. A drought had practically killed the grass, and the club went to considerable expense to prepare for the tournaments. Winter greens were also installed, and new pipes were laid through the whole course, in order to prevent future drought troubles.

The Greens Committee reported that the pro could not satisfactorily look after the greens, give lessons, and attend to the golf business. A greenskeeper and a professional were hired. In 1923, the golf professional's salary was one hundred dollars a month.

The privileges of the club were extended to some one hundred members of the National Furniture Warehouse Association in January, upon payment of regular greens fees. A party of Chicago golfers recommended by the president of the Illinois Central Railroad and the president and faculty of Southwestern College were also extended golfing privileges.

The president reported that the club was in good financial condition, that ten thousand dollars had been spent on improvements, and that, with the raise in dues, ten thousand dollars in indebtedness had been paid off.

The club owned about two acres of land at the corner of Southern and Greer, with a four-room cottage on the property, renting at fifteen dollars a month. Since the club did not use the property, the president proposed that it be exchanged for a piece of ground the same size fronting the golf course, lying between No. 2 green and the property of D. S. Weaver: "Any member who is given to slicing probably knows the land I speak of."

A lot at the northwest corner of Midland and the club grounds, fronting 100 feet on Midland by a depth of 236 feet on the country club grounds, was purchased for thirty-five hundred dollars. The men's Tap Room in the basement was redone. A debate about inviting nonmembers to events at the club caused great concern.

A special membership category was added in 1921 to develop young golfers. Twenty-five special memberships were added to encourage young men to take up the sport; those between the ages of fifteen and twenty-one paid fifty dollars a year, and those between twenty-one and twenty-five paid one hundred dollars a year.

In 1922, it was reported that L. A. Montedonico Jr. had played golf on several occasions with Porter, the caddy master. He was reprimanded, suspended for sixty days, and his father was notified.

In 1926, an accusation that the caddy master was selling golf balls was referred to the Greens Committee. The board also announced that employees of the club had been abusing the privilege of playing golf and that no employee was to be allowed to play golf at any time.

THE SWIMMING POOL

Throughout the early years of the 1920s, the question of a swimming pool kept coming up. When some complained that the pool would not be used by all members, the president pointed out that there were four hundred fifty members of the club, and only some two hundred of them played golf. Committee chairman C. O. Pfeil reported that a pool would cost between fifteen thousand and twenty thousand dollars, and members debated how to pay for it. Some thought that selling twenty-five additional memberships would cover the cost; others suggested a private subscription. In the end, a dues increase was approved, raising the dues to one hundred fifty dollars a year, with the increase going to build the pool.

A year later, the pool was still being discussed. Mr. S. M. Williamson complained there was considerable objection to the swimming pool among the members, but his proposal to return the matter to the membership for more discussion was voted down.

The pool was finally built, and the newspaper reported, "That swimming is not a mere passing fancy with society folk has been demonstrated by the building of many private pools and the new one at the country club without doubt will make the place more popular than at any other period in its history."

The "new natorium" opened on July 22, 1922. The two lifeguards, Joe Rice Dockery and J. Eugene Boulden, formerly of the University of Illinois Athletic Club, gave a display of fancy swimming strokes and dives.

More than three hundred members turned out for the formal dedication.

Most every one in society worthwhile who had not begun his or her summer vacation or who plan to keep cool in Memphis for the summer was there, and no more brilliant assembly was ever seen at the country club than the gathering that first partook of the elaborate menu in the club house and then informally gathered around the littoral of the limpid waters of the pool, watched the life guards go through some fancy swimming and diving, and after the stentorian announcement of J. M. Dockery, master of ceremonies, that the pool was formally opened, either donned bathing suits or repaired to the ballroom for the dancing which lasted till midnight. There was little ostentation about the opening, the whole affair being characterized by a delightful sense of camaraderie reminding many of the older members of the club as they expressed it of the old days when it was more like a big family.

The Milnor boys at the swimming pool.

The newspaper report continued, "Every table in the spacious ballroom was the center of a group of delighted members of the club and guests, almost every one of them being presided over by a host or hostess to specially invited guests. There were many unique and tasteful table decorations with summer blossoms rivaling in riot of color the bright hues of summer frocks."

Mrs. T. J. Turley, wife of the president, presided over a table of ten guests. The largest party was that given by Mrs. Rayburn Dunscomb at a beautifully decorated table near the center of the ballroom. Miss Frances Dockery was hostess to a gathering of members of the younger set, an even dozen girls enjoying her hospitality. A lively party of ten was at the table of Dr. and Mrs. Percy Wood. Mr. and Mrs. Edward G. Riddick entertained honoring Mrs. Thetus Sims, wife of former Congressman Sims, and her daughter Enid.

Now that the pool was built, there had to be rules. In 1922, a committee composed of Rowland Darnell, Nash Buckingham, and Charles O. Pfiel presented regulations for its operation, such as:

- The water in the pool was to be changed every three months, and the pool washed with Sapolio. The water was to be analyzed every thirty days.

- A vacuum cleaner of the type now in use by the Nineteenth Century Club was to be purchased, and the pool would be closed every Monday morning for cleaning.

- A Pool Master would be hired to serve as lifeguard, to give private swimming lessons for one dollar for a thirty-minute lesson, to sell or rent bathing suits and accessories, and to see that the pool was properly used at all times.

- No one was to use the pool unless the Pool Master was present, the hours were 8:30 A.M. to 11:00 P.M., every one must sign the register, and the club was not to be responsible in any way for accident, loss or service.

- Loud shouting, rough play, pushing one another, splashing, spitting, and unsanitary offenses would subject offenders to removal of pool privileges.

Bathing dress was an important issue, and here the board passed the buck:

Members of the Country Club and their guests will be permitted to wear any type or color or style of bathing suit they see fit. It is taken for granted that the members of the Memphis Country Club possess the proper discernment which marks the standing of their club. If at any time the choice of costume or conduct of any individual member offends, the swimming pool committee will receive in confidence, written, intelligent complaint and attempt correction intelligently.

At least one denizen of the new pool knew how to wear a bathing costume with flair. In 1921, the idea of a beauty contest occurred to city fathers in Atlantic City as a way to prolong the tourist season. They asked various cities to send a candidate, and the *Commercial Appeal* decided to sponsor a contest for the prettiest girl in Memphis. They invited all the season's debutantes to participate. At a pageant at Loew's Palace in August 1923, the winner,

Elizabeth Willins Mallory, dressed in white georgette trimmed with black velvet and rhinestones with gold beads, "glided through the evening's entertainment with a poise and dignity that was highly appreciated by the throngs who attended the presentation."

She was the daughter of cotton broker and MCC member Albert H. Mallory and his wife Laura Willins Mallory. Outfitted in a new wardrobe supplied by Gerber's, Bry's, Lowenstein's, and Goldsmith's department stores, with dresses for afternoon, evening, and dinner, as well as a complete bathing costume including cape, hat, hosiery, and undergarments, she had "all the exquisite finery so necessary to the girl who shall storm the citadel of America's court of beauty," according to the newspaper.

She was accompanied to Atlantic City by her chaperone, the wife of another country club member, Mrs. Hugh S. Hayley, and her whole family. The *Commercial Appeal* described the Miss America pageant as "a world conclave of feminine charm" on the famed Boardwalk. Elizabeth did not win the Golden Mermaid first prize, but she came home with three enormous trophies: first prize in the Bathers' Revue, Intercity Division, Southern Section; first prize in the Intercity Beauty Contest; and first prize in the Rolling Chair Parade.

In 1924, the annual income of the club was given as $64,477.95. The sources of income were dues, restaurant receipts, rental of rooms and garages, sale of cigars and soft drinks, locker room profits, transfer and greens fees, rental of the ballroom for entertainments, and miscellaneous items.

Expenses were listed as salaries; clubhouse operating expenses ($13,610.00); swimming pool operating expenses ($666.15); lights, fuel, water, entertainments, repairs, insurance, automobile expenses, magazines and stationery, tennis expenses ($191.25); taxes, association dues, laundry, legal fees, and interest on bonds and notes. The biggest expense was the golf course and the salaries of the caddy master and greens keeper ($15,514.61). Operating expenses totaled $58,047.01.

Other expenses were a new well and pump house; silver, china, and linen; new office furniture and fixtures; a new truck; and new decorations.

Miss Memphis Elizabeth Mallory (left) in the Miss America contest.

Mr. and Mrs. James Rogers Smith

Miss Eleanor Smith

Memphis Country Club

Thursday evening, May the twenty-seventh

at nine o'clock

Dancing   Please respond

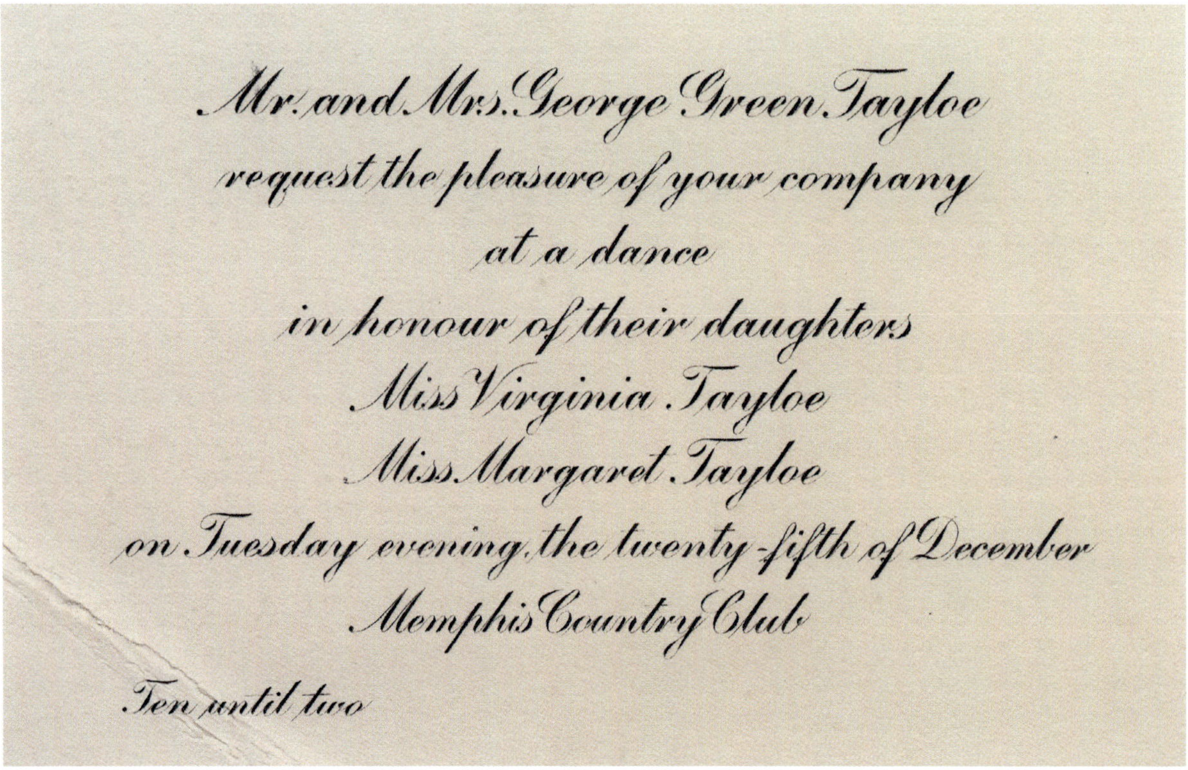

Mr. and Mrs. George Green Tayloe
request the pleasure of your company
at a dance
in honour of their daughters
Miss Virginia Tayloe
Miss Margaret Tayloe
on Tuesday evening, the twenty-fifth of December
Memphis Country Club

Ten until two

This page and opposite: Invitations to parties in the 1920s.

Jesse Peders Norfleet became president of the Memphis Country Club in 1926. He was educated at the University of Virginia and Vanderbilt University. In June 1899, Mr. Norfleet joined his father's firm, Sledge & Norfleet, and was with this company for most of his life. He held many positions in business and fraternal organizations: director of the National Bank of Commerce, the Memphis Branch Federal Reserve Bank of St. Louis, the Memphis Compress Company, a trustee of Vanderbilt University, a director for thirty-one years at Memphis Power & Light Company or its predecessors, until it was sold to city of Memphis. He was president of the Board of Education, Memphis City Schools, from 1914 to 1918.

Norfleet was chosen the second king of the Cotton Carnival in 1932. He married Elise Vance, who is credited with planting the first azaleas in Memphis.

On October 3, 1927, the *Commercial Appeal* announced that Mrs. Allie Starke Patteson had been chosen as hostess at the Memphis Country Club, the first lady manager. She was described by the newspaper as "a lovely lady of high social standing, gracious and efficient."

Born in 1875, she attended the Higbee School and Hollins College. She was one of the founders of the Vanity Fair Club, an elite social club, and was active in the Red Cross and the YWCA. She married James Patteson in 1896 and was divorced in 1924. They had seven children; the youngest, Elaine, was the first queen of Cotton Carnival.

She was hired at a salary of $125 a month, with a room and meals for herself and her daughter. Her salary was increased by $25 a month in 1928, when she was given the title of acting manager. She served as hostess and manager of the Memphis Country Club from 1927 until 1945. "Upon her retirement, the Board of Directors presented her with an honorary life membership in the Club in recognition and appreciation of the efficiency and faithfulness of her management and of her contribution to the social prestige of the Club."

Warfield Rodgers, a young man from Memphis, was a student at Sewanee during the twenties. When he came home for the holidays in 1928, he found many invitations, promising a busy social life for the college set. Many of the parties took place at the Memphis Country Club. The Girls Cotillion Club held a "Showboat Party" on November 20. Mr. and Mrs. George Green Tayloe entertained at a dance in honor of their daughters Virginia and Margaret on

J. P. Norfleet, president 1926–1928.

November 25. Phi Kappa Fraternity held a costume party, "The Big Circus," on December 26.

Rodgers was elected a member of the Yuletide Revelers. The stipend for membership was ten dollars. The Revel took place on December 24 at the country club, and he was instructed "in arranging to escort your Lady Fair, remember that only members of the Cotillion Club and the Girls Dinner Club, and their out-of-town house guests, are invited. Save embarrassment by respecting this rule." So that there would be no confusion, a list of the proper girls to invite was included. Shades of Peter Taylor's "The Old Forest"!

By 1929, the club's revenues totaled $77,002.06 from dues and fees, and $67,464.96 from the operation of the restaurant, rooms and garages, golf course, lockers and swimming pool. Expenses totaled $61,235.13.

Things were going well. Then came the Wall Street crash.

Allie Starke Patteson's Secret Recipe for Frozen Tomato Salad

A Memphis Country Club classic for over seventy-five years. Mrs. Patteson would never fully divulge the ingredients. Supposedly the secret was in the homemade mayonnaise.

- 1 quart can tomato juice
- 1 pint can crushed pineapple
- 1 (8-ounce) package of cream cheese or 1 cup of cottage cheese
- 1 pint homemade mayonnaise
- red food coloring
- seasonings: grated onion, salt, pepper, grated ginger

Mix the ingredients together and pour into two ice trays. Place the trays in the freezer. If preferred, the mixture may be frozen in an ice cream maker.

The Teens and Twenties

The Richmond McKinney Era

The sixth president of the Memphis Country Club, Dr. Richmond McKinney, was elected in 1928. He was to serve until 1941, the longest term of any president, and his tenure saw the club through some of its most difficult times.

Dr. McKinney took office at the end of the 1920s. He might have expected to preside over a gay and growing club. Instead, the Wall Street crash in 1929 plunged the country into the Great Depression. Across the nation, country clubs closed their doors as their memberships dropped.

Richmond McKinney was an eye, ear, nose and throat specialist. He had a busy private practice, was head of a division at the University of Tennessee Medical School, and served on the charity staffs of two hospitals. He was a past president of the American Bronchoscopic Society, and published articles in scientific journals.

In addition to all of this, he took on the presidency of the country club. It became another full-time job. The *Press Scimitar* reported in 1933, "Instead of accepting the club presidency as an unencumbered evidence of good will, as he might well have, he turned to it gladly and made it his hobby. Applying his brisk energy and intelligence to its problems, he went into it like a boy with a new puzzle."

Every afternoon, after leaving his office, he came to the club and strolled around, checking on every detail. He was affectionately known as "the Czar of Buntyn."

His kingdom was professionally surveyed in 1930. F. J. O'Leary, Valuation Engineer with offices in the Peabody Hotel, presented "An Appraisal of Memphis Country Club Buildings and Equipment as a Going Concern as of Oct. 20th, 1930." He surveyed the clubhouse, its heating, plumbing, electrical systems, awnings and screens, the swimming pool and equipment, the servants' quarters, the guests' garage, golf shop, pergola, summerhouse, sunhouses on the golf course, water works, and barn, with equipment and furnishings, tennis courts, fences, arbors, pavements, and sewer piping.

Dr. Richmond McKinney, the longest-serving president.

The inventory listed such details as a Hoover vacuum cleaner worth $75, a hand-operated dough mixer worth $26, a two compartment wooden laundry tub worth $60, a swivel stool worth $4, two hundred tablecloths worth $190, cocktail shakers worth $41, one lemon squeezer at $3, fifty-two hundred pieces of china at $850, and seventeen kitchen aprons at $14. Furniture included twenty Chinese red folding chairs, $40; a ping pong table, $12; a silver flower basket, $25; fifty-two cane seat bentwood chairs, $158; and one goldfish bowl, $6.

O'Leary figured the total insurable costs at $190,432, and the total replacement costs at $287,798.

According to the newspaper, when the Depression came, the country club was hit as was every part of society. "Panicky officials promptly raised the price of everything. Memberships were sold, attendance dropped off. 'It was like an old men's home,' a veteran clubman said."

Dr. McKinney moved swiftly. He cut prices and eliminated the charge for using the swimming pool. The moves were not universally popular. The newspaper reported that "the Old Guard began to grumble. 'He'll break the club. Doctors are bad businessmen. They can't even handle their own accounts.' Sure ruin was predicted on all sides."

But Dr. McKinney was convinced that lowering prices was the way to attract business. In his 1929 president's report, he said, "I should like to see the price of memberships remain at a low figure so that young men and women may join. The life of the club is youth."

Dr. McKinney planned more changes. He tore down an old wire fence and planted a hedge around the whole property. He announced plans for improving the clubhouse and modernizing the golf course. "We will then be in a position to invite some of the outstanding golfing events that should come this way . . . and do much toward making Memphis more conspicuous as a golfing center."

Cooperating with the newly organized Cotton Carnival, the club held a Women's Invitational Tournament in 1932. The Memphis Country Club was selected as the site for the Western Amateur Golf Tournament in 1933. It was reported, "Despite heavy rains, the tournament was an unqualified success and golf association officials were loud in their praise of the manner in which it was handled."

Dr. McKinney wrote, "The entry list was large, and represented the best golfing talent of the West and South, but the gods of the heavens frowned down on us, and never have we witnessed such a deluge as we had from the beginning almost to the end of the tournament. Even so, the participants in the tournament seemed to enjoy themselves, and . . . we have had the most complimentary expressions concerning the event and the manner in which it was handled by our club."

There were eight tennis courts, two of which were all-weather and one of which had floodlights for night play. There were plans for grandstands so that spectators could watch tennis matches. The annual Memphis Country Club Invitation Tennis Tournament was financially successful. Dr. McKinney wrote, "Our club is well known as one of the largest factors in the development of tennis in this section of our country, and has contributed largely toward making Memphis the tennis center of the South."

Bill Tilden played an exhibition match at the Stadium Court. A young Harry Wellford, the future federal judge, was a ball boy. It was considered a special privilege to be among those who picked up the balls and cleaned the court.

He recalls, "The attendance and interest was as high as for any tennis competition that I ever remember over many, many years . . . Tilden was past his prime but still a very skilled and colorful player . . . The old grandstand was full and there were bleachers and as many seats set up as could be accommodated (probably a couple of thousand people in attendance) . . . While Bill Tilden had slowed down, he still exhibited the flair and charisma that marked his long tennis career . . . As I remember there was considerable banter between Tilden, the umpire, and the linesmen, as well as the ball boys.

"It was an exciting occasion for the MCC, which always prided itself on being primarily a golf club."

The Press Scimitar *of August 9, 1934, featured ladies at the club pool: Mrs. Hubert Reese, Mrs. Pervis Milnor, Mrs. Caffey Robertson, Mrs. Malcolm Barboro, and Mrs. Richard Harding, and their swimming instructor, Miss Athenais Eichling, in 1935.*

Sunday night movies were instituted and equipment installed in 1929. Dr. McKinney picked the movies to be shown. The club had previously been empty on Sunday nights, now the Sunday night buffet and movie were popular events. The Red Room was opened in 1930 and became the heart of the club.

When the government raised the price of stamps from two cents to three cents, Dr. McKinney ordered that all club mail be sent in unsealed envelopes, saving half a cent per letter.

There were so many changes that it was feared that members might lose touch, so Dr. McKinney started a weekly letter to tell members of coming events. The newspaper said that the letter was distinguished by "its unassuming literary flavor, its subtle Scotch humor, and its solid good sense."

Five years after he took office, he was able to report that the club had not borrowed a cent, had reduced its bonded indebtedness by $8,000, and had assets of $33,410, up from $18,929 the year before.

A club operating in the black at this period was an unheard of phenomenon. Norman B. Freer, the newly elected president of the Western Golf Association, sent a letter to Dr. McKinney: "There is only one other club in the United States whose record is comparable with yours."

A change in the laws of the nation probably helped with the economics of the club. In

1933, the Twenty-first Amendment to the Constitution repealed the Eighteenth Amendment, and liquor and beer became legal again.

Entertainments flourished. Every May, the club honored the king and queen of Cotton Carnival with a party. The annual debutante ball resumed in November 1932, after a lapse of several years. It was called "an epoch in the social history of the city." Dr. McKinney reported that "It seems that our club has now become established as the launcher of the yearly output of debutantes upon the social sea." A Mardi Gras ball was initiated in February 1933. Tea dances during the football season were added to the social calendar.

One of the glittering private parties held was the debut of the Crump twins, Blanche and Sara, daughters of Mr. and Mrs. Frank M. Crump. It was a dance with a winter theme on December 22, 1933. The girls, wearing matching gowns of gold lame with mirror buckles at the shoulders, were escorted by Lovick Miles Jr., Emmet Joyner, Joe Gardner, and George Humphreys. There were other parties for the younger set.

The new, improved swimming pool opened in May 1935. Finished in aquamarine tile and surrounded by a cement terrace, it was 110 feet long and 10 feet deep, "which will permit all sorts of high diving and other spectacular feats in which the more daring swimmers like to indulge," reported the *Commercial Appeal*.

The opening was celebrated with an alfresco dinner and swimming party. Tables with gaily colored Deauville umbrellas surrounded the pool, "where members may sip cooling drinks between swims and dives. An orchestra will play for the guests on opening night, and those who do not swim may dance about the pool."

Alfresco dining on the pool terrace became a popular feature on warm summer days, for "it was always cool around the pool."

The *Press Scimitar* reported:

For emergencies like a long, hot summer at home, we submit a swimming club. Nine Memphis women have found it a happy idea—Mrs. Pervis Milnor, Mrs. Caffey Robertson, Mrs. Hubert Reese, Mrs. Malcolm Barboro, Mrs. Richard Harding, Mrs. Toof Brown, and Mrs. Harry Schadt.

Eleanor Abernathy won a two-inch silver perfume flask as a swimming trophy in 1934.

The Crump twins and the Condon brothers at a costume party.

During the hot weather, members of the club have been meeting at the Memphis Country Club pool each Wednesday morning, continuing instruction under Miss Athenais Eichling.

Mrs. Rees Lee's younger boys, Jimmy and Bayless, are often in the pool while their mother's swimming lesson is under way. Mrs. Barboro brings Julia and Lucy with her. Minor and Mary Ann Robertson can be found every Wednesday swimming at the deep end while Mrs. Caffey Robertson practices the crawl some distance away . . .

Mrs. Reese was swimming in a bright orange suit, with which she wore a white bathing cap trimmed with a Roman striped band. Mrs. Harding was in a suit of the same shade, and wore a white cap. Mrs. Barboro was diving in a black suit and white cap. Mrs. Milnor took several dives during the lesson. She wore a black suit with a Roman plaid bandanna and a white cap. Mrs. Robertson, another member of the "white cap crew," wore a brown suit with a brown and white top.

For teenagers, slipping into the pool after hours was a secret thrill. One member remembers that they would try to guess the time when the night watchman was coming by. Someone would give the signal, and they would all try to hang on to the ladder, go underwater, and hold their breaths until he had passed.

In the early thirties, Nina Robinson, Helen Abernathy, Helen Stout, and Bessie Campbell were having lunch together when someone suggested that they organize a study club to promote the knowledge of the cultural arts and world affairs. Each of the four invited three more people to join, and they began meeting for lunch at the country club. The Tuesday Study Club flourished, and others joined. But there came a time when everyone became so busy that the club nearly perished. Adele Orgill was elected president and pushed the club to more success by enlarging membership and recruiting outstanding speakers. The club continues to meet at the Memphis Country Club and, until 2000, held its annual new members' party there.

In 1936, Dr. McKinney announced more plans. The Tap Room was enlarged by a third and redecorated in knotty white pine paneling. A new five-hundred-foot well with a 250-gallon-per-minute capacity was drilled to supply the swimming pool, and seven hundred new trees were planted. Squash courts were also planned. Improvements were ongoing. Later two new all-weather tennis courts were added, and the men's locker room was improved.

When members and staff complained of the heat, two large exhaust fans were installed in the Red Room, two in the kitchen, two in the laundry, and two in the men's locker room, and ceiling fans were put in all the bedrooms. The Tap Room was provided four of the latest type of ceiling fans through the courtesy of a member.

In 1936, the club was faced with adding to the budget the new social security taxes. Dr. McKinney wrote in his annual report:

We are living in an era of the most extraordinary taxation the country has

Thursday Choice Score Trophy.

every known . . . Old age annuities and unemployment insurance are not merely theoretical, but are actually to be applied. Only those of our members who have looked into the matter can conceive of what these taxes will mean to any organization with a considerable number of employees. The system of record keeping is so complicated and exacting that for our club additional clerical services will be required, and since the amount of the taxation imposed increases in successive years, it is safe to say that ere [sic] long these taxes, together with the clerical expense involved, will amount to a large tax item for the club.

For the first time since the Depression began, all fourteen of the club's bedrooms were more or less constantly occupied. A new feature was a small nap room, where members "can find temporary surcease from their troubles in quiet naps." Those troubles probably included financial woes.

Some members complained that children had too many privileges at the club, citing other clubs where children were conspicuous by their absence. But Dr. McKinney said, "With the exception of occasional instances, the conduct of the children who use the club is quite good, and we have always had the cooperation of parents, when we sometimes have to call attention to misconduct on the part of their children, usually the result of youthful exuberance, in seeing that proper disciplinary measures are taken. After all, we must remember that these children are in a few years going to support your club, and I believe the purposes of a club of this kind are best served when we make it useful to the families of members."

Charlotte Stout Hooker grew up across the street from the country club. She was the daughter of Warda and Charles B. Stout, who purchased a Spanish-style home on Goodwyn in 1929. Her father was an avid golfer, and she learned the game as a teenager. She has written a charming account of her memories of life at the club in the 1930s.

There was no fence around the perimeter of the club and one could easily access the course and the large rambling gray stucco building. It was also open on the Southern Avenue side so one could walk between two tennis courts, under a rose arbor, all the way from the club entrance to that street and Buntyn's Station.

As with most Clubs having a pool, it was the center of children's summer activities with swimming lessons, meets and lunch there. All were required to wear their locker key on an elastic band when they swam. When freshly filled with Artesian well water, it was like ICE and the best way to enter was by a quick plunge. Between Memphis heat and many swimmers, it gradually warmed, and in a week needed to be changed. This was done every Sunday night and a special treat was a dip as the water was draining out. A return home in a wet bathing suit helped one get to sleep under a ceiling fan on a "sleeping porch" which *might* have a sultry breeze.

There were no walls between the Mens' and Ladies' dressing rooms, just a large bank of lockers. A fine maid named Gussie had full control of the Ladies' side and changes were made when she discovered something. On their side, boys could lie on the floor to peek under the lockers to study the reflections in the pools of water, thereby watching the girls dress and undress.

A trip to the "Caddy House" was a treat for you could get Moon Pies there, purportedly among "goodies" kept for the caddies. Another way for the young to get a treat that didn't go on Dad's chit was a quick run under the rose-arbor to just across the train-tracks to the Stanfell-Reitz drug-store for an Eskimo Pie. A big fat man (Bob, I think) was in complete charge of the caddies and he kept a large "cadre" of them at all times. When one's turn to carry came up, he bellowed out their name on his bull-horn, for using a caddy on the course was required. A player could ask for one of his choice . . . Some of them could teach you more about the game than the golf pro. No such thing as "pull" or "electric" golf cart in those days.

The Fourth of July was a big event for fireworks were shot out beyond the putting green for the spectators of all ages gathered under the ceiling fans of the big north porch. Sunday night buffets and "picture shows" were a great time for teen-agers to meet and get acquainted. Chairs and a screen were set up in the main lounge which also served as the ballroom for wedding receptions, formal debutante balls, Cotton Carnival functions, as well as high school formal sorority and fraternity dances. Bands like "Snookie Lanson's" were imported from Nashville and other cities, and rest assured, there were ALWAYS some parents chaperoning these special events. Some affairs in this room were lavishly decorated then other times it was just full of balloons and crepe paper twists.

Dances were held from 10 P.M. to 2 A.M. with an hour intermission from 12 to 1 A.M. This was a great time for a stroll on the golf course, or a quick run to Fortune's or Pig and Whistle for refreshments. It

The Phi Kappa dance, 1938:
Billy Webster, Heathy Butler, Peggy Webster, Bill Joe Denton, Virginia Adair Moore, and I. Runyon.

was the era of dressy, but not formal, "Tea" and "Backward" dances. For the latter, girls had to pick up the boys who frequently had been sent a carrot or onion corsage.

Besides the Presentation Balls, Debut teas were held in the main lounge. "Debs" were honored by friends sending her a gift or corsage for the event. The girls were frequently pinned with numerous orchids and gardenias as others were placed on a table near her where she stood in a receiving line. For teas, Mother and "Gran" were there with her and Mom and Dad held sway on Ball night. Hats and gloves, for teas, then long white kid gloves for the ball, were an absolute MUST . . .

Thanks to [her father] Charlie's golf, the Stouts were aware that during the steamy summer months, heavy dew caused edible mushrooms to sprout on the course. I doubt that many knew this, but if one got out quite early, before the grass was cut, an excellent mess could be gathered for dinner.

As time passed, the Club was no longer "in the country" and it became necessary to close it in from the public access, so a privet hedge was planted and this served well for many years. Time also took its toll on Charlie Stout and his golf game and so brother John A. Stout got Club permission to give him the first golf cart used on the Club course. It was a handsome one with a canvas roof that had a fringe which jiggled as he drove it like a little sultan, from his home through a special opening in the hedge, left just for him . . . At times he'd rest a bit and return on his machine for that VERY important 19th hole which included the best Planters Punch ever made anywhere . . . He seldom needed to buy balls for if the golfers on the ninth hole sliced the ball, it nearly always ended up in his front yard . . .

There must always have been a Red Room which was off base for all youngsters. Here the favorite Frozen Tomato Salad developed. The Men's Grill was never darkened by the presence of a woman, not even for special events . . .

It was a sad day when the old gray building with its large porches and ceiling fans on three sides, had to go, but its "Glory Days" had worn it out, and progress became a necessity. So, down it came and from its dust, the lovely brick building you see today rose. Now, nothing is the same, but the Memphis Country Club will always be a special place.

Another member, William Johnstone Britton, memorialized one of the holes on the Memphis Country Club golf course in a book of poems he published in the 1930s. Britton, born in Madison County, Mississippi, in 1880, came to Memphis and entered the cotton business in 1899. He operated his own cotton firm from 1919 to 1947 and served as president of the Memphis Cotton Exchange in 1921. His most famous poem was a tribute to Front Street. In the following poem he describes the thirteenth hole on the country club golf course.

William J. Britton with his grandson Dexter Muller.

Number Thirteen

*There's a tree down on the thirteenth hole,
    Luxuriant and green,
And no matter where you drive your ball,
    The tree provides a screen,
Which is death to all ambition for an eagle or
    a birdie,
And incidentally is the cause of many a dirty
    wordy,
And underneath and surrounding it is a deep
    and hellish ditch,
Which has caused full many a damn and
    many a "son-of-a-gun."*

Golf tournaments in 1935 were the Women's Invitational for the Marguerite Gaut Trophy, played in May, and the Buntyn Trophy Tournament, played in September.

The Fourth of July celebration at the club in 1936 saw the club at its most active. There were swimming races and tennis matches. Richard Harwood, Ed Russell, Dr. Jack Henry, and Billy Condon teed off in the annual golf tournament.

Lake Roberson and Parker Hall were members of the Ole Miss football team from 1938 through 1941. Roberson recounted that one of the highlights of playing for Ole Miss was coming to Memphis to play in Crump Stadium. The team, dressed in their best suits, would go first to the Memphis Country Club, where they went through their drill for the members on the lawn north of the clubhouse.

In 1937, the United States Women's Golf Championship Tournament chose the Memphis Country Club for its tournament in October. Dr. McKinney said, "We owe a lot to Mrs. Gaut for this coup. We sent her up to the National this year to try and get it and she certainly did a fine job. This will prove a great boon for Memphis as it will focus the attention of the entire nation on this city during the tournament."

That year, Dr. McKinney wrote about his devotion to the country club, "What began with me as a hobby has so grown into my thoughts and efforts to make this club a leader among country clubs that it now amounts almost to an obsession."

Dr. McKinney stated that "Debt to me is like the mythological Laocoön being choked by the coils of the serpent." In 1939, despite the economic conditions in the country, McKinney was able to report that the club showed a substantial profit for the fiscal year and that the club had shown physical and financial gains for many years.

The club was now a half million dollar operation, according to Dr. McKinney. "An abhorrence of debt, together with my Scotch instinct, causes me to be careful not to spend unless for necessary betterment of the club. 'Eternal vigilance is the price of success.'" In 1940, the club was now so successful that Dr. McKinney proposed that, although the majority of the members already contributed to the Community Fund, the sum of five hundred dollars be contributed by the Memphis Country Club.

In his 1941 annual report, Dr. McKinney reported, "In one respect this club is different from any that I have ever visited—that is in the privileges allowed children. In some clubs with which I am acquainted children are not allowed even on the second floor, and visiting these clubs, one misses the gaiety and happiness of youth. Doubtless, there are some of our members who feel that children have too many liberties in the clubhouse, but I have always maintained that the youth of the club should be encouraged in its use."

The McKinney era ended in 1941. He had kept the club financially successful and overseen improvement and growth. He had retired the bonds. The Board of Directors was so grateful that they voted unanimously to have his portrait painted and hung in the club.

VI
Cotton Carnival

During the dark days following the Civil War, the economy of the South had collapsed and political Reconstruction kept the region in turmoil. In 1872, the Memphis Mardi Gras was founded to boost the economy and raise the spirits of Memphians. The festival lasted through 1892, and in a diminished form until the turn of the century.

The same impulse stirred Memphis leaders at another time of economic hardship. In 1931, the Chamber of Commerce was unable to raise its $98,000 budget because of the Great

81

Van Vleet Memorial Trophy.

Depression. Various means to raise money and stimulate the economy were discussed.

Herbert Jennings, the manager of Loew's State Theater, had scheduled a showing of a movie called *Cabin in the Cotton*. He suggested having some sort of "Cotton Week" to promote the movie—and incidentally, promote the main cash crop of the region. He contacted A. Arthur Halle, president of the Retail Clothiers Association, who was enthusiastic about the idea for a celebration to promote Memphis and cotton.

Halle called Everett Cook, the new president of the Memphis Cotton Exchange, and they met with representatives of the Chamber of Commerce, Frank Grout and Walter Ackroyd. An association was chartered, officers were elected, committees were formed, money was raised, and plans were afoot to make all citizens cotton conscious—and to boost the Memphis economy.

The biggest dispute was over the name of the festival, planned for the first Monday in March. "Cotton Carnival" was finally chosen.

From the beginning, members of the Memphis Country Club were involved in all aspects of Cotton Carnival. Country club president Dr. Richmond McKinney chaired a secret committee which chose the king and queen. Membership in the committee was never revealed, and some people suspected that Dr. McKinney *was* the committee.

The theme that first year was "The Old South." The first queen of Cotton Carnival, Elaine Patteson, was the daughter of Mrs. Allie Starke Patteson, social secretary at the club. The first king was Frank Gailor. The royalty were honored by a parade, featuring eighty-six floats, designed by Mike Abt and made by his students at Tech High School.

A spring snow dampened that first Cotton Carnival parade, but a second carnival was planned for the next year, with the date changed to May. Towns in the surrounding area were asked to participate. A children's parade, a barge landing, and fireworks were added.

The Memphis Junior League put on a fashion show on a stage made of cotton bales, erected on the bluff by the Memphis Stagehands Union. The ladies discovered that it was hard to find party clothes made of cotton. Soon, local stores were demanding more clothes made of cotton.

The Mystic Society of the Memphi, which had run the old Memphis Mardi Gras,

The Memphi Midwinter Ball, 1965.

was revived, and other societies were formed to plan parties and festivities during carnival week.

The festival began to attract national attention. In 1934, the king and queen wore robes worn by Charles Laughton and Greer Garson in the movies. But when nationally syndicated columnist Westbrook Pegler pointed out that there was something odd about the king and queen of cotton wearing satin robes, special cotton robes were ordered for the next year by MCC member J. Everett Pidgeon.

In 1935, the Cotton Makers Jubilee began, with parades, midways, and activities for African-Americans. More parades and midways were added. In 1938, President Franklin D. Roosevelt punched a button in the White House to set off the fireworks beginning Cotton Carnival. Over the years, entertainers like Guy Lombardo, Tommy Dorsey, Gypsy Rose Lee, Eddie Fisher, Pat Boone, and Elvis Presley participated in carnival.

The annual country club carnival party became a favorite feature of carnival week. In

Memphi duchesses presented in 1965:
Palmer Brown, Lenore and Milton Binswanger, Jean and Hugh Sinclair,
George and Flora Stratton, and Daisy Fisher (sitting).

1940, when Lida Willey and Claude Crawford were king and queen of carnival, the *Press Scimitar* reported, "It wouldn't seem like carnival, of course, without Memphis Country Club's gala ball."

Climaxing the first evening of merrymaking and setting the mood for the week, hundreds gathered at the club for the annual event. Upstairs, downstairs, on verandas, in the Red Room, the ballroom and the dining room—gaiety everywhere . . . There was Mary Martin Dunscomb, club princess, looking lovely, with a coronet of gardenias adding a touch of the old South to her white and silver costume. There were the Queen and King, too. Every bit a royal couple—Lida in shining gold sequins, Claude regal in blue.

The *Commercial Appeal* reported:

Cotton really came into its own last night as lovely ladies arrayed not in silks and satin but bewitching cotton frocks danced away the hours at the Memphis Country Club ball given for Princess Mary Martin Dunscomb and Prince Sam Rembert.

Toof Brown and Everett Cook escort Queen Gaye Gillespie in 1968.

Queen Daphne Boyle, King Hallam Boyd, and Maid of Cotton Ellen Clark at the MCC party in 1977.

The Osiris Queen entertains the queens of Ptah, Aani, Memphi, Ptolemy, Kemet, Ennead, Ramet, and Sphinx, and Carnival King Bob Loeb and Queen Elizabeth Wilson at the Memphis Country Club in 2003.

Huckleberry vine with its dainty like blossoms will be combined with Jackson vine and other greenery in decorating the club. The entire lower floor will be transformed into a garden like setting, with the porches enclosed and bright with Japanese lanterns. The throne scene will be in the dining room . . . stately ivory peacock chairs with gold seats—all reflected in the deep mirror. Three graceful arches flanked by gold stands holding ivory peonies will face the throne.

The carnival was suspended during World War II, from 1942 to 1946. The year it resumed, the festivities were broadcast on NBC. In 1949, Cotton Carnival made the cover of *Life* magazine. In 1952, the Voice of America broadcast it behind the Iron Curtain.

In 1966, the MCC newsletter announced: "With festive heraldry and befitting fanfare, we shall honor our club Princess and her Prince, along with the King and Queen of Carnival on May 12." The court was presented at 7:30 P.M., there was dinner, and the Ray Stidham Orchestra played for dancing. The cost of the dinner dance was four dollars a person.

The secret society Memphi announced its duchesses at an annual midwinter ball held at the country club. In 1968, the theme was "Memphi on the Nile," and two pages in gold satin Egyptian costumes with towering turbans waved feathered fans as the duchesses made their entrances through gold silk curtains of a multicolored striped tent in the ballroom. They proceeded to a canopied dais banked with palm trees at the north end of the dining room. Pink pyramids decorated the tables. The next year, the Memphi ball ventured even farther than Egypt: the theme was "Way Out in Space."

In 1970, the Royal Club, composed of all former members of the Royal Court, held its party at the Memphis Country Club. The theme was "The Age of Aquarius," with decorations of shocking pink balloons, matching the dresses of the ladies of the realm.

In 1985, the name was changed to the Great River Carnival, then to simply Carnival Memphis. Each year a new facet of the Mid-South economy was featured, with trade shows, seminars, business meetings, and a school curriculum about the featured industry. Secret societies became known as Krewes and were still a major part of the festivities.

In 2003, when the Mystic Krewe of Memphi held its midwinter ball at the country club, the theme was Arabian Nights. A snake charmer with a huge "snake" writhed atop a table in the bar. The presentation of the duchesses was preceded by a parade of costumed acrobats. Guests dined on mixed greens with pecans, goat cheese and sundried cranberries drizzled in raspberry vinaigrette, black pepper filet with garlic mushrooms, lobster shitake, whipped potatoes, and grilled asparagus at tables decorated with calla lilies and gold candles.

For many years, the kings and queens of the carnival were always members of the Memphis Country Club.

The 1940s

VII

In September 1939, Germany invaded Poland. The hope of avoiding war in Europe disappeared, though President Franklin Roosevelt, in one of his "Fireside Chats" declared that the United States was neutral.

New Deal measures were still in effect. After the trials of the Great Depression, prosperity seemed just around the corner, largely due to the orders for military supplies that flooded the nation's factories. In 1940, Franklin Roosevelt won an unprecedented third term as president as the clouds of war loomed.

The Selective Service Act established the first peacetime draft for men between the ages of twenty and thirty-six.

The great success of 1939 was the movie *Gone with the Wind*. Clark Gable and Vivian Leigh turned Margaret Mitchell's novel of the Old South into an unforgettable picture of a world that never was. More realistically, John Steinbeck's *The Grapes of Wrath* pictured the tribulations of an Oklahoma family who lost their farm and were forced to become migrant workers. *The Yearling*, by Majorie Kinnan Rawlings, and *The Little Foxes*, by Lillian Hellman, were also popular.

Average life expectancy in the United States was sixty-four years, a major increase from forty-nine years in 1900. The first antibiotic was developed, but it was considered too poisonous for use in humans.

Richmond McKinney's successor as president of the country club was W. Lytle McKee. Born and raised in Memphis, he attended Vanderbilt University. He was in the cotton business. He married Marion Russell Kavanaugh and had four children. As a young man, McKee played polo but soon took up tennis as more economical. He played regularly with a group who called themselves the Royal Eyes.

When Dr. and Mrs. Shields Abernathy presented their daughter Eleanor to society at the Memphis Country Club on December 20, 1940, there were two parties, a reception in the afternoon and a ball at night. The newspaper described the parties in vivid detail.

A bower of red roses and banks of red poinsettias provided a background as the debutante and her parents greeted the afternoon guests: "Mrs. Clyde Denton in bright green, Mrs. W. W. Robinson in brown with bronze sequins, Mrs. Eugene Reynolds in scarlet jersey topped with a charming white feather hat, Mrs. Willis Campbell in a black frock encrusted with gold beading, and Mrs. Swayne Latham in a good looking suit of black and red trimmed with Persian lamb were among the guests."

The newspaper reported, "The outstanding costume was that of Mrs. Page Patterson, in black with a Mountie red coat and a huge envelope bag and umbrella to match. . . . Mrs. Worthen Agee in sables, sipped tea with Mrs. W. W. Simmons, stunning in gold and mink, with muff and hat to match . . . Miss Mary Hutchison and Miss Grace Hoyt paused to admire the table of gift flowers."

After the ladies had enjoyed tea, the younger set came to dance that night.

> Last night's dense fog did nothing to lessen the enthusiasm of the large crowd

W. Lytle McKee, president 1941–1942.

Decorations for Eleanor Abernathy's debut tea (above) and ball (below), 1940.

The wedding reception of Eleanor Abernathy and Dr. P. Thurman Crawford, December 3, 1941, four days before Pearl Harbor.

attending Miss Abernathy's presentation at the Memphis Country Club . . . Miss Hope Galloway, pretty in pale blue net with straps and bodice trim of royal blue brilliants, chatting with her three escorts, Belton Copp, Tunkie Saunders and Cress Fox. Miss Elizabeth Farnsworth, escorted by Cameron Mann, in one of the most stunning dresses at the party, pale blue trimmed with gold braid and a gold bracelet, distinguished by its simplicity. Miss Nancy Donelson, huge rhinestones in the belt and neckline ornaments of her deep rose crepe dress, escorted by Waddy West Jr.

Mr. and Mrs. Walter Armstrong Jr. hurried to greet the visitors, Mrs. Armstrong very attractive in a new hairdo and a stunning rose dress trimmed with a gold filigree design on the jacket. Miss Letty Brooks, an unusual ornament of ermine tips in her hair to match the trim on her black velvet dress, with her escort, Russell Wood. Miss Mary Mac Hines of New York and Memphis in a peach colored velvet fashion.

THE SECOND WORLD WAR

The Memphis Country Club was in good shape. But the world was about to go to war. After the Japanese attack on Pearl Harbor on December 7, 1941, the United States joined the Allies fighting against the Axis of Germany, Italy, and Japan.

After the attack on Pearl Harbor, the Yuletide Revelers changed the theme of their holiday party to the "Victory Ball." The brilliant wedding reception planned at the Memphis Country Club after the wedding of Margaret Ivy Bass and John Pervis Milnor Jr. was cancelled because of the national crisis. Instead, the bride's grandmother entertained at a small reception at her home.

From 1940 to 1946, the Second Army was headquartered at the Mid-South Fairgrounds, under the command of Lt. Gen. Ben Lear, who had entered the army as an enlisted man in the Spanish-American War and later served in World War I. He was a stern disciplinarian and was described as "tough as a nickel steak."

General Lear was playing golf at the Memphis Country Club one hot Sunday afternoon in July 1941. A convoy of forty-five army trucks, carrying some 350 soldiers returning from field maneuvers in Middle Tennessee to Camp Robinson, Arkansas, rolled down Central Avenue past the golf course. The soldiers spotted some attractive young ladies clad in shorts on the golf course and began saluting them with howls and whistles.

The women responded appreciatively, but General Lear was furious. Wearing casual civilian clothes, General Lear took off at a trot and hurdled the hedge along Central. He stopped the convoy and berated the commanding officer. All 350 men were ordered to turn around and go back to Second Army Headquarters where they camped for the night. That evening, Lear lectured the officers, calling the men's conduct a discredit to the company. The next day, he ordered the men to put on full packs and march the first fifteen miles on foot.

The "yoo hoo incident" at the Memphis Country Club attracted national publicity. General Lear was pilloried as a tyrant and acquired the nickname "Yoo Hoo Lear." Congressmen postured about abuse of "our brave boys." General Lear was later named commander of army ground forces in 1944 and served as deputy commander of the European Theater of Operations under Eisenhower. After the war, he retired in Memphis. The nickname remained with him.

McKay Van Vleet, president 1942–1943.

McKay Van Vleet, whose father had been the club's first president, became president in 1942. Educated at Hotchkiss and Princeton, he had also served as an officer of the Memphis Hunt and Polo Club. Upon his father's death in 1915, he became president of the Van Vleet Mansfield Drug Company, which had grown to be the largest wholesale drug company in the South. He served as president of Cotton Carnival in 1949.

His wife, the former Harriet Huger Smith, was the first president of the Junior League of Memphis. McKay Van Vleet served for one term, 1942–1943.

As the country prepared for war, the navy established the Naval Air Technical Training Center, an air base and a hospital, just north of Memphis in Millington. There was an army quartermaster supply depot on Airways and an air force depot on Jackson. The army hospital was built at Park and Shotwell, and the name of that street was changed to the more appropriate "Getwell" Street.

While Memphians planted Victory Gardens, saved tin cans and tinfoil, and became familiar with ration books, the young ladies of Memphis eagerly joined in the war effort. Bachelor officers stationed at military installations in Memphis and Millington were the guests of honor at the first Memphis Country Club party of the fall social season, on October 8, 1943. Seventy-two daughters of club members acted as hostesses, and an eight-piece military orchestra played for dancing at the tea dance, held from 5:30 P.M. to 8:00 P.M. in the spacious lounge. There was a soft drink bar, and appetizers were served.

Black was the fashionable color of the day, the newspaper reported. Miss Frances Gregg chaired the party, "a picture of fashion" in a black crepe dress with heaven blue trim and a purple orchid, and a tiny velvet beanie with a rhinestone clip, when she danced with Major Bob Snowden, stationed with the Marines in Pensacola, Florida.

Miss Sarah Barth wore black crepe distinguished by huge gold buttons, and Miss Betty Jane Kellogg wore black trimmed with touches of red outlined with a cross stitch of black thread. Miss Flora Williamson wore black with a bewitching pink bow, and Miss Laura Lake wore black with a blue yoke embroidered with pearls and threads of gold. Miss Nancy Donelson wore deep beige and gold. Miss Louise Clarke wore sky blue crepe with a pink rose at the V-neckline. Miss Mimi Galloway was "also in the popular black with an aqua ribbon threading the cobwebby lace yoke."

George Treadwell, president 1943–1945, and important figure in Tennessee golf.

Ensign Ainslie Pryor, on leave from an around-the-world cruise with the merchant marines, "was having fun greeting all his friends after a long absence." Several couples stopped to speak to Mr. and Mrs. Leslie Stratton, who were playing cards in the Red Room.

The party was judged a great success, with "scores of uniformed officers attending and rushing the daughters of country club members practically 'off their feet.'" It was such a success that it was announced that similar parties would be held later.

The ninth president of the Memphis Country Club was George Treadwell (1900–1987) who served from 1943 to 1946. He was one of the city's best golfers and held the club championship five times.

His nephew, Tim Treadwell, said that next to his wife and family, the Memphis Country Club and Calvary Episcopal Church were George Treadwell's great loves. He was senior partner in the insurance firm of Treadwell and Harry, which had been started by his mother and aunt, the first insurance agency in the country to be owned and operated by women.

At one point, Treadwell employed a secretary from Osceola, Arkansas. He recognized her talent and got her a job on a local radio station. That was only the beginning. The young woman was Dale Evans, who later married cowboy star Roy Rogers.

Dr. McKinney had warned of "the decrepitude" of the clubhouse in 1941. No sooner had Treadwell taken office than the furnace broke down, the machinery in the laundry and refrigerating plants failed, and a March hailstorm damaged the roof.

John R. Flippin was appointed to head a special committee to check the clubhouse. His report said, "As to the building—there is nothing I would advise you to do except patch work. Any major expense on this old building will be money thrown away. What you really need is a new Club House." But it would be many years before a major construction project could be considered.

George Treadwell was one of the organizers of the Memphis Golf Association in 1941 and was the first president, serving till 1946. He was active in the Tennessee Golf Association, the Southern Golf Association, and the United States Golf Association, serving as Sectional Affairs representative for twenty-five years.

His wide associations in the golfing world brought three national tournaments to the Memphis Country Club: the U.S. Amateur in 1948, the U.S. Senior Amateur in 1959, and the U.S. Women's Amateur in 1979.

Treadwell was a Memphis golfing icon. After the 1959 Senior Tournament, the director of the USGA wrote him, complimenting the Memphis Country Club, "You went far beyond the normal in what we regard as perhaps the most important aspect of major competitions—the spirit and general atmosphere in which the event is played. You and your fellow members provided a warm and gracious spirit from the moment your guests arrived at your door until the time they left."

Working with Treadwell was Thomas J. White (1890–1983). A cotton merchant originally from Jackson, Tennessee, he was president of the Tennessee Golf Association in 1937 and a director of the Southern Golf Association from 1940 to 1947.

He played in his first State Amateur Tournament in 1915, and consistently made the championship flight, winning in 1935. *The History of Tennessee Golf* says, "White and George Treadwell . . . were two of the most influential men in Memphis. It was a well-known fact that nothing happened at Memphis Country Club without their approval. In the 1930s, 1940s and 1950s they were two of golf's staunchest supporters in Memphis."

A letter written by a young man named Clarence Blakely to Newton E. Cartwright in 1940 describes Sam Snead playing at the Memphis Country Club. Written when Cartwright was twenty years old and in the naval signal corps stationed at Carmel, California, the letter is dated September 16, 1940. His daughter, Beth Dixon, found the letter among his papers.

> Yesterday (Sunday) Ralf Gualdual and Sam Snead came to play Jake Fondren, assistant pro at the Memphis Country Club, and Buck White, pro at Ridgeway. White won low ball with a 74, par is 70. Fondren shot a 75, Snead a 75 and Gualdual a 75. Snead made a 7 on number 8, a four par hole at Memphis Country Club. The admission was $1. I didn't pay but Dad (who was a member) took me out and we walked around 4 holes with them. We walked through the hedge. We, well at least I was scared, because everybody that bought a ticket wore them on their shirt. I didn't see anything so hot about them. Of course they weren't trying because they knew they were going to get the money promised them. There were 1,800 people attending . . .
>
> About three weeks ago the Memphis Country Club had a tournament. It cost $3 to enter. Elsworth Vines the tennis star is a swell golfer. He played with Snead and the pros all winter. He plays swell golf. He used a brassie on the ninth hole (301 yards) because if he uses a driver he will drive in the sand trap in front of the green. You can't drive the green. Vines made a two on the hole for a new record . . . I asked Vines for his ball at the end of the quarter final match and he gave it to me . . . I'll keep it and show it to you when you come home next.

During the war, another celebrity, Bing Crosby, played golf at the Memphis Country Club as part of a charity tour sponsored by the American Legion. The proceeds were to go to the "social, educational, and recreational benefit of military personnel of the 4th Ferrying Group, Air Transport Command," located at the Municipal Airport in Memphis. Advertisments said that admission was $1.81, with a tax of 19 cents, so tickets cost $2.00.

On May 23, 1943, Crosby arrived in Memphis to play a golf match with Bob Hope, only to discover that Hope's plane had been grounded by bad weather in Atlanta.

But the show must go on. Before a crowd of ten thousand, who had paid two dollars each, Crosby partnered with PGA tour player Byron Nelson to defeat Ed Dudley, Augusta National pro, and Jake Fondren, a local pro. Nelson shot 69; Fondren, 70; Crosby, 72; and Dudley, 73.

Jake Fondren was one of Memphis's best-known players. He turned pro when he was still a teenager and worked at Pine Hill and Overton Park golf courses. He was head professional at Colonial Country Club for a few years, then became W. C. Sherwood's assistant at the Memphis Country Club for six years. He then returned to Colonial until his retirement in 1969. He was known as "the

Tickets for golf exhibitions. Bob Hope didn't make it, but Bing Crosby did.

little pro," and carried a money clip engraved "To the Little Pro, from Bing Crosby."

E. William Henry remembers the match which he saw when he was a young teenager. He says:

> To young boys *Tarzan* movies were the rage and Johnny Weismuller, as the king of the apes, was a big star.
>
> A huge gallery came out to see "Der Bingle"; he was everybody's favorite. A mob surrounded the first tee box as he prepared to make his opening drive and spectators crowded the left border of the fairway. To be near the action, some enterprising youngsters had even climbed into the branches of the oak tree that still stands near the clubhouse at the corner of the current practice tee.
>
> Ever cool and relaxed, Crosby positioned himself over the ball, swung smoothly, and sent a respectable drive right down the middle. The crowd was restrained; a smattering of applause sounded briefly as he picked up his tee and began walking toward his ball.
>
> At that moment, a large limb of the tree holding one of the young spectators snapped loudly and plummeted to the ground amid a great flurry of leaves and branches. Without breaking his stride (and I was right behind him, so I heard and saw everything) the famous crooner looked toward the tree, shook his head, and muttered, "That Weismuller is everywhere."
>
> Bob Hope, had he been there, could hardly have topped that memorable one-liner.

Pairs Trophy.

After the match, Crosby sang for forty-five minutes to the adoring crowd, then went to Kennedy Hospital to entertain wounded soldiers before leaving on the 8:14 train for Washington.

The war meant many changes. Fifty of the club's regular members, as well as many sons and relatives, were serving in the armed forces. The club extended temporary membership privileges to some fifty army and navy personnel stationed in Memphis.

President Treadwell reported on one of the changes in his 1944 president's report:

> Some of you, no doubt, recall that we had "Children's Disease" this summer. In 1910 this Club was built for a "Country Club" in the suburbs of the city, with only a scattering of children in the neighborhood. Now the city has grown up around us and your Club, being in the center of our residential district, serves as both a "City Club" and a "Country Club." Therefore, it has become a children's playground. Shortage of servants and nurses has meant that more and more children use the Club and many are allowed to spend the day without the usual attendant parent, this placed a heavy burden on our staff. We endeavored in every way to give the children all of the privileges to which we thought they were entitled and we used our best means to control their activities. At first our efforts were absolutely futile, however, we are glad to report that in the latter part of the summer we had a Tennis Tournament and a Golf Tournament for them . . . It seemed to make the children realize that they were an important element in the Club life—and that we were interested in their well-being. Immediately their actions were much better controlled.

Another change was the servant problem: "Throughout the year, we had the same problems that all of you had at home which were: scarcity of choice foods and a shortage of servants . . . The shortage of the members' domestic servants naturally increased the number of persons eating at the Club and put more of a burden on our limited staff." It was necessary to increase food prices. The Club was operating close to the bone: of every dollar taken in, 98 cents was paid out in expenses, leaving only two cents to be added to the surplus.

In 1945, Treadwell proudly reported that "We served more people, did more business, spent more money and in spite of unusual conditions, were able, after depreciation, to show a net profit." Entertainment for large groups had been limited during the war, but over six hundred people attended the Victory Dinner Dance.

THE END OF THE WAR

The end of the war in 1945 brought monumental changes. The United States had once again asserted itself on the world stage and introduced the atomic age. The Cold War heated up as the Soviet Union and the United States faced each other across the battered battlefields of Europe and Asia.

Harry S. Truman, who had become president after Franklin Roosevelt's death, defeated Thomas Dewey to win his own four-year term in 1948. The Marshall Plan, aimed at rebuilding Europe and the GI Bill, enabled thousands of returning veterans to go to college.

As wartime rationing ended, rubber for tires and new automobiles were available again. Nylon stockings and Christian Dior's "New Look," with long swirling skirts, made fashion news after the skimpiness of wartime clothing. A Memphis girl, Barbara Walker, became Miss America in 1947.

Spiraling inflation and lack of housing greeted returning soldiers. But the mood of the country was positive. Veterans and their families looked to the suburbs for new housing, and dozens of new subdivisions were developed as Memphis grew into the surrounding farmland, and real estate development once again became big business. The first major suburban shopping center in Memphis was Poplar Plaza, built in 1949 at Poplar and Highland on the city's eastern edge, not far from the country club.

TENNIS AT THE CLUB

Joe Whalen was an early tennis pro at the club. He once won the National Professional Championship. Earl King recalls that Whalen was at the club only in the summers and lived in the locker room.

Jeanne Coors and baby Jeanne at the swimming pool in 1946.

In the late '40s and '50s the club had rubico courts. Before that, the surface was en-tout-cas, a clay surface with broken red brick particles in the surface. At the south end of the two main courts, there was a large permanent grandstand. It was a wood structure, painted forest green, with ten to fifteen rows of permanent seating under a partial roof. According to Alex Wellford Jr., the spectator was in an ideal spot to watch tennis—looking away from the sun, with the lowest seat at the base of the backstop. The tennis shop was under the stands, with an entrance at the west end.

The tennis pro, John Kraft, was a classic figure, Wellford says. "Following World War II, Bermuda shorts and tennis shorts had almost totally eclipsed the long white trousers previously required at most tennis clubs. Kraft always played tennis in long pants, even in the hottest weather. It was his trademark, just like member W. L. Taylor, who continued wearing long white trousers at the Club and his own court for the next fifty years. Kraft was polite, reserved, pleasant."

There was a single practice or teaching court located to the southeast of the present club entrance. Later it was converted to a platform tennis court, then to a teen lounge/snack bar.

There was no junior tennis training program in the early forties, although Kraft ran some tournaments for youngsters. Prior to World War II, member Ramsey Potts was a promoter of junior tennis, and his son, Ramsey Potts Jr. won the National Intercollegiate Doubles Championships and was one of the best players produced in Memphis.

Some of the junior players were Malcolm Saxon, Clara Saxon, Bickie McCallum, Sally Crump, Marie Louise Crump, Kate Harwood, Bill Butler, and Allen Malone. Wellford remembers that, at the age of ten, he played C. D. Smith in the finals of a tournament. "We had been evenly matched in practice. The day before our match, his mother, Maggie Smith, an intelligent player with classic strokes, taught C. D. how to hit a drop shot. The final was a rout."

Other players included Madeline Richardson, Dodie Cheairs, twins Peggy and Dottie Smith, cousins A. B. Potts and Ruth "Wootie" Beasley, Suzanne Ellis, Suzette Cathey, Josephine Lowrance, Sophie Woodson, B. Lee Mallory, Mary Ann Weaver, Dudley Weaver, John Bondurant, and Tom White.

Having finished a tennis lesson with Kraft, Robert Gooch Jr., age ten, grew tired of waiting for his mother to pick him up. He saw a train creeping along at Buntyn. Knowing that it would pass near his house on Grandview, several blocks farther east, he hitched a ride, planning to jump off when he got near home. By the time the train got to Grandview, it was clipping along at some thirty miles an hour. When the train finally slowed to a stop, Gooch was in Collierville. He had to face the music when he called home.

Among the women who played doubles regularly were Elise Morgan, Adeline Heiskell, Peggy Wellford, Libby Dudley, Nancy Aste, Peggy Smith, Maggie Smith, Audrey Taylor, and Elsie Burch. Frequent city champion Jean Dalstrom was often a guest. Betty Crump and Ada Norfleet Fuller were frequent players.

Men often on the courts included Martin Condon, Armour Bowen, Herbert Darnell, Robert Galloway, Allen Morgan Sr., Bunts Marshall, Ted Miles, Judge Sylvanus Polk,

Program for a tennis tournament, June 1946.

Van Pritchartt Sr., Tom White, Tom Price, Walter Lane Smith, Bobby Day Smith, Lewis McKee, Pervis Milnor, and John Stout.

College or junior age players included Van Pritchartt Jr., Frank Wilbourn, Jimmy Wetter, Frank Norfleet, Dunbar Abston, Frank Barton, Billy Dunavant, and Bill Leftwich (for whom the tennis complex in Audubon Park is named). Winston Cheairs and Buddy Stout were among the best of the younger players.

Earl King remembers that he and Giles Coors and other children of members acted as ball boys for ten cents a set for a regular doubles game with Julian Bondurant, Allen Morgan Sr., Lytle McKee, and General Everett Cook.

Alex Wellford Sr. was a well-known player. After winning a city and a state title, he sent in an entry to the Wimbledon Championship. At the age of forty-two, he was perhaps the oldest player accepted in the draw. His son recalls, "Before competing at Wimbledon, my father had never seen a grass court, so he arranged with Pat Abbott to hit some tennis balls on the practice green of the golf course.

"Earlier in 1953, I had watched him take a 5-2 lead in the first set in a match in Florida against Victor Seixas, who later that year won at Wimbledon . . . In those days there was not so much disparity between a solid club player and the top player in the world. How the game has changed!"

Tennis chairman Millsaps Fitzhugh pulled off a coup in 1946. On June 12–16, 1946, the Memphis Country Club presented the Southern Open Professional Tennis Tourney. Memphis had been promised the tournament in 1942, but wartime travel restrictions and the loss of players to the armed forces canceled it.

Several famous players—Bill Tilden, an "old master" at age fifty-three, Fred Perry of England, Frank Kovacs, Wayne Sabin, Welby Van Horn, and John Faunce—were among the contestants. Bobby Riggs played Don Budge before a capacity crowd for the championship. It was called "the most outstanding tournament ever held in the Mid-South."

One story tells that club members, including Swayne Latham Sr. and Van Pritchartt Sr., who had a regular Saturday doubles game, were none too happy when the courts were occupied by the tournament and their game was cancelled. They asked some friends, who were playing on a remaining court, if they could join their game. The friends refused, saying that Latham and Pritchartt weren't up to playing in their game. To get back at their friends, they planned a stunt and contacted well-known local aviator Vernon Omlie.

Spectators were settled on the bleachers watching Riggs and Budge play when they heard a noise getting louder and louder. A small plane flew over the club, the side door of the plane opened, and thousands of tennis balls rained down on the tennis courts. It was the revenge of the displaced players.

Sugar and butter were plentiful again after wartime scarcity, and people set out to enjoy themselves. At the first debutante ball since the war, on December 27, 1947, twenty-one young ladies were presented to society wearing long white dresses and carrying bouquets of red poinsettias. The ballroom was decorated with a row of white-flocked Christmas trees and clouds of shimmering material in the alcoves.

Parties and meetings kept the club busy. The Glass Collectors Club installed its new

The 1947 Debutante Ball:
Ellen Ramsay, Carroll Russell, Amelia Russell, and Betty McCadden.

officers at the country club on May 5, 1948. Fragrant gardenias decorated the tables. The retiring president, Mrs. William R. Atkinson, wearing a chic suit of black faille highlighted with gold costume jewelry, turned the gavel over to Mrs. John Quincy Wolfe, the new president, who looked smart in a tailored two-piece dress of dove gray crepe and a big black straw hat. New members were Mrs. Berry Brooks and Mrs. Carrington Jones.

When the Tuesday Study Club held its first luncheon and lecture for the 1949 season at the Memphis Country Club in October, Dr. R. B. Gibbs, pastor of the First Unitarian Church, was the speaker, on "The Significance of the Great Books." President Mrs. A. C. Treadwell Beasley presided, and program chairman Mrs. Charles Gerber introduced the speaker. Mrs. Joe Davis and Mrs. Harry Schmeisser were luncheon chairmen and saw that the dining room was decorated with "autumn blossoms in tones of bronze, gold, and burgundy."

Edward P. Russell was club president from 1946 to 1948. He grew up in Mississippi, attended the Webb School, Phillips Academy at Andover, Massachusetts, and received his law degree from the University of Virginia in 1921. He entered the law practice in the firm of Canada, Williams and Russell, which became Canada, Russell and Turner in 1940. He specialized in railroad and corporate law.

For many years he was chairman of the board of the Hutchison School and headed the fund drive that resulted in the school's move to its present home on Ridgeway Road. He served as president of the Memphis and Shelby County Bar Association, the Tennessee Club, and the University Club, as well as the Memphis Country Club.

One of Russell's first jobs as country club president was to report on the condition of the clubhouse. A nationally known architect reported that a new clubhouse, at least 20 percent larger, was needed, and would cost one million dollars. At war's end, scarce building materials were going for veterans' housing, and construction costs were high. Inventories of glassware, silverware, and linens were depleted and had been impossible to obtain during the war. It was decided to clean up, paint up, patch up—and get along for the time being.

With the end of the war and increased activities at the club in 1946, President Russell was able to report that the number of meals served in the last year had increased 25 percent. Bar and restaurant sales totaled $160,000. The club had operated only a "milk bar" since 1944,

Edward P. Russell, president 1946–1948.

so bar receipts were down, but there was a large inventory of beverages for the future. No club yearbook had been printed since 1942, and a new yearbook was welcomed in 1946. Mrs. Allie Patteson retired in 1946, after eighteen years as hostess.

The gross income ballooned from $193,576.73 in 1944 to $324,501.52 in 1947. In November 1947, the club had 450 regular members, 50 nonresident members, 120 lady members, 73 special members, 14 clergy members, and 6 army-navy members, a total of 713 members.

Even with a dues increase in 1947 and full membership rolls, high costs, raised salaries, and special expenditures meant an operating loss of nearly ten thousand dollars in 1948. Dues were raised again, to three hundred dollars a year.

Many young people coming back from the war felt the country club dues were too high, and some left to join the University Club. Junior memberships were instituted so that younger people could continue using the club at more reasonable rates.

In an effort to keep young members using the club, Tunkie Saunders invented a huge martini, served in something like a small vase, which sold in the Red Room for one dollar. Music was added on every Saturday night. Before long, Saturday night at the country club was a "must do." No matter where you had been earlier, you stopped by the club on Saturday night.

POST-WAR ACTIVITY

There were no Women's State Amateur Golf Tournaments during the war, but when the tournaments resumed, a Memphis Country Club player was a star. Margaret Gunther began playing golf in 1935 when she was twelve years old. Country club pro W. C. Sherwood taught her the basics, then famed player Marguerite Gaut took her under her wing. With her encouragement, Margaret won her first tournament at age eighteen. She attended Southwestern (now Rhodes College) and the University of Alabama during the war years.

After the war, she played in all the major women's tournaments and in 1949 became the first Tennessean to win the Women's Southern Championship since Mrs. Gaut. She married real estate man Shelby Lee and raised four children in Memphis. Mrs. Lee remembers that at the beginning of every hole there was a bucket of sand and a bucket of water. Instead of using a wooden tee, golfers made a little mound of wet sand to place their ball on.

In 1963, at the Memphis Country Club, Margaret Gunther Lee won her sixth State Amateur. In September 2003, she was inducted into the Tennessee Golf Hall of

The team from the Memphis Country Club won the City Pro-Am Tournament in 1948: Charlie Kittle, Ray Terry, Pat Abbott, and Hugh Francis Jr.

*New Year's Eve, 1949:
unidentified partygoer, Jean Anthony, John Fargason, Ellen Ramsay,
Nell Fargason, and Reed McPhillips.*

Fame. The citation called her "the bridge between Tennessee's first and second generations of great women players."

Pat Abbott (1912–1984) became head golf professional at the Memphis Country Club in 1947 and held the position for thirty-four years. According to *The History of Tennessee Golf*, "In addition to being a fine player, he possessed the credentials necessary for being a great club professional. He was a good teacher. He ran a good shop. He was personable and his members loved him."

Abbott grew up in Pasadena, California, and his first tournament victory was the 1935 Southern California Amateur. He won again in 1938 and 1941, becoming the first golfer from a public course to win the event. After moving to Tennessee, he won the Tennessee Open in 1949, 1954, 1955, and 1962, and the state PGA in 1969, 1971, and 1974.

He was also an actor. When he was young and living in California, he had an actor's guild card. He and his wife Charlotte performed in many Memphis stage productions, and she served on the board of Theater Memphis.

Abbott was inducted into the Tennessee Golf Hall of Fame in 2002. A Pat Abbott Future Champions Fund was established. When he was young, Abbott had received an invitation to play in the first Masters Tournament but had to decline because of the financial costs of traveling to Augusta. The fund named in his honor will make sure that no junior player is denied the opportunity to play in a championship or national event for lack of money.

The Labor Day weekend in 1948 saw the Forty-eighth Annual Championship of the United States Golf Association played at the Memphis Country Club. There were 1,220 entries. George Treadwell was chairman, and his connections in the golfing world got the tournament for the club. He wrote in the program, "Ever since the club was founded in 1905 there have been tournaments at our 'Old Buntyn' course, local ones at first, then bigger and bigger events as time went on, building up to a magnificent present."

The golf course was the club's pride. Other clubs frequently inquired how the Memphis Country Club was able to maintain such "a high standard of perfection" without large expenditures of money. The president gave credit to the chairman and Greens Committee and greenskeeper, for keeping costs at $25,366.92 a year, or $2,113.83 per month, or approximately $1,410 per green.

W. Groom Leftwich, president of the country club in 1948–1950, was born in Aberdeen, Mississippi, in 1896, and died in Memphis in 1966. A Sewanee graduate, he was married to Mattie Howard Scape in 1925. After serving in the army, he moved to Memphis and was active in the investment business, with the firm of Leftwich, Ross, and Crisler. He was the president of Cotton Carnival in 1936.

W. Groom Leftwich, president 1948–1950.

His son, William Groom Leftwich Jr., a lieutenant colonel in the marine corps, was a hero of the Vietnam War. He was killed in a helicopter crash on November 18, 1970, at the age of thirty-nine. A Spruance-class destroyer was named for him in 1978, and the marines award the Leftwich Trophy for exemplary leadership. The tennis facility in Audubon Park is named for him.

According to one member, the menu for the regular Sunday night buffet had a distressing sameness: chicken ala king and congealed salad every Sunday night. If you wanted a steak, you had to go to the Red Room. The Red Room had twin fireplaces with portraits above the mantels. An observant eye would note that the portraits were not just a pair, they were identical. On the Fourth of July, 1949, 882 people were served, a club record.

According to the president's report, weather interfered with club use in 1950. Rain and cool weather kept down usage of golf, tennis, and pool facilities. But restaurant and bar service continued to increase. The club was able to reduce its indebtedness from $115,000 to $103,000. After the privations of the war years, club members looked forward to a prosperous decade.

VIII
The 1950s

At the beginning of the decade, the country found itself at war again. This time American troops were sent to Korea in an undeclared war against Chinese and Korean Communists. In Washington, J. Edgar Hoover and Senator Joseph McCarthy were finding homegrown Communists under every bed.

The space race began in 1957 when the Soviet Union fired an unmanned satellite into space. Although the United States had been beaten in an area where it thought it was supreme,

109

Sputnik jokes abounded: a Sputnik cocktail was two parts vodka and one part sour grapes.

But the main mood of the country was complacency. Smiling, avuncular Dwight D. Eisenhower was in the White House. Before long there were television sets in every living room. It was the era of *Father Knows Best* and *Ozzie and Harriet*.

Broadway hits were *The King and I, Damn Yankees,* and *My Fair Lady.* John F. Kennedy's *Profiles in Courage* won a Pulitzer Prize. People flocked to the movies to see *High Noon, From Here to Eternity, Mr. Roberts, Gigi,* and *Around the World in Eighty Days.*

A young man from Memphis made musical history. In 1956, Elvis Presley had several hits on the charts: "Hound Dog," "Heartbreak Hotel," "Don't Be Cruel," and "Love Me Tender." In 1957 he bought a mansion in Whitehaven. That December, he received his draft notice. Young girls sobbed as Presley went off to the army.

James E. Harwood Jr. served as president of the club from 1950 to 1953. He had joined the American Snuff Company in the production part of the business in 1924 and became executive director of Conwood Corporation, as the company changed its name in 1965 to reflect a combination of his name and that of Martin Condon III, the then president.

He was a 1927 graduate of the Memphis Law School. He served as a director of the Tennessee Manufacturers Association, the Memphis Area Chamber of Commerce, the Memphis Community Chest, the Memphis Cotton Carnival Association, and was chairman of the 1973 Governor's Conference, held in Memphis.

Work done included remodeling the Cocktail Lounge, Main Lounge, Children's Snack Bar, and bedrooms; rewiring the entire club; installing a concrete motion picture projection booth, a paddle tennis court, and new caddy facilities; and purchasing an automatic dishwashing machine.

Interior of the cocktail lounge.

Adele Orgill, with her brother Joseph Orgill Jr. and her cousin Edmund Orgill, entertains the French consul, Lionel Vasse, in November 1951.

Monthly club dances were an addition to the social schedule. Sunday night movies continued to be one of the club's chief attractions for families.

In November 1951, a reception at the country club honored Mrs. Adele Orgill. She was awarded two high honors by the French government—the Legion of Honor and the Legion of Merit—for her work as the Memphis chairman of CARE. She had seen the postwar plight of the French people on a trip to France and threw herself with "boundless energy and enthusiasm" into raising money to send CARE packages.

Mrs. Orgill entertained at a buffet dinner after Lionel Vasse, the French consul general in New Orleans, awarded her the decorations. Hundreds of guests attended. Towering arrangements of large snowball-type chrysanthemums were in the lounge. "On the twin mantels, tall ivory tapers held in antique brass candelabra sent shafts of sparkling light upward, with central bouquets of white flowers," wrote the *Press Scimitar*. In the dining room, the long buffet table, "laden with festive food and centered by bright fruit and deep-toned flowers in gold, bronze and wine, with green grapes extending in garlands from the bouquet and even clustered against the turkeys . . . The Thanksgiving theme was repeated in a great gilded horn of plenty on the table under the mirror . . . fruit, vegetables, and fall flowers cascaded from the cornucopia . . . The beauty, the glowing warmth of the scene, was really indescribable."

Adele Orgill and Mrs. William E. Oates both wore stunning Paris models. Mrs. Orgill's was a Sophie original of black Chantilly lace with panels embroidered in midnight blue sequins. Mrs. Oates wore a Patou frock combining a black satin skirt and bodice of cream satin. Mrs. Joseph Orgill Jr. was smart in navy blue, with a short jacket of navy blue and gold metallic threads and jeweled designs on the shoulders. The jacket had been woven and made by Mrs. Adele Orgill. Mrs. Edmund Orgill wore slate blue taffeta and Mrs. Kenneth Orgill wore white chiffon and lace.

The wedding reception of Giles Coors and Sophie Woodson, 1952: Del Voltz, Elinor Colbert, Mayrene Dillard, Frances Deupree, the groom and bride, Susan Harris, Sue Walton, and Sara Humphreys.

Consul Vasse mentioned "the long love affair between her and France, and as you know, I represent France." Then he kissed Mrs. Orgill on both cheeks, the French custom in presenting awards.

Mrs. Joseph Orgill Sr., in blue lace, was quoted as saying, "When that Frenchman kissed Adele, he really demoralized the party . . . Everybody started kissing everybody around!"

Beginning in the fifties, a group of members formed the Pendennis Club, a club within the club, which met every Friday night for bridge and poker. Jimmy Dobbs, George Coors, Ferd Heckle, Tim Treadwell, Frank Norfleet, Tommy Price, and Paul Gillespie were some of the regular players. Their wives came for dinner on Friday nights and played bridge. One wife remembered, "Then we'd wait for the men—and wait, and wait." Sometimes till one or two in the morning. Also, during the fifties, Mrs. Paul Abel came from Clarksdale, Mississippi, on a regular basis to give bridge lessons at the club.

James Edward Stark became president in 1953. A native of Memphis, he was educated at Memphis University School, Culver Military Academy, and the University of Pennsylvania. He went into the lumber business upon the death of his father in 1922, and continued to own and operate the mill which bore his name until 1960, when he sold it and entered the wholesale lumber business, in which he remained active until his death in 1976. He served as president of the Southern Hardwood

Traffic Association and the Lumberman's Club, as well as the Memphis Country Club.

Stark was able to report: "It has always seemed to me that the best test of the value of an organization such as ours is the use the members make of it. With this in mind, we are gratified indeed to note that the use of the club during the past year was again at the highest level in the club's history, restaurant and service sales reaching a total of $294,373."

The limit of regular resident memberships was raised from 450 to 500, so that junior members could become full members when they reached the age of thirty. Lady memberships were also increased. Improvements in 1953 included the installation of air-conditioning units in all the bedrooms and offices.

In 1953 an Employees' Benefit Fund was created, "for use in lieu of insurance to aid worthy qualified employees in distress because of illness or accident." The fund was created by reserving 3 percent of the total annual payrolls. The first year the fund amounted to $4,955.85.

A committee composed of the six living past presidents was formed for long-range planning and to explore the need for a new clubhouse. The immediate past president, James E. Harwood, was the chairman. When work on the new clubhouse began, Harwood was said to keep such close accounts that he counted the nails.

Greenskeeper Jimmy Hamner was recognized for producing "the finest golf course the Southern Golf Association has ever played on." After the USGA Senior Amateur Championship was played there in 1959, the *Journal of Turf Management* called the Memphis Country Club "one of the fine homes of American golf . . . the most hospitable home possible."

GOLFING GREATS

Meanwhile, a Memphis golfer was making a name for himself. Cary Middlecoff was state

Cary Middlecoff returns to Memphis after winning the 1956 U.S. Open.

The 1950s

Gaut Short Game Trophy.

amateur champion for four straight years, 1940 to 1943, while he was still a student at the University of Mississippi and the University of Tennessee Dental School. When he completed his dental degree in 1943, he was commissioned a second lieutenant in the army. He was stationed part of the time at Fort Oglethorpe and Fort Gordon, near the Augusta National Golf Club, and was able to play there many times.

In 1946, he played in the National Amateur Tournament, then he turned professional. From 1946 through 1959, he won forty tournaments, including two U.S. Opens in 1949 and 1956, and the 1955 Masters. He was the leading money winner on the PGA tour for the decade of the 1950s and won the Vardon Trophy in 1956 for the lowest scoring average on the tour. He is tied for seventh on the PGA's career victory list.

Middlecoff's victory in the 1949 National Open in Chicago was front-page news in Memphis. He had a two-over-par score of 288 to beat Sam Snead, Byron Nelson, and others. He was described as "Having more color than a circus bandwagon and the strokes with which to back it."

Despite several conditions which impeded his playing—severe hay fever, an eye injury incurred while filling a tooth, and back trouble—he developed a unique, measured style. He was inducted into the World Golf Hall of Fame as well as the Tennessee Sports Hall of Fame. *The History of Tennessee Golf* says, "Cary Middlecoff set a standard for golf far above that of any other Tennessean . . . a golfer from the Volunteer State will probably never duplicate his three major victories and forty PGA Tour titles."

After his retirement from professional play in 1963, he was associated with *Golf Digest* for many years and was television's first golf analyst. Middlecoff was first a member of Colonial Country Club. In the early 1950s, he became affiliated with the Memphis Country Club and listed that as his home club. In the early 1960s he became a regular member. *The History of Tennessee Golf* says, "For the last twenty years of Middlecoff's life, his favorite place was the men's grill at the Memphis Country Club. Here was where he was most comfortable, talking with friends." He died in 1998 at the age of seventy-seven.

Golf stories abound. Two fondly remembered groups played at the club regularly, though their styles varied greatly.

The Greer Gang was a group of golfing buddies who gave rise to many stories in the 1950s. The original Greer Gang consisted of Rip Greer, George Treadwell, Henry Taylor, Alex Wellford, Dunlap Cannon, and Tunkie Saunders. Dr. Blasingame and "Skinny" Russell filled gaps as needed. In 1959 Dan Canale became a regular as Saunders tapered off his regular play. Lewis McKee and Richard Leatherman filled in later as time started taking its toll.

Nicknames were the rule of the day. Greer was known as Ripper (Jack the Ripper), Treadwell as Gorgeous George (always groomed), Taylor was Sweetie Pie (the gang's "gentleman"), Wellford as Bear (the group's enforcer), Cannon as Sky King (skyward drives, often landing near the tee box), Saunders as Shotgun ("Vance Alexander can explain"), and Canale as Daniele (the Italian gambler).

Dan Canale described the group's heyday (referring to himself in the third person): "Canale's first round of golf with the Gang defined its strict, uncompromising standards. He arrived on the tenth tee (always the starting hole) and was introduced to Rip Greer, the only one he did not know. Without looking up, Greer said, 'Hello, son. What kind of game do you play?' Canale began, 'Pretty good, but I've had a bad cold and . . .' Greer interrupted firmly, 'Son, if you're looking for sympathy, go in the club house, get the dictionary, and you'll find 'sympathy' between 'sex' and 'syphilis.' Now tee off.'"

With no wager, Canale teed off. It was tough golf, and for the next forty-five years, the game never changed.

> Rip was the "organizer"; he made up the game, determined who would play, and supervised the wagers. He was a self-made golfer who had never played before his late 30s, and with no natural golf form or finesse, became a very competent machine-molded player. In his late 70s he became the oldest golfer to qualify for the United States Senior Amateur Championship, played that year at Hilton Head, South Carolina. Although he was single, he was married—to golf. It permeated his very existence and he contributed much to the game at the MCC.

Joe Irby, now the MCC men's locker room attendant, started as a caddy for the Greer Gang. He remembers one day on the number eleven tee, it seemed that everyone had teed off. As they started down the fairway, Rip Greer asked his caddy, "Did you see my ball?" Irby replied politely, "You ain't hit yet, Mr. Greer."

Dan Canale continues his description:

> George was a "handshaker," an insurance salesman through and through, and when spotting a prospect out on the course, even a fairway away, he would slice or hook as required and get the handshake and sales pitch attended to.

> Henry was kindness personified, a true sportsman at somewhat of a disadvantage with this Gang. But he was fine golfer and quietly collected a majority of his bets over the years.

> Alex was impatient with the slow, deliberate play of Greer. He would finish a hole, hurry to the next tee and be almost on the next green by the time the rest of the Gang teed off. When Greer "acted up," the Enforcer would restore order—with firmness—usually bodily picking Greer up and depositing him off the green.

> Dunlap was the clever member of the Gang. Each time he knew who he wanted to be his betting partner and he maneuvered, always "innocently," to achieve his

goal. He was a tenacious competitor and an excellent putter, especially under pressure. Tunkie was a [sic] egotist, supremely confident and always anxious to tell you about his abilities. But he usually backed up his proclamations and most often opened his wallet to deposit rather than to withdraw any money.

We played by "Greer Rules." They were simple: Once off the tee, you played your ball where you found it or put it in your pocket, no relief allowed. A souvenir from the Peabody Hotel Skyway Room, a mock *Commercial Appeal* front page headlined: "U.S.G.A. to Adopt Greer Rules." His rules upset U.S.G.A. Committeeman Treadwell, but they stood, no exceptions . . .

Time has wilted many of the group's games and has erased many participants but the war on the links will be cherished and fondly remembered though now "Gone with the Wind."

Another group which began in the late forties and flourished in the fifties, sixties, and seventies was called the Mafia. The members were mostly veterans of World War II and

The Mafia:
Cousin No No, Bug Eye, Woodie, the General, Folkie, Sweetmeat, Billy Boy, and Greyhound.

were raised in the Great Depression. They played golf every Wednesday afternoon, and Saturday and Sunday mornings. Before long they, too, had nicknames.

One of the instigators of the group was Phil Canale, who was Shelby County attorney general. Because he was of Italian descent and charged with upholding the law, he was known as the Godfather or the General, and the group got the name the Mafia.

Humphrey Folk Sr. was called Folkie or the Hawk. Paul Gillespie was known as Old Blue or Blue Boy, because of his Yale affiliation. Phil Pidgeon was known as Neander, because his shots looked like those of a Neanderthal.

Tommy Price was called Sweetmeat. Jim Manire was the Nose. Bill Roberts was Billy Boy. Tim Treadwell was Bug Eye. Larry Thompson was Pops, because of his many children, or Greyhound. Malcolm Aste was Nasty. Jim Welch was the Giant. John Shea was the Ear, and Martin Shea was Cousin No No.

Russell Wood was Woodie. Gene Hill was Clean Gene. Hugh Sprunt was Cotton Man, or Ghost. Hal McGeorge was McJock, and became a leader of the group after some others had gone to their reward, the Masters Tournament in the Sky, according to Tim Treadwell.

The nicknames could cause occasional confusion. Ben Harrison left a message with his secretary, to her consternation, about setting up a game: "I don't think the Ghost will come, but Sweetmeat and Greyhound have said they'd be there at 1:30."

Some of those who joined the game occasionally were known as "nonresident members": Henry Wetter, Ben Harrison, DeWitt Shy, Billy Webster, Richard Allen, John Heiskell, Ed Lawler, and Jim Miles from Jackson, Tennessee. Eugene Pidgeon was too good a golfer to join the Mafia but would play occasionally when he couldn't find another game.

The group developed its own set of rules. First, you could tee up your ball anywhere you wanted. It was customary for Phil Canale to tee his ball, even in sand traps. Second, you could move your ball any legal distance from where it was lying; this was known as a tree limb. This insured that no one ever had a bad lie. Third, it was optional if you wanted to call a ball out of bounds. You were never penalized for going out of bounds; losing your ball was considered penalty enough.

The Mafia played in sleet and snow, using red balls. They putted at the tee markers when the greens were frozen. "Winter rules" developed into a game barely recognizable as golf. Phil Pidgeon took a free flowing attitude toward winter rules, but it was said that he would never improve his lie more than ten club lengths.

They had a way of hand signaling to the foursome or fivesome behind to let them know what score they had to beat. If the group's lowest score was a bogey, a hand was held up. A hand held horizontal meant par. A hand pointed down to the ground meant an eagle. The most famous cry was "Pocket!" If a player had hit the ball four times and still wasn't on the green, the rest of the group would yell "Pocket!" meaning "Put the damn ball in your pocket and stop taking up our time."

The most amazing shot belonged to Paul Gillespie. He hit a ball over the hedge on number six. It hit the top of a bus, bounced back, and hit the fairway, right in front of the green.

The group sometimes traveled together. Jim Manire tells the story of one trip to Point

*Three men at the bar:
General Clyde Beck, Percy H. Wood, and Dr. Giles Coors.*

Clear, Alabama. When they were ready to tee off, a newlywed couple appeared, and the Mafia members asked them to play through, but the newlyweds declined, "You gentlemen go ahead."

Price, McGeorge, and Manire made decent drives. Phil Canale, who was not awake yet and was wearing small black sunglasses that made him look like the Mole in Dick Tracy comic strips, took a mighty swing with his driver, and dribbled the ball right into a fishpond. Canale hit some of the worst shots ever seen. He would pop up, pocket the ball, and shoot forty-five to ninety degrees off course.

When the newlyweds passed by on a parallel fairway, Manire went across and told them, "You see the guy who dipped it in the pond? He was twice Amateur Champion of Tennessee. Now he is blind. We take him along because he enjoys being in the fresh air and hearing the click of the ball."

That night, the bride came over and said, "George and I think you are the sweetest men we ever saw to treat your golfing companion with so much patience."

There were many other stories about the Mafia. The players didn't take the game too seriously and never played for much money. But after the game was over, there was great competition in the Tap Room—rolling the dice to see who would end up with all the chits.

On one occasion, Pep Allen hadn't played with the Mafia but was in the Tap Room. He was a great sportsman, playing all games—"he'd play ice hockey in the Sahara." He hadn't ordered a drink, but he saw the dice game and borrowed a chit just so he could play. Needless to say, he ended up with all the chits, about forty dollars worth.

Sometimes the Mafia would come in from the golf course at one or two o'clock, and not leave the club until five. Someone was always promising that this was the last roll—the Grand Old Roll. Then the loser would insist on one more—the Grand Old Grand Old Roll.

Jim Manire remembers, "There was a time in the mid-nineties when many members of the Mafia died one after another. The Mafia played out . . . I think all of us knew that the golf game was a gift from the Lord above."

Martin Condon III became president of the country club from 1954 to 1957. His grandfather had been president in the teens. He was born in Pelham Manor, New York. The family moved to Memphis when his grandfather became president of the American Snuff Company. He was educated at Lawrenceville School and Princeton, where he graduated Phi Beta Kappa. He served as a first lieutenant in the navy during World War II.

After the war he became president of the American Snuff Company, later renamed the Conwood Corporation. He was a board member of Union Planters Bank, Plough Incorporated, and Dobbs Houses. He served as president of the United States Industrial Council, vice president of the National Association of Manufacturers, board member of both the Memphis Chamber of Commerce and Le Bonheur Children's Hospital, and Tennessee Chairman of Radio Free Europe.

Martin J. Condon III, president 1954–1957.

DINING AT THE CLUB

A 1955 dinner ticket shows that thirteen people could eat a full dinner, complete with shrimp cocktails, roast beef, filet, mixed grill, and lamb chops, for $60.65. That was from the regular menu. But other, grander choices were available.

On October 27, 1956, the chairman of the House Committee, J. T. "Tunkie" Saunders, sent a letter to the membership, with a long

The 1950s

list of elaborate dishes. "It is the opinion of the food committee that many of the members would prefer something different when dining out; for one of the main purposes in eating out is to have food which is not generally prepared at home.

"As you know, most of the best dishes of the world's leading restaurants require more or less elaborate preparation and much time and effort . . . With this in mind, your food committee has prepared the following 'Order in Advance' menu . . . supplemental to our regular 'A la Carte' menu, which contains dishes that can be prepared in a short time."

Members could provide their own game, or the club could obtain certain items—pheasant, deer, chukar partridge, Scotch grouse, Canadian sturgeon, or fresh malossol caviar—on three or four days notice.

The choices that could be ordered in advance were elaborate, lovingly described, and sound overly rich to modern tastes steeped in fears of cholesterol and triglycerides. The list was long; some of the choices were:

Algonquin Special Soup: A chicken curry soup thickened with egg yolk and cream. The prize recipe of the Algonquin Hotel chef, given by the courtesy of the maitre d'hotel Georges.

Pilaff De Crabs: Crabmeat served with rice and a mixture of chopped ham, bacon, onions, tomato paste, white wine, rum and heavy cream. Recipe from "Le Relais des Isles" restaurant, Paris. Patron—M. Jacquest, who was originally from the West Indies, where this recipe is well known.

Lobster Arciduc: The lobster is boiled live, the meat removed and sauteed in butter and later mixed with a cream sauce heavily seasoned with brandy, port wine, whiskey and cayenne pepper. French recipe. This dish has an elusive flavor.

Fine Fat Pullet: The breast bone is removed and the bird skewered, then cooked with shallots, mushrooms, and various condiments and vegetables; allowed to cool and wrapped with fat back of pork; hermetically sealed with six sheets of white paper and cooked for one hour. Sent to the table in sheets. What an ineffable flavour when the sheets are opened!

Canard aux Ananas: Roast duck served with sautéed pineapple. When the duck is removed from the pan the juice from the pineapple is poured into the pan and reduced, at which time white wine, vinegar, and demi-glace is added. The duck is blazed with Triple Sec before being served and the sauce poured over it. This recipe is from the Gafner, by M. Jean Borrin and is also a good way to prepare Long Island duck, and should be a pleasant change from the usual methods of preparation.

Gigot la Clinque: Leg of mutton which is marinated for a week in old red wine and olive oil. Injected into the leg daily is a mixture of fresh orange juice and brandy . . . Served with a venison sauce, to which has been added just before serving, two tablespoons of the blood of a hare . . .

The food might be grand, but the surroundings left something to be desired. The story was told that mice were so plentiful in the old part of the building that they brazenly ran up and down the drapes in the Red Room. President James D. Robinson even had names for the mice: "There goes Jack. Here comes Jill."

The forty-five-year-old clubhouse had outlived its usefulness. Despite the continual

*A festive evening at the club:
Mary Budd Bodine, Dr. Giles Coors, Marguerite Turner,
Toof Brown, Dr. J. J. McCaughan, Louise Dewey, Dick Bodine, Ida Brown,
Dr. Carroll Turner, and Gertrude Coors.*

repairs, repainting, and redecorating, it had to go. The committee of past presidents presented its report. A building program was approved at the annual meeting in October 1955. Plans for a new million-dollar clubhouse were announced.

Club member Walk C. Jones Jr. was the architect. He announced that the new clubhouse would have a Deep South flavor. It was to be a red brick building with white trim and full-length windows facing the golf course.

Best of all, it would be fireproof and completely air-conditioned.

On March 28, 1956, members received a plan for financing the construction, based on long study and consideration of the recommendations of members. Many means of financing had been considered, and the board had studied the matter carefully before making this proposal.

To finance the first stage of construction at $500,000, membership sale price was to

Tearing down the clubhouse, from the Press Scimitar, April 4, 1958.

increase to $2,750, and each regular member would pay an assessment of $250, at $25 per month over the next ten months, beginning in May 1956. In addition, fifty more regular memberships would be authorized.

Members were informed that the loss of interest on $250 during the term of membership was estimated at about 60 cents a month, "a very low cost per member."

Work began upon approval by the membership. In 1957, cost was estimated at eighteen dollars per square foot. Erich Schmied, also a member, was general contractor for the building.

The east end of the existing clubhouse was demolished, and the first stage of construction began with the men's locker room, ladies' locker room, Red Room, Tap Room, golf shop, and kitchen. The building proceeded in stages, so that the club never completely closed down.

Meals were still served during the construction, and the Buntyn train stop was still active. Ellen Ramsay Clark remembers having Sunday night supper at the club, then crossing the street to board the train, the *Tennessean*, with a group of students at Virginia schools—Randolph Macon, Sweetbriar, UVA, and Washington and Lee—who were going back to school after vacations. Boys going to Camp Carolina also boarded at Buntyn, escorted to camp by Dottie Gillespie.

When the Junior League held its playday at the country club in 1955, Dottie Gillespie, the new president, received the gavel from Mrs. H. Duncan Taylor. Members played golf, tennis, and bridge, and enjoyed a luncheon featuring Chicken Suzette. Mrs. William Leatherman and Mrs. Edward Lawler won the golf prizes, and Miss Connie Austin won the tennis prize.

The Junior League helped sell tickets for one of the top golf tournaments when the Western Amateur Best Ball Championship was held at the Memphis Country Club on October 6–9, 1955. Even before the official ticket sales began, Dr. Cary Middlecoff was pictured buying tickets from Nancy Cook and Barbara Sprunt.

Mrs. Sam Rembert won a mink stole as top salesman. A cocktail party and dinner was a feature of the tournament, and Junior League members sold soft drinks and sandwiches from a booth on the course.

In June 1957, two Hollywood stars were entertained at the country club. Danny Thomas and Jane Russell were in town for a benefit for St. Jude, and Edward F. Barry, chairman of the St. Jude Fund, led them in singing.

Property adjacent to the practice tee was owned by Miss Christine Tate, daughter of one of the founding members, Robert F. Tate. Over the years, Miss Tate and the club had gotten crossways, and she would not let people come into her yard to pick up the balls that had been sliced there. The club built a tall fence to try to solve the problem, but golf balls still ended up in her yard. Richard Leatherman Sr. rented some property from her in Tunica County, so he was put in charge of dealing with Miss Tate. Apparently he pacified her, although she never allowed the caddies to enter her yard.

In 1955, she bequeathed two acres of her property, adjoining the number one fairway, to the club. Her property became the location of two new tennis courts, as the new clubhouse took the old ones. The Tate Room, located just off the main entrance in the new clubhouse, was named for her.

On January 20, 1958, the first phase of the new clubhouse was finished, and work on the next phase could begin. A picture in the *Press Scimitar* on April 4, 1958, was captioned "It Looks Like the Work of a Tornado—It's Really the Work of a Bulldozer." The newspaper continued, "It proved more economical to tear down the building, even breaking the big glass windows (some children had fun throwing rocks thru them) than to take it down and salvage the material. . . . The first part has been finished.

The interior of the Grill Room: Dunlap Cannon, Dr. George Coors, Rip Greer, and James D. Robinson discuss the Tennessee Open Tournament to be held at the club in April 1959.

President and Mrs. James D. Robinson in the ballroom of the new clubhouse.

Now two-thirds of the old building is being knocked down."

When James D. Robinson became president in 1958, he had to report that although the work on the building was going steadily, operating with reduced facilities caused many problems. Restaurant sales were down 23 percent and bar sales down 6 percent Many capital purchases, unconnected to the building budget, were necessary, and new furniture, decorations, and landscaping were not included in the budget. An assessment for the building fund was levied on regular resident members. It was an unusual year, the president admitted, "All in all, I think we have done as well as could be expected under the circumstances."

Robinson was born in New Orleans and educated at Cornell. He moved to Memphis in the 1930s, and served in the navy during World War II, flying planes in the South Pacific. He was the inventor of the first practical and efficient commercial dishwashing system and founder of the company that bore its name, Auto-Chlor System, Inc. The company was purchased by Unilever in 1995.

Robinson donated the original tennis lounge to MCC. He was 1951's Ouro of the Grand Krewe of Memphi. He and his wife are buried in the St. John's Episcopal Cemetery which he bought, refurbished, and donated to the church before his death in 1983. He was elected a member of the Society of Entrepreneurs in Memphis posthumously. Robinson Residence Hall at Rhodes College was dedicated on December 17, 1989, in his memory. The James Dinkins Robinson Memorial Library at Trezevant Manor in the heart of Memphis is also dedicated in his honor.

The new clubhouse was completed and fully opened in July 1959. Entertainment picked up considerably. The new cocktail lounge proved popular, and Sunday night movies were again under way. Billy Buxton worked many hours on the new sound system, making tape recordings.

Members admired the view of the golf course from the pastel yellow dining room. The ballroom featured two crystal chandeliers and indirect lighting, which "could be reduced or brightened to suit different tastes."

The cocktail lounge had scarlet red walls, a jet black bar, glass-topped tables, and leather chairs. It was said to be modeled on Maxim's in Paris. An ash-paneled curving corridor led from the auto entrance to the cocktail lounge.

The new Red Room was for mixed groups in golf or tennis attire, "or in what the clubhouse rules refer to as 'field costume.'" The Tap Room was restored to its men-only status after having served both men and women during the construction period.

The new golf pro shop opened with dark paneling and exposed beams. Golf bags were now to be stored in upright racks, which would eliminate scuffing, instead of the old horizontal racks. In January 1959, several members, Dunlap Cannon, Dr. George Coors, J. Ripley Greer, and president James D. Robinson met to discuss the Tennessee Open Golf Tournament which was to be held at the country club in April.

The newspaper reported on the golf fashions at Ladies Day at the club in April 1959.

The new clubhouse opened on July 3, 1959.

The 1950s

The Commercial Appeal *covered golf fashions on April 9, 1959:*
(Top left)—Mrs. John J. Corrigan.
(Top right)—Mrs. Clifford Merrin.
(Right)—Mrs. J. W. McDonnell Jr.,
Mrs. Edward Cook, and Mrs. James R. Welsh.

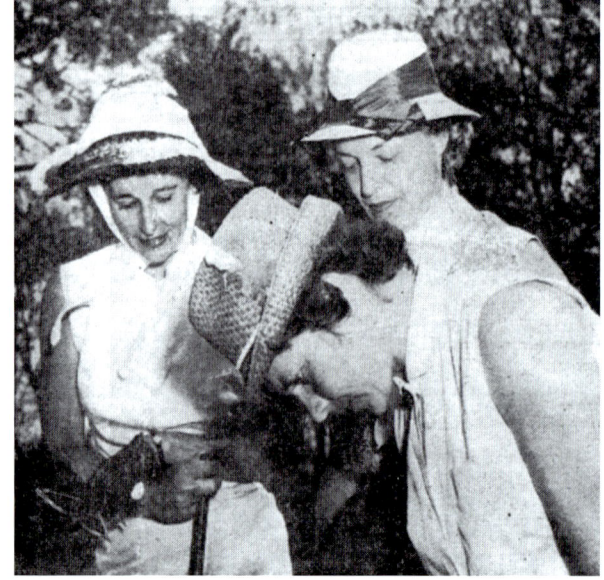

Mrs. John J. Corrigan wore a wide-brimmed straw-style hat anchored under the chin with a scarf threaded through. Mrs. Clifford Merriman coordinated her plaid-trimmed blouse with a matching hatband and wore a pin shaped like a golf club. Mrs. J. W. McDonnell wore her good luck hat, a red straw with feather trim; Mrs. Edward W. Cook work a rippled straw in ombre shades; and Mrs. James R. Welsh wore a natural straw with a bright blue band and perky bow.

The new clubhouse was formally opened over the Fourth of July holiday. The *Commercial Appeal* wrote on July 3, 1959, "The Memphis Country Club, capstone of Mid-South society almost since the beginning of this century, enters upon a new era today with the formal opening of its elegant new clubhouse on its historic site on Southern at Goodwyn . . . In a manner of speaking, its features combine the wisdom of the ages, having been built under the direction of a building committee, comprising the living past presidents of the club, to whom are traditionally brought all complaints and suggestions by the membership down through the years."

The newspaper effused, "Nowhere nearer than Atlanta, if there, does it have a peer. Its members refer to it as 'our million dollar clubhouse.' Actually it cost substantially more than that."

Mortgage payments of forty-five hundred dollars a month were a burden, but it was hoped that increased activity at the club would prove profitable. The close-knit membership was commented upon: "Generally half or more of the vacancies are filled by sons or sons-in-law of members."

Three charter members were still on the rolls to see the third building: J. P. Norfleet, John Sneed Williams, and Robert M. Metcalf. Homer K. Jones, who joined in 1907, and McKay Van Vleet, who joined in 1909, also remembered the original structure, as the new building opened to the delight of the members.

IX
The 1960s

After the complacency of the 1950s, the 1960s were a decade of turmoil. Relations with the Soviet Union worsened after a U.S. U-2 reconnaissance plane was shot down inside the USSR in May 1960.

The first televised presidential debates occurred in September 1960, between the Republican candidate Richard Nixon and Democrat John F. Kennedy. Kennedy won the election but did not live to serve out one term. His assassination in Dallas, Texas, on November 22, 1963, stunned the country.

Under his successor, Lyndon Johnson, Congress passed civil rights legislation, Medicare for the elderly, and tax reduction. As the United States became more deeply involved in the conflict in Vietnam, protests against the war gained strength at home.

Sometimes it seemed as if half the nation had taken to the streets. There were marches opposed to the war and in favor of civil rights. The Poor People's March, led by Dr. Martin Luther King Jr., brought two hundred thousand people to Washington in 1963. Freedom Riders rode buses through Mississippi. Dr. King led a march from Selma to Birmingham, Alabama, in 1965.

It was a violent decade. Civil rights leader Medgar Evers was shot in Mississippi in June 1963. A church bombing in Birmingham killed four young black girls. Kennedy's killer, Lee Harvey Oswald, was shot while in custody of the Dallas police while the nation watched on television in 1963. Malcolm X was killed by a rival Black Muslim faction in 1965. James Meredith was shot and wounded on a march from Memphis to Oxford, Mississippi. Racial riots in Watts, Miami, Newark, and other cities occurred. A student at the University of Texas went on a shooting spree from a campus tower, killing thirteen and wounding thirty-three in 1966. Presidential candidate Robert F. Kennedy was killed in Los Angeles in June 1968. Hurricane Camille killed more than three hundred people in Mississippi, Louisiana, and Alabama. Casualties mounted in Vietnam, and protests multiplied in the United States. And in Memphis, Dr. Martin Luther King Jr. was assassinated on April 4, 1968, setting off a wave of rioting and protest across the country.

The United States launched a chimpanzee into space and recovered him successfully in 1961. Lieutenant Colonel John Glenn became the first American to orbit the earth in 1962. On July 16, 1969, Neil Armstrong became the first man to set foot on the moon, fulfilling President Kennedy's pledge to put an American on the moon in a decade.

The Surgeon General's Report in 1964 found that the use of cigarettes "contribute substantially to mortality."

To Kill a Mockingbird won a Pulitzer Prize in 1960, and Gregory Peck won an Oscar in 1963 for his role in the movie. Charles Van Doren and other quiz show contestants were arrested for fixed outcomes on the popular TV shows. Television was called "a vast wasteland" by Newton Minow, chairman of the Federal Communications Commission. Folk music became popular, with the Kingston Trio; Joan Baez; and Peter, Paul and Mary topping the charts. The Beatles caused a riot on their arrival in New York in 1964. Elvis Presley served in the army in Germany and was about to head home.

The decade of the 1960s was one of increased use at the Memphis Country Club as the membership took advantage of the new clubhouse. It was also one of increased costs. President James D. Robinson pointed out in November 1960 that utility costs had doubled and property taxes had increased by nearly as much.

In January 1960, the Red Room was the site of a surprise birthday party for two members of the young married set. Lawrence Rainer and Renny Pidgeon shared the honors. The party was the idea of Betsy and Chappy Weaver, who told guests to bring "crazy" presents.

A party planning meeting around the pool for the Symphony Ball: (Foreground)— Mrs. William L. Roberts, Mrs. Lester Samelson, and Mrs. Paul Gillespie.

The *Press Scimitar* reported, "The usually quiet Sunday evening dining was thrown into an uproar when Lawrence opened her present. It was a lizard, at least 2½ feet long, according to one eye-witness. (Next week someone will swear it was a dragon) . . . The little guinea pig given to Renny by Jimmy Beck and Linda and Scrammy Wade seemed tame in comparison. He spent the evening quietly chewing parsley." Among the guests were James Boone and Josephine Lowrance, Cullen and Jane Kehoe, and of course, Bobby Pidgeon and Jim Rainer.

Memphis Country Club golfers participated in the first international Pro-Am Golf Tournament in Scotland. John Sheahan, Hugh Allen, Charles Kittle, and pro Pat Abbott were among forty teams who journeyed to Gleneagles. Sheahan reported that it was a thrill to compete: "In Scotland you don't play golf, you live golf."

In 1960, Ben Hogan and Gene Littler tied for second in the Memphis Open, now known

Twins planning the Sinfonetta Ball, October 12, 1960: Mrs. Emmet Joyner Jr., Mrs. Phil Pidgeon, Mrs. Swayne Latham Jr., and Mrs. George Humphreys.

as the FedEx St. Jude Classic. Hogan practiced at the Memphis Country Club and stayed in the guest rooms.

What was to become a long-term golfing group known as the Saturday Morning Dogs began in 1960 with Richard Austin and Jac Crisler. Before the end of the decade, Walter Scott, Henry Jones, Jack Gordon, Ed Walthal, Bill Gerber, Tommy White, John Austin, Craft Dewey, and John Salmon had been added. Fred James, John Adamson, John Marshall, Jeff Mann, John Malmo, Ed Bennett, George Clarke, John T. Stout, Dr. Peter Quinn, Scott Fisher, Richard Leatherman, Bailey Wiener, John Kenney, Kevin Kenney, Jim Daughdrill, Dick Bodine, Charles Cobb, Bill Milnor, Dr. Peter Ballenger, John Collier, Jim Harwood, Tom Hutton, Bill Maury, Blair McDonald, Lucian Minor, John Cawthon, Bob Fallis, and Willis Willey were among those who played with the Dogs.

The group held a "Come as Someone Else" party in 1968, and in 1975, they held the first awards party, with posters as prizes. By two years later, in 1977, several awards categories had been created—Articulate Adjective, Wildest Woods, Putrid Putter, and Infamous Irons—and the prizes were plastic trophies. By the seventh annual awards party, black tie was *de rigueur* and the prizes were silver bowls. A Most Improved award, voted on by the players, is awarded. The Dogs have continued to play for over forty years, every Tuesday, Thursday, and Saturday.

The club continued to be the location of choice for fund-raisers and parties for many organizations. The ladies planning the Symphony Ball were photographed around the pool in the early sixties. The newspaper said, "Planning a party is fun—especially if the planning is done in 'party fashion' with coffee and cokes around a big pool. An event of such magnitude as the Memphis Symphony Ball requires much work from many people."

For the first ball in 1959, Marguerite Piazza Condon agreed to perform her successful

The Saturday Morning Dogs—Then: (Standing)—Fred James, Ed Walthal, Jac Crisler, Jack Gordon, Bill Gerber, and Richard Austin. (Seated)—Henry Jones and Walter Scott.

The Saturday Morning Dogs—Now: (Standing)—Jack Gordon, Henry Jones, John Austin, and John Salmon. (Seated)—Richard Austin, Walter Scott, Jac Crisler, and Ed Walthal.

A party group:
(Standing)—Billy Buxton, Mary Buxton, and John D. Canale. (Sitting)—Norma Willey, Mary Treadwell, Peggy Canale, Nancy Cook, Heloise McKee, Lewis McKee, Sam Rembert, and Scottie Rembert.

musical act. A friend from New York brought professional lighting and sound designers for the event. The ball became an annual event on the Memphis social calendar.

The Duration Club held its annual Charity Ball at the country club on February 20, 1960. The Duration Club was formed for the "duration" of the war to brighten the existence of those who fought in World War II. After the war, the club remained in existence to provide entertainment for veterans and patients in the military hospitals, and later opened a school for mentally handicapped children. About six hundred people attended the fund-raiser, when the ballroom, dining room, and Tate Room were decorated in an Oriental theme.

When the Tennessee Dental Association held its meeting in Memphis in May 1960, the Dental Auxiliary luncheon was held at the Memphis Country Club. The theme was "A French Salon," and four hostesses dressed as French maids walked among the guests passing out favors. The unusual table decorations were the main feature, according to the *Press Scimitar*. Some 275 "exotic and original whimsies" created from paper plates, ribbon, and straw were mounted on hat stands. A ribbon led from each hat to the plate to show each lady which hat was hers. Hats were swapped back and forth to coordinate with each lady's costume. Gerber's Department Store presented a fashion show. Models passed through columns banked with palms, and gold and white period tables were piled high with gay hat boxes with hats tumbling out in colorful profusion.

The Josephine Circle presented its eight new members at a luncheon at the country club on May 4, 1960. Table decorations were spring flowers in pastel colors accented with green, and the new members received gift corsages.

Laclede's Ladies Shop presented a fashion show at the luncheon of the Women's Council of the Real Estate Board. Country club members Mrs. Giles Coors, in an evening gown of red satin, and Mrs. Howard Willey, in golden silk chiffon, modeled.

A festive after-theater party for Diamond Horseshoe patrons of Memphis Opera Theater, the cast of *Don Giovanni*, and Memphis Opera Theater officers was held on November 12, 1963 at the country club. Mrs. Edward W. Cook, Harry McCoy Jr., and Mrs. James R. Welsh were chairmen of the elaborate event.

A special event for club members was planned around the "much discussed multi-million dollar movie *Cleopatra.*" On June 28, 1963, cocktails and dinner were served at the club, then an air-conditioned bus took people to the Crosstown Theater, where seats were reserved in the center section. The cost for the evening was ten dollars. Club member Berry Brooks also showed his movies about African safaris at the club.

The 1960s dining room menu, with a dark green cover and the MCC monogram, looks very much like today's menu—except for one major difference: the prices. An actual meal check from September 4, 1960, shows that four diners enjoyed a meal consisting of one cup of vichyssoise, two shrimp cocktails, two filets mignon en brochette, and two eight-ounce filets. For all this, W. D. Mathis Jr. paid a total of seventeen dollars.

Other menu items included oysters on the half shell, 85¢; seafood cocktail of lobster, shrimp, and crabmeat, 85¢; white rose madrilene with sour cream and caviar, 40¢; broiled lobster tail with drawn butter, $3; Delaware shad roe with broiled tomato and bacon strips, $3.50; Rocky Mountain rainbow trout amandine, $2.75; roast prime ribs of beef au jus, $2.75; ten-ounce filet mignon, $4.50; bacon-wrapped lamb noisettes, $3.25; omelet with mushrooms, bacon, ham, or seafood, $1.25; brandied macaroons with coffee ice cream, 45¢; homemade pies, 25¢; a la mode, 35¢. The most expensive item on the menu was Chateaubriand for two at $9. Beverages offered were coffee, tea, milk, or Sanka for 15¢, but if your bill totaled more than $1.00, no charge was made for beverages.

In 1963 the house on the property that Miss Christine Tate had bequeathed to the club was removed, and tennis courts and a tennis lounge were built there.

Lewis McKee Sr. served as president in 1961–1963, twenty years after his father had been president. During World War II, he served as a fighter pilot in the South Pacific. After the war, he returned to Memphis and entered the family cotton business. He joined National Bank of Commerce, becoming president. He became president of the Federal Company, which changed its name to Holly Farms. In the

The swimming pool.

1980s, he became an Episcopal priest and served at Calvary Episcopal Church.

The Board of Directors studied possible changes in the club rules. President McKee sent a letter saying that the conclusion was that few changes were necessary, but many rules needed to be reemphasized.

> Your attention is directed to the House Rules under the paragraph styled "Dress." This will be henceforth changed to read: "Members in field costume may be served food or drink in the Red Room only on special occasions. Field costume not permitted in any of the main dining rooms or in the Club House Lounge and coats may not be dispensed with therein which includes members, guests, and also including minor children of the members. A state of partial dress is not permitted on the Club grounds, nor in the Club House, except in locker rooms and in the Snack Bar."

Guests were not allowed on the tennis courts, golf course, or pool more than once a week, and not on Saturday afternoons, Sundays, or holidays; guests were required to be accompanied by a member, who was responsible for guest fees.

Samuel S. Rembert Jr. was president from 1963 until 1965. The first of his family to come to Shelby County arrived in its earliest years. Andrew Rembert settled on a Revolutionary War grant near Woodstock in 1819 and named his plantation Seven Hills Plantation. His son, the first Samuel S. Rembert, was an inventor. Among his inventions was a bed on pulleys attached to a clock that rose slowly during the night, reaching the ceiling at midnight and slowly descending to the floor. He wrote a book in 1876, called *The Science of Life for the Wife at Home in Her Kitchen, Chamber, and Parlor, or Hygienic Philosophy*. In it he offered advice to women in the kitchen, with recipes and household hints; in the parlor, with hints on how to be an interesting conversationalist; and in the bedroom, with delicately worded sexual advice.

The fourth Sam Rembert attended Princeton and served in the navy in World War II. He farmed cotton and soybeans in Arkansas and Mississippi. He served as president of the country club from 1963 to 1965. He died in 1997, at the age of seventy-eight.

Improvements in 1963 included sprinklers for the golf course and tennis courts, and a new swimming pool and well. The new swimming pool was roughly 40 percent larger than the old one. A brick wall was built around the pool area the next year.

President Rembert called 1964 "a year of the usual crises." But the next year he was able to report that the club was in sound condition, with an operating profit of $19,000. The mortgage obligation was $54,000 yearly, and the club instituted a plan of regular maintenance and improvements.

The golf course irrigation system was a source of pride—and of irritation. The company which had installed the system went bankrupt. It took a couple of years to work out all the details satisfactorily. For members, the charge for cleaning and storing clubs went from $1.50 a month to $2.00, the first increase in cost in over twenty years.

Thanksgiving dinner in 1964 included shrimp on ice; caviar; prime ribs of beef; roast turkey and dressing; bourbon flavored sweet potatoes; tiny onions in cream sauce; green peas, buttered; bing cherry mold; cranberry mold; stuffed celery; deviled eggs and olives; hot mincemeat pie; pumpkin chiffon pie; and salted nuts and mints. The cost of all this bounty was four dollars.

What was to become a major annual event began in 1963: the Member-Guest Golf Tournament. Parties were as much a part of the weekend as golf. In 1966, the whole weekend cost one hundred dollars, and included "refreshment, food, refreshment, entertainment, refreshment, special events, and refreshment," according to the tournament committee. A block of rooms had been set aside at the Admiral Benbow Inn for guests, with shuttle service provided.

The 1965 Debutante Ball featured the Russ David Band from St. Louis, magnificent decorations, and a gourmet supper. The president assured the membership that the parents of the debutantes were charged to cover the additional costs, two hundred dollars per debutante. The fee included the presentation, two escorts, flowers, a favor for the girl, invitations for the parents, refreshments, and a midnight supper. Parents were urged to invite as many friends as possible at fifteen dollars each.

Selected stags, two for each debutante, were invited to form a Floor Committee. A letter said, "For to a great degree your cooperation can make this just another party or a great one. It is expected, therefore, that as a member of this functioning floor committee you will make it your personal responsibility to assure each Debutante has a good time. It is not necessary to tell you how to do this—*you know*. Make sure the Debs have a good time; you'll have a good time and assure the success of the party."

Sunday night movies were a favorite tradition. In 1965, parents were urged to make sure that their children went directly to the movie after eating: "Too many children have been using the Club as a gathering place and *never* attend the movie at all. In fairness to all concerned, we ask that if you send your young people to the Club for supper and the show, that you so instruct them, otherwise the Club Management will ask them to go to the movie or else please go home." Movies included *Seven Brides for Seven Brothers*, *Annie Get Your Gun*, *Gun for a Coward*, *The Big Land*, *Colorado*, *Meet Captain Kidd*, *David Copperfield*, and *Premature Burial*.

The club newsletter in the 1960s was called *Tate Room Tattler*. It announced the first MCC gin rummy champion in 1966: Hugh Sinclair, with Dan Canale as runner-up. Another new event was Cinema Horse Races. Guests were given programs detailing facts about the horses and jockeys, and an envelope containing scrip money for wagers. When the master of ceremonies declared the Tote closed, a sealed box carrying the film was opened, and films of five races were shown. The winning bettors were rewarded, and a buffet diner was served, all for five dollars a person.

A Spring Dance for ninth, tenth, and eleventh graders featured a rock and roll band, "Coat and Necktie mandatory for boys and appropriate dress for young ladies will be required."

The Ball Room became a dinner theater in October 1966, with the south dining room converted into a stage. An Atlanta theater group called The Wits' End Players presented *Let Yourself Go*.

Albert Austin III, who served as president from 1965 to 1968, was a third-generation member of the Memphis Country Club. A graduate of the United States Military Academy at West Point, he served in the air force from 1949 to 1955, leaving the service with the rank of captain. He joined Boyle Investment Company in 1955, and retired as vice chairman of the

*Marguerite Gaut
Senior Women's Invitational Trophy.*

Sam Rembert Jr., president 1963–1965, with Mrs. Edward J. Lawler, Mrs. Eugene Pidgeon, and Mrs. Paul Gillespie, planning the Member-Guest Tournament, 1963.

board in 1989. He joined the country club as a junior member in 1955 and became a regular member two years later.

He was active with Hutchison School, the Boys' Club, the Mid-South Coliseum Board, Future Memphis, and the Med; served on the board of Union Planters Corporation; and then became chairman of Cannon, Austin and Cannon, with his son-in-law, Henry Cannon, and his successor as club president, Dr. Bland Cannon.

He first served on the Memphis Country Club Board in 1964 and was in charge of installing the first irrigation system for the greens and fairways. During his time as president, the first Health Club was added.

When Health Club facilities were first suggested, the idea drew opposition, particularly from members who were doctors. They reasoned that health was a matter for professionals, not for amateurs. The first health and athletic addition was completed in 1968, however. Separate facilities for men and women offered sauna, steambath, whirlpool, and sunlamp facilities; exercise machines; squash and handball courts; and sleeping rooms.

In 1966, President Austin reported that a study showed that the total amount of tips received in the Red Room and dining room averaged only a little more than 8 percent, and he urged members to increase the waiters' renumeration. In 1967, a 15 percent tip was added to each bill.

The sixtieth anniversary of the Memphis Country Club was celebrated with a gala black-tie party on March 5, 1966. Cocktails at 7:00 P.M. were followed by a buffet at 7:30. After dinner, Berl Olswanger's band played for dancing, and singer-comedian Shearon Elebash was featured in a floor show.

The serpentine buffet table had a red, black, and gold cover. A large ice carving of the letters MCC centered the table. A suckling pig was at one end of the buffet and a decorative lobster at the other. Flower arrangements of

A Memphi Midwinter Ball in the mid-1960s:
Paul Gillespie, Martha Doggrell, Helen Crawford, Carl Stanton, Pat Martin, Mary Stanton,
Frank Doggrell, Buddy Keesee, Mary Alice Martin, Beverly Pettey, John Pettey,
Emily Keesee, Pat Crawford, Virginia Graves, and Paul Graves.

white carnations, yellow acacia, and red tulips were in the center of the tables, and the presidents' table featured a black runner beneath the flowers.

The living past presidents were recognized. Three were in Florida: George Treadwell, Martin J. Condon III, and James D. Robinson. Those in attendance were seated together: Edward P. Russell, W. Groom Leftwich, James E. Harwood Jr., James E. Stark, Lewis McKee Sr., and Sam Rembert Jr.

Women golfers were entertained with Playtime 1967 at an April Dutch Treat luncheon. The Lucky Swingers—Minnie Lee Allen, Joy Austin, Inez Boone, Martha Canale, Esther Klyce, Irene Orgill, and Aggie Turley, with Ruth Marie Cobb, accompanist—provided music. Helen of Memphis staged a fashion show, and Pat Abbott presented a monologue. Everyone received a golf ball favor, with a gold putter as a door prize. The cost for the gourmet luncheon was two dollars.

Berl Olswanger played for a Splash Party on June 2, 1967, to celebrate the opening of the pool. The menu was an international buffet, featuring Szekely Gulyas (Hungarian sauerkraut and pork), Italian cannelloni (stuffed pancakes with bolognaise sauce), sauerbraten (German pickled beef with dumplings), scampi a la Venice (red scampi in garlic butter), filet of sole pompadour (in hollandaise sauce), and coq au vin (chicken French style in red wine). There were special prizes for costumes: the "mod-est man" and the mini-est mini skirt. The cost for "dinner, dance, decorations, swimming . . . come rain or moon shine" was $4.75.

Income decreased in 1968, and President Austin gave several reasons. First, the club had been closed during the riots in the spring of 1968 following the death of Dr. Martin Luther King Jr. Operating costs were up, $23,500 in salaries alone. The Board of Directors had instituted a policy curtailing the number and size of non-social, organizational parties and meetings. Another factor was the change in enforcement of the "liquor by the drink" laws. The cost of doing business was going up.

Dr. Bland W. Cannon served as president from 1968 to 1970. Born in Brownsville in 1920, he was educated at Southwestern (now Rhodes College) and received graduate and medical degrees from Northwestern University. He served in the army in Munich, Germany.

He was a neurological surgeon, a clinical professor, and vice chancellor for academic affairs at the University of Tennessee Medical College. He was a founder and president of the Congress of Neurological Surgeons, the world's largest neurological surgeons' society.

He served as president of the Tennessee Medical Association; a founder of the Mid-South Medical Center Council for Health Planning; and on many boards and advisory committees, winning many awards for service.

He retired from the active practice of medicine in 1980 to pursue businesses, including Associated Health Consultants and Cannon, Austin and Cannon, real estate development.

During Dr. Cannon's term, the club manager was terminated, and Elgin Scott, the associate manager, served as acting manager. A wall along the southern club property was built, the health and athletic facility was equipped and furnished, and color TV and radio were added to each guest room. Property at 576 Tate Lane was purchased for fifteen thousand dollars. Two

Mrs. and Dr. Bland Cannon, president 1968–1970, at the club's Cotton Carnival party.

The 1968 Member-Guest Tournament: (Standing)—Pat Abbott and Dr. George Coors. (Seated)—Cary Middlecoff, and Byron Morse from Little Rock.

new tennis courts were built, and the parking lot reconfigured.

A survey of comparable clubs in southern cities revealed that the Memphis Country Club supported a broader base of activities than other clubs, and few clubs offered such a wide range of facilities for all types of activities. The dues were below the going rate. Again, MCC was called "a combination City and Country Club . . . one of the few clubs with a fine golf course right in the heart of the city."

President Cannon thought it necessary to warn the membership in February 1970: "Your Board of Directors requested that I again bring to your attention the policies regarding liquor sales and consumption. The loss of our liquor license would seriously affect the operation of the club and would impose a great inconvenience on all the members." No member was to have in his possession liquor that was not purchased from the club, except at a private party at the discretion of the manager. Hours were to be strictly enforced, and minors were not to be served.

A long-lasting tennis group began in the late sixties. Margaret and Buddy Krausnick and Diana and Richard Allen were the nucleus, and the group grew to include Dorothy and Kemmons Wilson, Sue and Cooper Robinson, Sally and Palmer Brown, Ellen and Larry Thompson, Flo and Bobby Snowden, Bab and Tom Quackenboss, Betty and Charlie Russell, Peggy and John Canale, Elizabeth and John Stout, Katie and Bill Roberts, Peggy and Frank Jemison, Dottie and Wallace Pennepacker, Edie and Ralph Hand, Jane and Ewing Carruthers, Jan and Roy Bell, and Libby and Jim Daughdrill.

After the games, they had dinner in the Red Room, until they were told that tennis

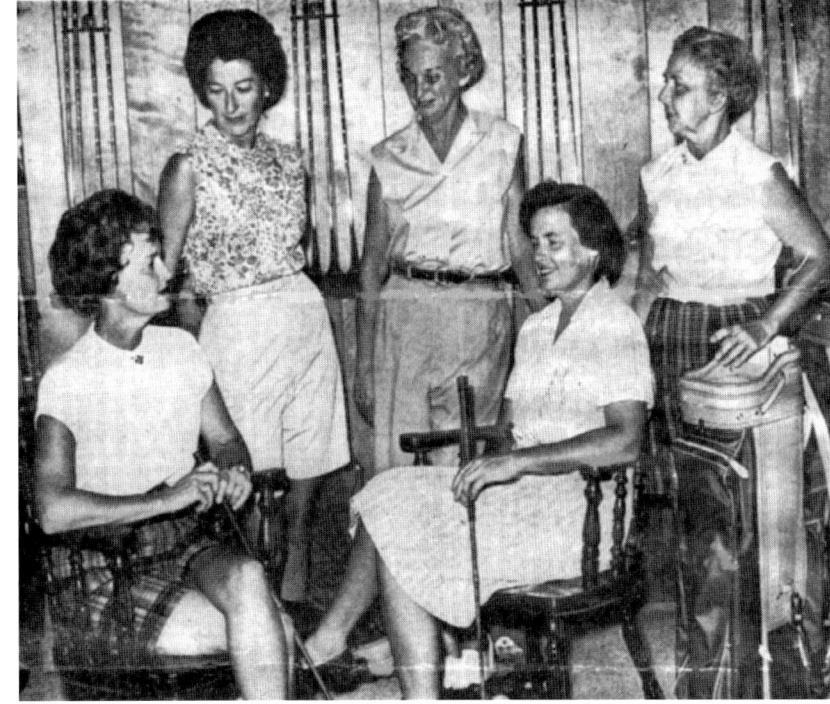

Planning for the Women's City Golf Tournament to be played at the Memphis Country Club: Mrs. J. V. Montedonico, Mrs. Paul Gillespie, Mrs. Frank Aycock Jr., Mrs. Shelby Lee (Margaret Gunther Lee), and Mrs. Robert Cooke Jr.

attire was not "proper." So the party moved to the tennis lounge, with Joyce Jones in attendance for drinks and short orders. She has served in this capacity since 1975. From April to Thanksgiving, for nearly thirty years, the group has played on Thursdays.

The 1970s

The seventies began with the dreaded word "recession" in the air, with rising inflation and joblessness seen as serious problems.

The government used the word "incursion" to describe the movement of fifty thousand U.S. and South Vietnamese troops into Cambodia. It sparked a nationwide shutdown of colleges and universities. At Kent State University in Ohio, four students were killed when National Guard troops fired at demonstrators.

The Holiday Ball debutantes, 1970:
(Standing)—Katherine Petree, Carla Kittle, Tempe Adams, Charlotte Saunders, Peggy Miller, and Mary Lee Bartlett; (Seated)—Jessie Howard, Agnes Dixon, and Dee Turley.

President Richard Nixon stunned the world when he announced that he would visit Communist China, a first step toward normalizing relations. In 1972, Nixon became the first president to visit the USSR since Franklin Roosevelt. He was reelected in a Republican landslide in 1972.

A year later, the vice president, Spiro Agnew, resigned after being charged with receiving kickbacks while he was governor of Maryland.

During much of the decade, the public was consumed by the Watergate Affair. What was at first called "a second rate burglary" of the Democratic Party headquarters in June 1972 resulted in televised congressional hearings, journalistic sleuthing, the revelation of a White House taping system, a series of high-level resignations, prison sentences for White House officials, and the threat of an impeachment trial for the president. The climax came in August 1974, when President Nixon became the first U.S. president to resign.

Gerald Ford, who had been appointed vice president after Agnew's resignation, became the thirty-eighth president, and chose Nelson Rockefeller as vice president. Ford pardoned President Nixon for any crimes he may have committed, saying he wanted to end the divisions caused by the Watergate Affair.

The war that had divided the nation finally ended in April 1975, with the airlift of the last U.S. citizens out of Saigon.

Jimmy Carter of Georgia became president in 1977. A major concern for his administration was the availability of energy, with long lines at gas stations and rising prices. In 1979, Islamic revolutionaries toppled the Iranian regime of Shah Reza Pahlevi. In November, the revolutionaries seized the U.S. Embassy with sixty-five American hostages inside.

The decade ended with a ray of hope in the troubled Middle East when President Anwar Sadat of Egypt and Prime Minister Menachem Begin of Israel signed a peace treaty at the White House.

Thomas H. Hutton Sr. was president of the Memphis Country Club from 1970 to 1972. Born in Sioux City, Iowa, he graduated

The dance floor at the Debutante Ball.

from Central High School in Memphis in 1921, and Northwestern University in 1943. He served in the navy, in the Fifth Amphibious Force, making five landings. After the war, he joined Chuck Hutton Company and became president in 1961.

Hutton was a dealer and financial participant in twenty-seven auto dealerships or parts companies; a senior vice president and director of Memphis Bank and Trust Company; and director of First Federal Savings and Loan, Arrow Office Supply Company, Guardian Central Life Insurance, and Guardian Discount Company. His community activities included the chairmanship of Shelby United Neighbors, the presidency of Memphis Rotary Club, and the 100 Club. He has served on the boards of the Memphis Arts Council, the Salvation Army, Memphis University School, and the William R. Moore School of Technology. His father became a member of the Memphis Country Club in 1940.

The officers continued to worry about the financial status of the club and worked to improve efficiency. The golf course continued in good condition, despite the loss of many trees, "one to the saw and twenty-nine by wind and lightning," Tom Hutton reported. "Typical of a private country club, the operation of the restaurant and bar facilities continued to suffer from lack of regular use. There is a great fluctuation in business from day to day with no predictable pattern." The Health Club grew in popularity.

E. C. Krausnick, president 1972–1974.

In 1970, cart paths were added to the golf course in areas of heavy traffic, and in 1979 the paths were covered with asphalt. Greens superintendent James Hamner retired after over half a century at the country club.

The 1970 Holiday Ball presented twenty-five debutantes in a glittering mid-winter setting of glistening icicles and flocked trees. The girls, in long white dresses, were presented gifts of silver and cascade bouquets of white poinsettias and feathery silver-glittered leaves. President Hutton announced each girl, who appeared through a forest of white trees and was met by her father at the foot of the stage and escorted through a path outlined with white ribbon to a glittering gazebo at the opposite end of the ballroom.

E. Carl "Buddy" Krausnick Jr. became president of the country club in 1972. He had succeeded his father as president of the Tennessee Brewery in 1953. The brewery was established in Memphis in 1877. Three Germans from St. Louis bought it in 1885 and added the splendid castellated building on the South Bluffs. One of these men was Krausnick's great-grandfather, Casper Koehler.

The brewery's most famous beer was Goldcrest 51. In 1952 and 1953, Goldcrest television ads featured famed golfer Cary Middlecoff. When the brewery closed in 1954, Krausnick went into the insurance business.

Among the capital improvements in the seventies was the addition of a fence around the club property. A new golf equipment barn was built. The tennis lounge and pro shop were doubled in size. Restaurant sales went up, but spiraling food costs and the increase in the minimum wage negated profits.

A foursome from the Memphis Country Club came in second at the International Four

The Memphis Country Club team came in second at the International Four Ball Tournament, Gleneagles, Scotland, 1973: Pro Pat Abbott, Richard Leatherman, and club presidents William A. Webster (1976–1978) and Al Austin (1965–1968).

Ball Tournament played at Gleneagles, Scotland, in 1973. The team was made up of pro Pat Abbott, Richard Leatherman, Billy Webster, and Al Austin. For several years, pro Pat Abbott led an annual expedition to Scotland for golfers.

Giles A. Coors Jr. was president of the club in 1974–1976. His family had been members since 1932. He graduated from high school in 1943 and attended Ole Miss for a year, then when he was eighteen, he went into the army air corps. He was in training when the war ended and he was discharged. He then attended the University of Virginia. He was an officer of Union Planters Bank and active with the Boys Club, Junior Achievement, the Salvation Army, and many other community organizations. He served as president of the Memphis Board of Trade and was king of Cotton Carnival in 1972.

When he married Sophie Woodson on June 30, 1953, the wedding reception was held at the country club. The bride and groom had gone up to dress for going away when a fire broke out in the men's locker room. The automatic sprinkler system went off, drenching the formally dressed guests. The bride and groom left with a fire engine escort.

The major objective of the officers was to bring the financial condition of the club under control. Coors reported, "Club operations are extremely sensitive to changes in the economy as well as the costs associated with inflation." The key was to increase club usage of the restaurant and bar.

Giles Coors, president 1974–1976.

In the early '70s, a pesky nematode damaged the golf course, but dogwoods, pines, and other decorative trees were planted. Seventy children participated in the swim team. The tennis courts and the new patio on the south side of the tennis house were so popular that a plan to build three new indoor courts was proposed. A guard service now patrolled the grounds day and night. The kitchen was renovated, and a modern telephone system was purchased.

In 1975, Mrs. George (Sara) Humphreys became social secretary and served for ten years. One of the first crises she had to face was a planned Election Day party that went awry. The day of the party someone informed her that no liquor could be served at a public place on the day of election. The law covered bars and restaurants—and private clubs, too. Guests were already arriving when a solution was found: the party was held in the upstairs bedrooms with private hosts.

One day as she drove into the club parking lot, she saw a police car leaving, only to discover that the police were taking the chef

Mike P. Sturdivant dances with his daughter Ygondine at his son's wedding reception, July 6, 1974.

Mike and Jan Sturdivant leave their wedding from the golf course, July 6, 1974.

away. He had no green card. The rest of the staff managed to cope.

Another crisis involved girls unfastening their halter tops to sunbathe at the pool, to the great embarrassment of the teenage lifeguards. Mrs. Humphreys was called to intervene.

The library was called Alaska because it was so cold in air-conditioning season. Mrs. Humphreys kept a collection of sweaters to lend to people who shivered.

Sara Humphreys remembered planning many parties. One year she recruited decorator Bob Ruffin to drape the ballroom in red velvet and jewels for an Arabian Nights theme for the annual debut party. It was a great success, but some people complained: it had always been called the Holly Ball, with Christmas decorations.

Flowers for most club functions were not in the budget, so she called upon her friends to help. Sarah Ann Varner and Jane Wynne stepped into the breach. Sara Humphrey's twin sister Blanche Thompson decorated for a Hawaiian party.

One group of women who played bridge together regularly had a particularly noisy game, shouting at each other over the play. Once a trio came to rehearse for the night's entertainment in the Red Room. The ladies yelled so loudly at the musicians that they refused to come back that night for the party.

Easter has always been a big event, with children looking forward to the Easter egg hunt. John Phillips III was a faithful Easter Bunny for years. One year Mrs. Humphreys was hiding eggs early on Sunday morning when she was horrified to find one of the mothers following her, spotting where the eggs were hidden. "I just wanted to help my children out," the mother said.

The club initiated a Christmas Children's Party in 1975 in the snack bar. By the next year it had grown so much that Santa Claus greeted children in the ballroom from 4 to 6 P.M.; a children's buffet was held in the Red Room with hamburgers, fried chicken, and ice cream sandwiches; and parents dined in either the Red Room or the dining room. A movie was shown in the ballroom from 7 to 8 P.M. Even as secretary, Mrs. Humphreys was never allowed in the men's card room.

William A. Webster served as president of the Memphis Country Club from 1976 to 1978. His chief memory is that the board managed to build a lake on the eleventh hole overnight, to the amazement of members. Over one hundred dogwoods, pines, and other decorative trees, donated by two members, were planted.

Wiener Golf Improvement Trophy.

Webster's father was an early member of the country club, joining around 1910. William A. Webster was a graduate of Culver Military Academy and Washington and Lee. He served in the naval air corps until 1945. He joined the Webster Company, started by his father in 1898, and served as president and chairman until 1973. Then he became general manager of the Webcon Division of Alcon Labs until 1978, was a realtor with Wilkinson and Snowden, then a stockbroker at Robinson Humphreys from 1980 to 1985.

Raises in wages and in medical insurance, and increases in the cost of food, power, insurance, and maintenance were causing concern. Security was also a problem. A guardhouse was erected to identify those entering club property, and television monitors were installed in storerooms and sensitive areas.

Tennis was growing in popularity. It was estimated that between three hundred and four hundred people played tennis at the club. Those enthusiasts wanted more facilities, especially indoor courts. Architect Walk Jones III estimated that a building for three courts would cost about $350,000. The board decided that such a building would not need heating or air-conditioning, only fans and blowers.

Parties in the 1970s.

Name bands provided entertainment on weekends, but members were also called upon to display their talents, from piano to organ to banjo. Hugh Smith, Owen Tabor, Roger Fakes, and Toof Brown performed.

A Washington's Birthday Backgammon Tournament, bingo in the Red Room with Bill Geralds as caller, and a ski party were winter events. In March, the club celebrated St. Patrick's Day with green decorations, shamrocks, green derbies and leprechauns, and an Irish buffet ending with Irish coffee. Elvis Presley Night and Pat O'Brien Night were other March events.

The club celebrated the nation's bicentennial in patriotic fashion. In June 1976, an out-of-town repertory company performed *Heroes and Hard Cases*, a bicentennial song and dance with comic routines, following a buffet dinner.

The Fourth of July celebration that year included red, white, and blue hats and decorations, and a champagne toast to Uncle Sam at midnight.

The Member-Guest Golf Tournament provided the excuse for much entertainment. In 1977, a tennis tournament was added. There was a black-tie dinner on Friday night, with Jim Johnson's Orchestra playing. In addition to golf and tennis on Saturday, there was a luncheon and fashion show for the ladies. A yellow and white striped tent adjoining the golf course was the luncheon gathering spot for the players. Saturday night was disco night with an informal buffet and the awarding of prizes. Flower arrangements in fall colors of gold, orange, and avocado filled the club.

W. Neely Mallory Jr., president in 1978–1980, is a third-generation club member. A graduate of Yale, he served as a pilot in the U.S. Air Force.

He is CEO of the Mallory Group, a family business involved in farming, cotton and general merchandise warehousing, international

The Men's Card Room: (Playing)—Richard Harwood, Malcolm Aste, James Robinson, and Billy Leadsinger. (Seated in rear)—Ted Lewis and Tom White. (Coming in the door)—Ray Williams.

The Member-Guest Tournament, 1976:
Billy Webster, Jack Hilton of Bay Point, Dan and Martha Canale,
Bethel Edrington, Marie Webster, and Lucy Hilton.

freight forwarding and customs brokerage; and managing partner of Mallory Farms in Chatfield, Arkansas. He has been president of the Cotton Warehouse Association of America, the Memphis Cotton Exchange, the National Cotton Council, and Future Memphis. He was king of Cotton Carnival in 1970. He has served on the boards of National Commerce Bancorp, the Memphis Hardwood Flooring Association, the Memphis Uniport, the Dixon Gallery and Gardens, the Plough Community Foundation, Le Bonheur Hospital, and Memphis University School.

When Mallory took over as president in 1978, the first order of business was to find important new staff members. Rodney Lingle was hired to replace longtime greens superintendent James Hamner. Educated at Ole Miss, with a degree in turf grass from Mississippi State, he and his staff did the work of renovation and planting without hiring outside assistance.

The 1970s

The Evening of Champions, July 16, 1979:
Mrs. William Carrington Jones, tennis; Mrs. George Early, nine-hole women's champion;
Lee Cheairs, men's golf; Mrs. Edward Lawler, women's eighteen-hole champion;
and Judge Harry Wellford, squash. (Seated)—Thomas J. White, the oldest living golf champion.

Lew Frank was hired as general manager. He was a graduate of the Cornell Hotel and Restaurant School and had worked for the Dinkler Hotel chain, the Waldorf Astoria, and with the catering division of American Airlines. He was with Dobbs Houses in the food service business for eighteen years before coming to the Memphis Country Club, where he served until 1999.

The USGA Women's Amateur Golf Tournament was held at the club in August 1979. The Memphis Area Women's Golf Association Invitational was also held at the country club that year, with a field of ninety-six golfers. Country clubs represented included Bella Vista, Chickasaw, Colonial, Farmington, Ridgeway, Whitehaven, and Windyke.

One of the problems facing the board was membership. President Mallory said, "If there are 'good' problems, we have one, for there are more Special A members reaching the age of Regular Resident Membership than certificates available." This meant few openings for those outside the family.

The club started a new tradition in 1976—a party honoring new members. The husband received a bottle of champagne and the wife received flowers. In 1979, President Mallory said, "This is a great opportunity for new members of the club to meet other members, whom, ordinarily, it might take five or six years to become acquainted with. Oftentimes members that are primarily tennis players don't get to know the golfers for years. This way, at least faces, if not names, become more familiar."

In 1978, the country club held An Evening of Champions as part of its Independence Day celebration. Trophies were presented to the winners of golf, racquetball, handball, and squash tournaments at a dinner dance. In the past, trophies had been presented at the end of each tournament. "After each tournament is over, the only ones left are the winner and the runnerup. There's no one else on hand to witness the award-giving," said Sara Humphreys, social secretary. So the banquet was planned to recognize the winners in public.

Trophies were awarded to golf champions Lee Cheairs and Jim Haygood; Middlecoff fourball winner Claude Crawford; Joyner Memorial Scramble winners Jack Hays and Jim McDonnell. Van Vleet Tournament winner was Dwight Drinkard, and 1978 father-son golf champions Dr. Sam Raines and his step-son Bill Mueller.

Tennis winners were Billy Dunavant and Allen Morgan Jr.; doubles winners were Billy Dunavant and George Dunklin Jr., and Carroll Todd Jr. and Barham Ray. Squash champion was Harry Wellford.

Women's golf winners were eighteen-hole champion Liz Lawler and nine-hole champion Betty Cunningham; spring handicap tournament winners Gig Pittman and Alice Malone;

The Clark family at the tennis courts: (Standing)—Ken and Ellen Clark, Ken III, and Marshall. (Kneeling)—Ellen, Allison, and Ramsay.

Letter from an Unknown President

The officers of the country club have to deal with many problems. Here is one response. Unfortunately, the author and the date are unknown, but many presidents undoubtedly shared the sentiments.

We have certainly had our share of cold weather lately, which is no doubt the reason why the weather seems to be the most popular topic of conversation these days. Many of our good members sometimes advise us that the various rooms in the club are either too hot or too cold and I guess it is only natural that when the weather is unusual that we get even more good advice from these various members. Now this may seem to be a simple matter, but I believe that some talented person could write several volumes on this subject and still not cover the subject adequately. I certainly won't attempt to do this, but I will say a few words about one very important phase of this subject, which is the thermostat. A thermostat is a very common device and probably the average home contains at least seven or eight thermostats on various pieces of equipment such as the refrigerator, stove, heating and cooling systems, etc.

I am sure that everyone is familiar with a thermostat, but I am also confident that probably no more than one person in 50,000 actually has the vaguest idea of how to use a thermostat. For instance, I have been trying to explain this rather simple subject to my good wife for many years, but I have been unsuccessful. She still thinks that if the room is a bit chilly the only answer is to shove the thermostat up to eighty degrees and then she can't understand why the room gets too hot. Now unfortunately some people seem comfortable at seventy degrees, but others are chilly unless the temperature is up to 73 or 76 degrees, and even these people vary somewhat in their feeling, and this also varies somewhat according to the outside temperature. Therefore, when even two people occupy a room one of them is probably going to be too hot or too cold. Now the experts agree that 72 degrees is a good compromise, and consequently we set the thermostats in all the various rooms of the club at this figure. However, on various occasions we get complaints and our engineer raises the temperature slightly, and then we get just as many complaints about it being too hot, so he comes back and lowers the temperature slightly, and round and round we go. I certainly wish we could find some way of pleasing all these people, but so far the only suggestions I get is that it is either too hot or too cold, and I can't figure out which is right.

Many people have this same problem, and I did have one friend that worked out a pretty good solution. It seems that he completely remodeled his office and he put a thermostat adjacent to every desk and the various girls who worked in the office could push the thermostat up or down at will, and this seemed to make them very happy. Of course, these thermostats were only dummies and had no effect on the heating system, but I sometimes think that we would have been wise to use this system at the club. At the present, however, I can't think of a really satisfactory solution, but a member can engage a bedroom which has an individual thermostat and could then have the privilege of pushing the thermostat back and forth, which no doubt would be most enjoyable.

Not long ago I read about one other possibility, but unfortunately it is still in the development stage. It seems that some company is working on thermostatically controlled underwear and they would merely plug it into the nearest wall socket and would have the supreme enjoyment of being able to play with their own personal thermostat. Anyway, I will keep you informed of any late development, and we can only hope for future success. Personally, I am leaving for Florida next week, and I am certain that it will be delightfully cold and rainy there.

The Greer Gang still going strong in 1979: George Treadwell, Dan Canale, Rip Greer, Alex Wellford, and Dunlap Cannon.

tennis winners were Allison Garrott and Peggy Jones, Libby Dudley and Peggy Jones, Jane Carruthers and Jan Bell.

On July Fourth, swimming races and pony rides were offered for youngsters, there were luncheon and dinner buffets, and fireworks capped the evening.

The Member-Guest Tournament in 1978 was cut short by rain on Saturday. The golfers played eighteen instead of thirty-six holes, and the tennis matches had to be rescheduled at various indoor facilities around town. Everyone who played received a handsome gift, a print of a watercolor by Dr. Allen Hughes, signed by the artist, showing the seventh hole with the columned club in the background.

One of the memorable parties of the seventies honored Rip Greer and his devotion to golf. At age seventy-five, Greer played eighteen holes of golf every day that weather permitted. George Treadwell, his longtime golfing buddy, said, "There are practicing attorneys and practicing doctors, but Rip is the only practicing golfer I know."

About 250 guests attended the black-tie party. Greer was the developer of the Chickasaw Gardens subdivision, but his golf was the focus of the evening. Berl Olswanger's Orchestra played for dancing after dinner, then there was a roast and the presentation of gag gifts. Greer and George Treadwell began playing regularly in 1943, and others joined them to form the Greer Gang, a foursome plus two, or a "gangsome."

In September 1978, an Evening in Rome party was a great success. It was followed in February 1979, by an Evening in Paris dinner dance. The menu featured such French specialities as escargot, vichyssoise, onion soup, pâté, coq au vin, duck a l'orange, and beef stroganoff, with chocolate mousse and crêpe suzette for dessert. Tall white chef's hats with red and blue rosettes decorated the tables.

Weddings and private parties filled the club evenings. One of the most unusual parties honored a bird dog. When Richard and Carroll Leatherman's pointer, Miss One Dot, won the National Bird Dog Championship at Ames Plantation in Grand Junction, Tennessee, her owners celebrated with a party at the country club on March 21, 1979.

Miss One Dot wore a collar of pink and white flowers when she was toasted with silver goblets. The newspaper reported that the guests had a splendid time and that Miss One

Richard and Carroll Leatherman and Miss One Dot.

Past presidents at the seventy-fifth anniversary party:
Katherine and James E. Harwood (1950–1952); San and James Edward Stark (1952–1954);
Scottie and Samuel S. Rembert (1963–1965); Louise and Dr. Bland Cannon (1968–1970);
Wister and George Treadwell (1943–1946); and Ginger and Albert Austin III (1965–1968).

Dot appeared bored by the proceedings, but was too well-bred to show it.

The decade closed with an anniversary party. The club celebrated its seventy-fifth anniversary on August 30. Berl Olswanger, who had entertained for fifty of those years, led his band for dancing. When club president Neely Mallory introduced him, Mr. Olswanger remembered that Mallory's parents had been among his earliest patrons. When he wasn't old enough to drive, the Mallorys would pick him up and drive him to the party at which he was to perform.

The 1970s

The 1980s
XI

As the decade of the eighties began, Ronald Reagan swept into the presidency in a Republican landslide. The Iranian hostage crisis ended at the same time that he was being sworn in. The Soviet invasion of Afghanistan caused a deep freeze in U.S.-USSR relations in 1980. Peace in the Middle East was elusive as Israelis advanced into Lebanon in response to Palestinian attacks. Some eight hundred marines were sent to Beirut. The American Embassy was bombed in 1984.

Sandra Day O'Connor became the first woman justice on the Supreme Court. Astronaut Sally Ride became the first U.S. woman in space. Democrat Geraldine Ferraro became the first woman candidate of a major party to run for vice president.

Mount St. Helens in southwestern Washington State erupted and set off a series of fires, mudslides, and floods. *Gandhi* won the Academy Award in 1982, and *Cats* opened on Broadway. The Metropolitan Opera abandoned its national tour after 1986; the Met's spring performances in Memphis had been an important part of the Memphis social scene since 1946.

Elvis Presley's Graceland opened to tourists in 1982 and became one of the most-visited house museums in the United States. Beale Street began to be developed as a tourist attraction the same year; after some fits and starts, by the end of the 1990s it was a busy restaurant and entertainment venue.

John Hull Dobbs served as president of the Memphis Country Club from 1980 to 1982. A graduate of Duke, he served in the air force. From 1957 to 1970, he was with Dobbs Houses, serving as president and chairman of the board. After Dobbs Houses was sold in 1966, he went to work to reestablish the Dobbs family in the automobile business and acquired twenty-five separate franchises, as well as twelve Anheuser Busch distributorships. The company sold the automobile dealerships in the 1990s but retained other assets, including Wendy's franchises. The family also operates a health maintenance organization in Pennsylvania. He was inducted into the Society of Entrepreneurs in 2004.

John Hull Dobbs, president 1980–1982.

In 1980, the assets of the Memphis Country Club were listed at $2,282,523. Cable TV came to the club in 1980, and the club purchased its first computer in 1982.

Friday night gourmet dinners for parties of ten or twelve began in January 1980. "Fresh flowers, candlelight, and impeccable service make this an evening to remember," said the newsletter.

One menu featured chilled cream of avocado soup garnished with toasted almonds; fresh Maine lobster salad in shell; a choice of spring lamb persillade, stuffed filet mignon with sauce Perigourdine, broiled sweetbreads and Virginia ham Eugenie, or filet of sole Veronique; pommes Parisienne and fresh asparagus tips hollandaise; and frozen rum chestnut bombe or Grand Marnier soufflé with vanilla sauce, for $18.50 a person.

A party scene.

The first Anna Morrow Memorial Tennis Tournament for girls eighteen or older was held in 1980.

David Nenon was the swim team coach in charge of more than forty youngsters in the summer of 1980. The soon-to-be-senior at Georgia Tech was in his sixth year of coaching; his two older brothers had preceded him and his younger brother Chris took over the next year. His rule—everybody who shows up swims—made for controlled chaos and wet but happy swimmers.

A Las Vegas Night was held in April 1981, with games of chance, music by the River City Six, a buffet, and prizes. The cost was $10.00 a couple and $8.50 a person. The members wagered with play money and won prizes.

Pat Abbot retired on March 1, 1981, as head golf professional after thirty-four years. More than 350 club members attended a retirement party for Abbott, with cocktails, dinner, a roast, and dancing. John A. Stevens wore a kilt in honor of the yearly trips to Scotland on which Abbot had led golfers.

Tim Rush started working as assistant golf professional in 1980 and succeeded Abbott as head golf pro. He reports that he has seen the golf course go through two renovations. In one, the bunkers and tees were reworked to bring the course back to its original Donald Ross style. In the other renovation, the grasses on the fairways and greens were updated with playable types of zoysia and champion Bermuda.

Rush says that his twenty-plus years at the club have been a fulfilling experience. He has particularly enjoyed seeing youngsters who were junior golfers when he began grow up to be outstanding members and players.

The *Press Scimitar* featured a story about longtime Memphis Country Club head waitress Bea Frye. "Working in the club is different from working in a commercial restaurant because you get close to the people," she was quoted as saying, "I've been here a long time, so I know all the members. It's just like a home. It's a lovely place. It's no point in me ever going anywhere else. I just like it here best."

Commenting on her twenty-nine-year career at the club, she said, "When I first started, there wasn't as much planned activity. Now there is. Whole groups come for tennis, mah-jongg, or bridge. Ladies didn't do as much golfing then as now. Tuesday Study Club, Little Garden Club, Ikebana all meet here."

When asked how she kept her cool when serving crowded balls and dinners for over one thousand people, Mrs. Frye replied, "Working a larger party, like during Cotton Carnival or the debutante season, is much easier because there are so many people they don't pay any attention to what you are doing. I think, too, we waitresses see others happy and really have fun working. We feel we are helping them in their happiness and good times by giving good service."

In the 1980s, the board noted a problem with the annual Debutante Ball. It was felt that the younger stags tended to treat the night as a free booze and food night and did not really mingle with the debutantes. In 1982, the board decided to make the Debutante Ball an event for sophomores in college, and since there would be no ball that year, to have a Welcome Home Christmas Tea Dance for college students.

Joseph Orgill III became president in 1982 and served until 1984. Educated at Pentecost-Garrison in Memphis, the Taft School in Connecticut, and Yale University, he is chairman of Orgill Incorporated and a director of First Tennessee National Corporation and the Mallory Group.

His civic activities included the Dixon Gallery and Gardens, the United Way,

Dorothy and Kemmons Wilson and Natalie and Davant Latham.

LeMoyne Owen College, the Downtown Ministry, the Children's Museum, St. Mary's and Hutchison Schools, Rhodes College, and the Shelby County Hospital Authority. He was a member of the Sectional Affairs Committee of the United States Golf Association and a member of several golf clubs around the country.

His family had long been members of the country club. His wife's parents, Mr. and Mrs. S. R. Leatherman of Robinsonville, Mississippi, used the club as their Memphis residence.

During his term, over half a million dollars was spent on capital improvements beyond normal maintenance. The membership was full, with a waiting list. Food and service were called excellent.

Manager Lew Frank wrote a letter to the staff at the end of 1982: "It has been a difficult economic year for the nation. It has also been a tough year for the Memphis Country Club in that we took in less operating dollars than we spent. Other businesses call this a LOSS . . . Let's all help to make 1983 a turn around year."

When Scott Fisher chaired the male Member-Guest Tournament in June 1983, participants were given a package including a score card, rule sheet, three golf balls, a shirt, a golf bag identification tag, an activity schedule, and a list of the 112 participants and wives.

The weekend began on Friday, June 17, with a casual party at poolside with music by the Settlers, followed by a buffet and dancing indoors to the music of Flash Back. While the men had breakfast in the Tap Room and played golf on Saturday, their wives enjoyed a luncheon and an Albert Nipon fashion

April 22, 1984: sisters Estelle Corrigan and Martha Jane Cobb have celebrated Easter at the club for seventy-five years.

show, presented by Dottie Gillespie. On Saturday night, there was a black tie seated dinner and dancing to the music of T. O. Earnhardt's Band. While the men had a breakfast buffet and the final round followed lunch on the porch on Sunday morning, the women attended a Bloody Mary brunch in the Ladies Lounge. The cost was three hundred dollars, and included breakfasts, lunches, dinners, entertainment, prizes, and greens fees. A Ladies Member-Guest Tournament was also held in June.

Food prices seem low in comparison with today's menus. In September 1983, a special Breakfast at Brennan's featured four kinds of eggs; four shellfish entrees; three meat, fish, or chicken entrees; salads; vegetables; crepes Fitzgerald, bananas Foster, or French caramel custard; and ramos gin fizzes; all for $12.50.

The Friday night buffet offered an even greater bargain: fried chicken, barbecued chicken, or chicken and dressing; vegetables; cornbread; and fresh cobblers, $3.95. In August, Wednesday family suppers offered a burger and shake night, a fish fry, a country kitchen menu, and pasta night, for $6.50.

An August party for MCC MCs (male chauvinists) featured a mini gin tournament and a mini backgammon tournament, a super steak dinner, and drinks specially priced at $1.50 from 6:30 P.M. on.

Sisters Estelle Corrigan and Martha Jane Cobb celebrated Easter at the country club just as they had done for the last seventy-five years by singing the "Easter Time" song: "Easter is the time for eggs / And the time for eggs is the Easter Time!"

Michael McDonnell served as president of the Memphis Country Club from 1984 to 1986. He graduated from Yale, started his career at Union Planters, then moved to Little Rock with Little Rock Furniture Manufacturing Company in 1964. He returned to Memphis in 1968 when he and his cousin Joe Orgill went into partnership in the Orgill Company, in holding companies West Union and the Rock Island Corporation.

He serves on the board of Shelby Farms, the MOST scholarship program, and Rhodes College. He is a part owner of the St. Louis Cardinals.

The new swimming pool was constructed during his term. Turmoil in the insurance industry and the high risk associated with alcohol-related accidents increased the cost of insurance coverage for the club in 1986. Directors and managers were indemnified.

A Rock Night in April 1985 featured Tony Barrasso's Band playing hard and soft rock. A buffet of fried chicken and barbecued ribs "with all the trimmings" cost $7.75. A Bavarian buffet in October featured lentil soup with frankfurters, Liederkranz cheese, leichter kartoffglsalat (potato salad), serreriesalat (celery knob salad), gurken salat mit sauer sahne (cucumbers in sour cream), Westphalian ham, herring in red wine and herring in sour cream, sauerbraten, wiener schnitzel, bratwurst, knockwurst, potato pancakes and potato dumplings, red cabbage, applesauce, hot apple strudel, and Black Forest cake with an assortment of German beers. It cost $12.50 per person.

Michael McDonnell, president 1984–1986.

*The Senior Member-Guest Tournament, October 1988:
Dr. Bland Cannon, Henry Goodrich of Birmingham, Fletcher Johnson, and Billy Webster.*

The bountiful Thanksgiving buffet cost $12 for adults and $5.50 for children under six. A summer cold buffet, with cold soups, salads, cold meats, and ice creams cost $6.75. The cost of the Member-Guest Tournament in 1984 was $350.00

The Memphis Country Club made the front page in a surprising way in 1986. In October, Malcolm Fraser, the former prime minister of Australia, was the featured speaker at a dinner of the Economic Club of Memphis, held at the club. Fraser, prime minister of Australia from 1975 to 1983, had a distinguished career as a politician, and his speech to the business leaders of Memphis was a serious event.

Fraser was staying in the guest rooms at the club. After the evening meeting was over, he decided to see the other side of Memphis. Apparently he called a cab to take him to Beale Street. Sometime between midnight and one in the morning, he

*You are cordially invited
to participate in the Memphis Cotillion
to be held at the Memphis Country Club
under the direction of
Mr. Jon D. Williams
(please open for calendar inside)*

The Memphis Cotillion invitation.

checked into the Admiral Benbow Inn at 1220 Union under an assumed name and paid with a one-hundred-dollar bill.

He was scheduled to have a breakfast meeting the next morning with the executive committee of the Economic Club at the country club. Instead, he woke up at the Admiral Benbow, minus his pants and his passport, apparently the victim of a prostitute's Mickey Finn. He appeared in the motel lobby wearing nothing but a shirt, a tie, and a towel; borrowed an ill-fitting pair of pants; and called for a cab to return him to the country club. As the Admiral Benbow desk clerk told a reporter, "He didn't look too prominent at 7 o'clock in the morning."

James Hallam Boyd Jr. was president of the club from 1986 to 1988. He was with National Bank of Commerce from 1966 to 1994, becoming senior trust officer and chairman of the Board of Commerce Capital Management Corporation. Among his many civic activities are the chairmanships of the Memphis Heart Association, Family Services, Duration School, and the University of Tennessee Medical Group Pension Fund. He has served on the boards of the Plough Foundation, the Memphis Rotary Club, Trezevant Manor, the Boy Scouts, the Boys Club, Le Bonheur and St. Jude, Bridges and United Way. He was king of Cotton Carnival in 1977.

At the November 1987 annual meeting, the membership ratified the board's recommendation for a three-year capital plan to include an indoor tennis facility, replacement of the slate roof for the clubhouse, renovation and remodeling in the clubhouse, and the first significant golf course renovation in over forty years.

The board held a special meeting on the roof to approve plans for a total reroofing project. When construction costs exceeded the budget, Kemmons Wilson and Palmer Brown kindly offered to fund the new bathrooms in

Memphis Cotillion dancers.

The club in the snow.

the tennis facility. The improvements were to be covered by an assessment so that there would be no bank debt at the end of the three-year period.

After much discussion and a trial period, the Tap Room was open to the general membership—no longer men only—after 6:30 P.M.; it was the beginning of informal dining at the club.

Lewis "Mac" McKee Jr. became the third generation of his family to serve as president of the Memphis Country Club. His grandfather, W. Lytle McKee, was president in 1941–1942, and his father, Lewis McKee Sr., was president in 1960–1963. A graduate of Memphis University School and the University of Virginia, he has been in the real estate business since 1974 and started McKee and McFarland in 1982.

During his term as president in 1988–90, the first significant golf course renovation in over forty years took place, restoring the golf course to its original Donald Ross features. Golf course architect John LaFoy was hired to supervise, with the stipulation that the original Donald Ross design be retained.

Members were able to play at Colonial, Chickasaw, Farmington, and Ridgeway Country Clubs during the construction. Despite sixteen days of rain in June, the work proceeded. The official golf course reopening was celebrated with a two-man member scramble on July 28. Dinner and dancing capped the day; a lobster dinner was $22.50, while steak cost $17.50.

The Member-Guest Golf Tournament, scheduled for September 15–17, was so popular that it sold out and had a waiting list one day after it was announced. The fee for the tournament, including greens fees, meals, entertainment, and prizes, was $425.

The Senior Member-Guest Golf Tournament and the Senior Tennis Invitational were also popular.

Major renovations of the clubhouse were completed, and at last, the construction of the much-discussed indoor tennis facility. The first year of the indoor tennis facility was a huge success and scheduling for the time slots was highly competitive. The manager reported to the board that, since the opening of the indoor tennis courts, there had been a huge increase in play. But the loss of towels was staggering. The club had an inventory of over 2,500 large and small white towels; by March 15, 1989, there were fewer than 150 towels in reserve.

In 1989 there was a dues increase of approximately 6.5 percent and a new policy

MCC Memorial Tournament Trophy.

for quarterly food minimum. President McKee warned members that the Memphis Country Club was a strictly social club and would accept only personal checks, no business checks or checks from a nonmember.

Social activity picked up. Jim Johnson's Orchestra played for Stone Crab Night and the Holiday Ball, and Reba and the Portables played for an Italian buffet. There was a Country/Western Cookout in May for families. Burgers for Li'l Cowpokes were five dollars, and T-Bones for Big Ranchers were fifteen dollars.

On November 17 gin rummy finals were held, and Jason D. Williams entertained on

November 18. Thanksgiving dinner, a bountiful buffet, cost sixteen dollars for adults and five dollars for children under eight.

Hugh "Blackie" Allan challenged Tommy Keesee that he could beat him at tennis, even if Allan played barehanded against Keesee's racquet. The rules allowed Allan ten seconds after catching the ball to return it. Keesee said, "It looks as if the man with racquet should win, but that is deceiving. That tennis ball slows down quite a bit after it hits the ground. I aced him four or five times, but those he got his hands on he caught . . . he would give me a fake one way, fake a lob another way, then get me all out of shape and throw it over the net in another direction." Allan won, 7–5.

Throughout the decade, dressed-up youngsters arrived at the club on late winter afternoons for dancing class. Dance instructor Jon D. Williams came to Memphis weekly for the Memphis Country Club Cotillion.

For eight winter weeks, students from Presbyterian Day School, St. Mary's, Hutchison, Grace St. Luke's, and St. Agnes came to learn manners and dancing.

Williams taught classes for fifth and sixth graders in cities like Dallas, Denver, Fort Worth, and Middleburg, Virginia.

Girls were required to wear party dresses, white gloves, and flats or little heels. Boys wore suits, or slacks and jackets, with ties, dark socks, and dark polished shoes. They learned the Cotton-Eye Joe and the Texas Two Step as well as the foxtrot and the waltz. Cookies and punch were served, and the boys learned to ask the girls politely for a dance, in preparation for future debutante parties and Saturday night dances.

Ode to MCC ~ Christmas 1982

'Twas the night before Christmas and all through the Club,
    We were busy as bees; Ah, now there's the rub.

Members coming and going as gay as can be,
    And the switchboard's all lit up like "Ye Olde Christmas tree."

Sara's telephone calls, they outnumber a score,
    Think I will scream if she gets just one more.

Barbara's trusty typewriter is clickety-clackin',
    While down in the storeroom Albert still is unpacking.

Now Baxter is dashing from pillar to post,
    And Curtis's kitchen is serving the most

Elegant fare one could ever conceive,
    While Wayne's super cocktails are hard to believe!

Then down from below Rex's shouts we can hear.
    "No, you can't have a pencil, you've had one this year!"

On Patty! On Polly! On Kinkle and Nancy!
    Take care of your duties, don't try nothin' fancy.

Just sit in your cage and keep doing your thing,
    Don't go to the girls' room, the switchboard might ring.

On Lucille! On Tammy! On Roscoe and Bea,
    Now work away, work away, let's earn our fee!

Well, we've worked all year long, without too many flaws,
    Now we're weary and tired, is there no Santa Claus?

When out of his office bounds a fella named Lew,
    Shouting "Merry Christmas to all, the Club closes at two!"

                                            Nancy Davis
                                     MCC Switchboard Operator

Into the Twenty-first Century

Downtown Memphis experienced a renaissance in the last decades of the twentieth century. Riverfront views and urban living drew people downtown. Luxurious homes bloomed on Mud Island and at South Bluffs. Old warehouses and office buildings were turned into apartments and condominiums, and for the first time in many years there was a large population of people living, as well as working, downtown.

Commercial developments at Peabody Place and Beale Street prospered. The Lorraine Motel opened as the National

Civil Rights Museum in 1991. Vintage trolleys began carrying passengers in 1993. The decaying Central Station was revitalized as a transportation hub in 1999, with trains, buses, and trolleys.

The Memphis Symphony made its home at the new Cannon Performing Arts Center, Broadway plays came to the revitalized Orpheum Theater, the Power House behind Central Station exhibited contemporary art, and South Main Street became a neighborhood of galleries, shops, and artists' studios.

The popular Wonders exhibits moved to the Pyramid, which opened as a basketball arena in 1991. By 2003, another, larger basketball arena was being built in the south side of town to house the Memphis Grizzlies. A state-of-the-art baseball park, AutoZone Park, opened on Union Avenue in 2000 as home to the Memphis Redbirds. A new public school opened in 2003 to serve the growing downtown population.

Memphis music, which had swept the world, began to get its due at home. The Rock 'n Soul Museum, a Smithsonian presentation located at the Gibson Guitar Factory south of Beale Street, opened in 2002. The Stax Museum of American Soul Music and the Stax Academy opened in the heart of a neglected South Memphis neighborhood in 2003.

Dr. Willie Herenton became the first black mayor of the city of Memphis in 1991, and in 2002, A. C. Wharton became the first black mayor of Shelby County

Jackson W. Moore Sr., who served as president of the Memphis Country Club from 1990-1992, says that he is "the first son-in-law to be elected president," having been proposed for membership by his father-in-law, Kemmons Wilson. A native of Clanton, Alabama, he graduated from the University of Alabama.

He is chairman of the board, president and CEO of Union Planters Corporation and its lead bank subsidiary, Union Planters Bank N.A.

He has served as a trustee of Vanderbilt, Asbury Theological Seminary, Samford University, and the University of Alabama. He teaches a Sunday school class at Christ United Methodist Church, and served on the Memphis/Shelby County Sports Authority and the Chickasaw Council of Boy Scouts.

Jack Moore, president 1990–1992.

In *Golf Digest's* 2002 ranking of the nation's best CEO golfers, he was ranked tenth. The *Commercial Appeal* quoted him as commenting on his high ranking: "I think I'm the only guy who turns in all my scores . . . I've always said that with every birthday ending in zero, you've got to give up a sport: touch football, basketball.

But you can keep playing golf." His father, a doctor in Alabama, still plays regularly at the Clanton Country Club at age eighty-seven.

During his term there were renovations to the locker rooms, the card rooms, and the dining room, and a modern HVAC system was installed throughout the club. The new River Room Cocktail Lounge was located at the west end of the club between the library and breakfast room. The redecoration was supervised by a secret committee of three wives of club members. The Club purchased a duplex on Terrell Place near the tennis courts. The Health Club was renovated and new equipment was purchased.

Fred Schaeffer, president 1992–1994.

Social activities were in full swing. February saw a Valentine party featuring the David Humphreys orchestra from Nashville, a stone crab feast, and Duck Gumbo Night, using the members' ducks. In April, members were urged to celebrate Secretary's Week by bringing their Gal Friday to a luncheon with flower favors and a fashion show. Mike Sheehan called the numbers on Bingo Night, and bands played for dancing on certain Friday and Saturday nights.

The swimming pool opened on Memorial Day with a BBQ cookout. One of the reports given to the president described the apprehension by the night guard of a young couple skinny dipping in the pool. The male suspect asked the guard to turn around so his date could dress. When the guard turned back, the couple had run away. The incident report concluded sternly, "This will not happen again."

Broadway came to Memphis in August 1990, when a touring company performed *Tintypes*, a musical celebration of America from the 1890s to the 1920s as seen through the eyes of a European immigrant. Dinner and the show cost $19.50.

In November, the Club presented an art show by its members. Thirty-two members displayed their talents in paintings, sculpture, wood carvings, ceramics and pottery in the Café des Beaux Arts, while Edwin Hubbard's trio provided music and cocktails and complimentary hors d'oeuvres were served.

Frederick C. Schaeffer, Sr. was another son-in-law president. Born in Lancaster, Pennsylvania, he spent most of his teen years in Swarthmore, Pennsylvania. After graduation from Washington and Lee, he married Josephine Phillips and moved to Memphis where he joined the New England Mutual Life Insurance Company, of which his father-in-law, John Phillips III, was a general agent. He formed the Schaeffer Company, which represented New England Life and other insurance carriers.

Happy golfers: Dr. Owen Tabor, Pepper Allen, Mike McDonnell, Fred Schaeffer, Allen Morgan Jr., Claude Crawford, Fred Ridolphi, Dr. Ferrell Varner, Robert Tayloe, Dr. Randy McCloy, Dr. Jim Varner, and Dr. Tom Morris.

He was board chairman of the Hutchison School and Presbyterian Day School, and a trustee of Memphis University School, the Dixon Gallery and Gardens, and the Children's Museum. He died of cancer at age fifty-five in 1997.

Fred became a junior member of the Club in 1964, and served as president from 1992 to 1994. He was a 14 handicapper in golf, and shot a career best 74 in the Van Vleet Tournament in 1993. His regular golf partners began wagering on exactly where his 74th shot would fall in each day's round. The golf shop staff invited all his friends to participate, recording the bets on the days that Fred played; his normal times were Thursday afternoons and Saturday mornings.

Major renovation took place during his term. In November 1994, he was able to report that the cost of the recent renovation was $3,153,000, and the Club had been able to retire nearly one-third of the indebtedness. The renovation was the largest single project undertaken since 1958. The plumbing, heating, and cooling equipment was replaced, and the Men's and Ladies' locker rooms were redone. The renovation of eating areas in the Tap Room and the Red

Room and a new menu meant that business went up. The Club remained open throughout the work.

The Mother's Day buffet in May cost $15.00 for adults and $5.00 for children. Members could have cocktails and early supper and take a bus to the Catherine the Great Wonders exhibit at the Pyramid. The Fourth of July featured golf, tennis, swimming, pony rides, and fireworks, with a cookout and cold buffet in the Tennis Lounge. When the Rams played the Oilers in Memphis in August, members could have cocktails in the Red Room, take a bus to the game, and order a box lunch to take along.

The First Annual MCC Ryder Cup Invitational was held in August 1991, a "more golf oriented tournament" where members could pick their guests in any age or location bracket.

The newsletter boasted Strawberry Season in April 1992. The kitchen supplied strawberry tartlets with crème anglaise, moist strawberry cake, strawberry shortcakes, or strawberries and Chantilly cream. At the bar you could order strawberry daiquiris, cream coolers, fizzes, or margaritas.

In October, the Club sponsored Murder Mystery Night, an evening of intrigue and suspense—and cocktails and dinner. Halloween saw The Night of the Great Pumpkin, when MCC employees competed with pumpkin carvings, and pumpkin muffins and pumpkin pie were served with dinner.

Gourmet dinners began again on Saturday nights, back by popular demand. This time the price was $30. A typical menu featured a choice of cold smoked salmon, pâté de maison, or lobster raviolis; mixed green salad with goat cheese and walnuts or Bibb and bacon salad; Chateaubriand Bouquetiere with sauce Bernaise, rack of lamb Dijon persillade, breast of duckling a l'orange with Grand Marnier sauce, or pompano en papillote with vin blanc sauce; wild rice, sautéed spinach, or fresh asparagus; individual crème brûlée, chocolate macadamia torte, or frozen peach cordial.

Different styles for different folks. Some preferred formal gourmet dining while others wanted more casual meals. In the fall of 1993, experimentation began: "Informal dining seems to be more popular than ever, so one night each week we will have a change of atmosphere in the Red Room. Semi-casual attire—adults only—no reservations."

The River Room Lounge, on the west side of the main hallway, opened for drinks Wednesday through Sunday after 5 P.M. But it never caught on, and was reserved for special occasions. Members were reassured that "You can have your cocktails in the Red

Broken Racket Trophy, awarded to Bruce Taylor, 1997.

Room and Tap Room as you have done for years."

Parents were repeatedly asked to keep their children in tow while dining in the Tap Room.

A tennis tradition that dated from the 1940s was still going strong. Drop In Tennis started in 1946. The only requirement was that you had to be male, and show up between 1:30 and 5:00 P.M. on Saturday and Sunday, and on Thursday between 4:00 and 6:30 P.M., rain or shine.

The players through the years included Judge Sylvanus Polk, Stanley Snow, Norman Blake Jr., Hugh Cunningham, Alex Wellford Sr., Ward Archer Sr., Allen Morgan Sr., Bill Morgan, Dr. Phil Lewis, Tommy Price, Kemmons Wilson Sr., Cooper Adams Sr., Sid Stewart, Dr. Bland Cannon, Phil Burnett, Billy Britton, Jim Shannon, Gene Hill, Dr. Tom White (known as the Dean of Memphis Tennis), Ewing Carruthers Jr., Frank Jones, Toof Brown, Arthur Fulmer Jr., Jim Harwood, Joel Hobson, Davant Latham, Carroll Johnson, Guy Erb, John Stevens, John Bondurant, Carroll Todd Jr. and Sr., Jimmy Wetter Sr., Neely Mallory, B. Lee Mallory, Dr. Allen Hughes, Bill Butler, Roy Bell, Bill Gerber, Dr. Sidney Wilroy, John Maxwell, Martin Thompson, Bruce Hopkins, David Simpson, Hubert Turley III, Casey Bowlin, Cary Whitehead, Palmer Brown, Jack Jones, Jim Daughdrill, Van Pritchartt, Clyde Patton, Bruce Taylor, Tom Johnston, Marty Pryor, Hal Crenshaw, Ralph Hand, Bill Purcell, Jim Witherington Jr., Jim Rainer III, Ed Morrow, Giles Coors Jr., Dunbar Abston, Bill Coolidge, Wayne Pyeatt, Herbert Rhea, Bill Maury, Bob Smith, Steve Rhea, Martin Shea, Bobby Snowden, Bill Carrington Jones, Alex Wellford III, Brig Klyce, Lee Wiener, Kent Wunderlich, Joe Morrison, Wallace Witmer Jr., Billy Yandell, Will Yandell, and Phil Zanone.

On a normal spring weekend, there will be six courts going outside. When the weather is bad, two of the indoor courts are reserved for Drop In players on weekends, and one on Thursday afternoons.

The Tennis Group, which started in the sixties, is still going strong in 1993.

The Revival of the Buntyn Cup, 1997:
(Above)—Bobby Weaver, Allen Morgan Jr., Steve Morrow, Trow Gillespie,
Reggie Barnes, and Scott Fisher.

(Below)—John Dicken, Jimmy Smith, Haywood Henderson, DeWitt Shy, Jack Moore,
Michael Babb, and George Kirk.

Bruce Hopkins remembers, "Until 1988, when the three new indoor tennis courts opened, Drop In Tennis was played exclusively outside. The only thing that hindered our playing was the weather—if it rained or snowed or was bitterly cold. We used to play when it was spitting snow in January, or when thunderous storms were swirling overhead. The great thing about Drop In Tennis is that all you have to do is show up, everyone gets to play, the ages can run from 20 to 85 on any given weekend, and many a young child has been forced into play when we needed a fourth for the 'fifth or sixth' set and there were only three men left."

The annual MUGS doubles and singles tournament held every summer is closely associated with Drop In Tennis. Doubles pairings are done by a secret committee. Beginning in the '90s, a number of "Drop Ins" have taken a winter tennis trip to Florida, Arizona, California, or Puerto Rico to play at different clubs. Since the late '90s, the MCC tennis pros have arranged a Men's Tennis Clinic at Hidden Dunes in Destin, Florida.

The Drop In Players frequently have an evening party to which wives are invited, and many trophies are awarded, including the coveted "Broken Racket" awards.

The ice storm in February 1994 was responsible for much damage to the trees on the golf course. Capital expenses included the purchase of four wheelers for transporting the golf course crew, two way radios, a grinder to sharpen mowers, and a stump grinder.

Banquet manager Bea Frye retired after forty-seven years. Rex Galloway, who had been business manager for thirty-seven years, retired. Patty Magsig was a switchboard operator from February 14, 1975 until her death from cancer on December 15, 2002. She knew every member simply by the sound of the voice. She was the first one the members saw as they entered the club and always had a beautiful smile and a charming greeting.

Tommy Adams Jr., president 1994–1996.

The Buntyn Cup golf tournament had started in 1921, but was later discontinued. It was re-established in 1994 by Trow Gillespie and Haywood Henderson as a one-day, invitation only, golf tournament. The late DeWitt Shy and Cary Middlecoff were selected as the Cup's first honorary captains, and Gillespie and Henderson were elected permanent co-captains. Much like the Masters, participation is based on a very secretive process. Participants rotate each year, depending on a rigorous selection process, including, but not limited to, such criteria as golf prowess, social grace, and respect shown to the permanent captains.

Cocktails and team drawings on Friday night kick off the tournament, along with hoisting the customized flag adjacent to the 18th green. Saturday's thirty-six-hole competition utilizes a modified Ryder Cup format and is hotly competitive. An elegant awards dinner, to which wives are sometimes invited, occurs on Saturday night, and the festivities are concluded with the winning team drinking from an ancient silver cup and singing the Cup's official song, "We Won Today."

Thomas C. Adams Jr., president from 1994 to 1996, was born in Memphis but moved to Houston at an early age with his family. He lived in Houston for seventeen years, but returned to Memphis and graduated from Memphis University School. He graduated from the University of Mississippi and received an Executive MBA from the University of North Carolina at Chapel Hill. He is executive vice-president of First Tennessee Bank in charge of the Funds Management Division.

He has served on many community boards, including the Memphis Junior League Advisory Board; the Emanuel Episcopal Center; the Dixon Gallery and Gardens; and the Ole Miss Board of Trustees of the School of Banking and Finance.

President Adams stated that the club had, on average, fifteen membership openings a year. Ten of these traditionally went to sons or sons-in-law, with five memberships going to people with no family relationship to the club.

The constitution of the club was amended to allow for the election of women members and to remove any reference to gender for all categories of membership. Members were assured that the change was not a response to "political correctness" or a way to sneak in objectionable sons-in-law. President Adams said, "They are not some

Ladies who lunch: Jane Pierotti, Donna Kay Bridgforth, Jean Anne Wiener, Babs Ducklo, Susan Crawford, Caroline Whittle, Dorritte Early, and Ann Barton.

Into the Twenty-first Century

Card players: Catherine Smithwick, Anne Stokes, Cecil Marshall, and Nancy Erb.

type of social activists who want to play golf at 9 on Saturday, and then sit in front of the Tap Room tube for a burger and a few beers. These are our daughters, they grew up here."

To reassure members, "Men only" rules continued in the Tap Room and the men's card room, and for Saturday preferences on the golf course and tennis courts.

There had been a decline in member dining. The number of people served in 1995 was 24 percent lower than the number served in 1990. The Board of Directors discussed various ways to build club usage. More contemporary menus featuring fresh pastas, fresh seafood, and grilled steaks and chops, and an enlarged selection of wines by the glass were suggested. A soft-serve yogurt machine in the Tap Room offered low-fat flavors. Pasta of the week was featured.

In September, more changes in dining were announced. Formal dining was moved to the South Dining Room. The Tap Room welcomed families for informal dining with children. Informal adults-only dining was tried in the Red Room, now called the Red Room Grill, "No coat or tie required, but please no shorts or field attire." The Red Room offered more entertainment: Tony Barrasso, Hudson and Saleeby, Beth Carson, and Ron Smith.

In the Red Room, a ten-ounce New York strip steak coast $17.95, farm-raised catfish was $13.50, grilled lamb chops were $20.25, and veal liver sauté was $12.95. Florida pompano, Norwegian salmon, or red snapper was $15.00. The dessert specialty was the fresh baked fruit cobbler of the week for $4.00; for another dollar you could add ice cream.

When the USGA announced new rules and guidelines governing handicap and registration in 1994, the Club announced that it would implement the new procedures beginning on January 1, 1995. In 1994, the Club had thirty-nine golf outings, of which thirty-eight were handicapped events.

Dues were increased, for regular resident members the monthly dues was set at $275 a month. Greens fees were increased to $50 for eighteen holes; $25 for nine holes; Junior eighteen holes, $17.50; Junior nine holes, $10; and Outings, $65. The cost of presenting a debutante daughter rose to $2,000.

On New Year's Eve, members had two choices: dinner of beef tenderloin or red snapper with champagne could be enjoyed in the early bird version from 6:30 to 9:30 P.M. in the Red Room for $35, or the full event starting with dinner at 8:30 P.M. and going on through black eyed peas, coffee, and donuts at 12:30 in the morning, for $50. Rene Koopman's orchestra played.

W. Reid Sanders served as president from 1996 to 1998. A graduate of the University of Virginia, he was co-founder of Southeastern Asset Management and Longleaf Partners Foundation. He has served on the boards of the Dixon Gallery and Gardens, Rhodes College, the Hutchison School, and the Campbell Clinic Foundation.

His father, Edward Harvey Sanders, was a member of the Memphis Country Club from 1937 until his death in 1957. His stepfather, Dr. Hugh Smith, was a member from 1956 until his death in 1989.

During his term as president, a significant increase in the golf course budget was passed, with the goal of improving the course and regaining the club's previous rank in the state. Golf cart paths were redesigned and resurfaced with concrete. More decorative flowers and trees were planted. Additional staff and equipment were added. The ranking of the course within the state rose from eighteenth to tenth.

Symphony on the grounds, 2003: (Back row)—Eb and Camille LeMaster, Barbara and Bill Prest, and Tom Whitman. (Front row)—John and Jane Dulin and Howard and Loring Byers.

Peter Pettit, president 1998–2000, at Dinner in the Kitchen.

On April 30, 1997, the Club purchased the Buntyn Restaurant building, adding 0.30 acres to the east parking lot. The cost was $350,000, a steep increase since the Club's first land purchases in 1905: over sixty acres for $15,640. Parking decals were issued for members for increased security.

The club began funding a formal retirement plan, with a pension plan for all members and a 401K-type savings plan for those choosing to participate. Approximately half of the 130 employees of the club had been with the club for five years or more.

The tennis program continued to grow. Some eighty-five children were in the junior development program, and approximately eighty ladies competed in regular leagues. A men's league with about twenty players was organized. The Tennis Awards Banquet featured Wimbledon and U.S. Open Champion Stan Smith as speaker.

On Valentine's Day, 220 people were served. A concert by the Memphis Symphony Orchestra, with shrimp and tenderloin box suppers for the grown-ups and snack packs for youngsters, was held on the golf course on September 6, 1996. The Club held a tailgate party before the University of Memphis–University of Tennessee football game.

The end of the summer was celebrated with a joint party with the University Club. The symphony on the golf course continued to be a popular family-oriented event. A special dinner commemorated the famed Justine's restaurant on October 5, with oysters Mimi, crabmeat Justine, filet with béarnaise sauce or pompano Claudette, and desert Justine. It was such a success that the evening was repeated a second time in November.

Peter R. Pettit served as president from 1998 to 2000. A graduate of the University of Virginia, he was a lawyer with Canada, Russell and Turner, then with Malone and Hyde distribution company, and then with Bass, Berry and Sims. During his tenure, the golf course was converted to zoysia fairways and Bermuda greens.

New York architect Craig Smith and Memphis architects Looney, Ricks and Kiss were hired to analyze the clubhouse and facilities for a long-range plan. Renovations included new men's and women's health and exercise facilities, the pool snack bar, and dressing rooms. A $3.8 million master plan was adopted. The project hit a major snag when the fire marshall demanded a $250,000 firewall between the card room and the health facilities. But the work was completed in summer of 2001 by Montgomery Martin Contractors.

In 1999, Lew Frank retired, and a party honored his more than twenty years of service to the Memphis Country Club. Michael Babb, who had been clubhouse manager, was promoted to general manager. Babb was born in Oak Ridge, Tennessee, and attended the University of Tennessee and Memphis State University. He began working at the Memphis Country Club in October 1991 while attending Memphis State, and decided to pursue a career in the hospitality industry.

Lew Frank taught him the club business. In 1996, he was promoted to clubhouse manager/assistant general manager. Babb has served on the Board of Directors of the Club Managers' Association of America since 1997 and served as state president in 2002.

W. Cary Whitehead III was the president from 2000 to 2002 as the Memphis Country Club entered the new millennium. His father-in-law, Tom Price, had served as club attorney for many years. Whitehead graduated from Memphis University School and Ole Miss, and entered the commercial real estate field in 1971. His developments include International Place and Southwind Office Center. He lists hunting, fly fishing, skiing, tennis, and golf as his hobbies.

During his tenure, a day care center opened. The idea had been discussed for many years prior to the opening, but some members

The Health Club.

Swimming races.

Swim team winners Robert Gooch, Natalie Magness, and Sherman Tabor.

The crawfish boil, 2001.

had opposed the idea. The center, located in the old girls' swim locker rooms downstairs by the business office, was open on Tuesday, Wednesday, Friday, and Saturday from 9 A.M. to 2 P.M., and on Thursday from 9 A.M. to 9 P.M., and during certain club functions. Up to ten children from three months to ten years could be cared for at each session. Parents were required to be on the grounds at all times when their children were in the center.

Technology reared its ugly head and the board responded in April 2000 with a policy to prohibit the use of cell phones on all Club property. An article was added to the by-laws: "The purpose of the Club is for the social gathering, entertainment and recreation of its members, their families and their guests. The Club is not to be used for the conduct or promotion of business activities." Vibrating pagers could be used, but anyone using a cell phone would be fined one hundred dollars. The club began communicating with members by e-mail as well as through the monthly mailed newsletter.

In the spring, the Club announced that every fourth Saturday night, there would be special events planned for kids, following in the tradition of the now-abandoned Sunday night movies.

On March 24, the MCC Mini-Masters provided an indoor putt-putt course. On April 28, a Hulk Hogan Hoagie party featured a twelve-foot long sandwich, and on May 19, the Dining Room Derby constructed a race track for remote control cars.

Johan Svenssen, formerly professional at the Dallas Country Club, was hired as the new tennis director, and tennis activity increased. An annual memorial golf tournament, honoring MCC golfing legends began. The first tournament, in July 2000, honored Fred Schaeffer. The second annual Memphis Country Club Memorial Golf Tournament, on June 29 and 30, 2001, honored Tom Adams Sr.

In 2001, the new health club was completed, with substantially expanded men's and women's exercise rooms and locker rooms, an aerobics room, an international squash court, massage rooms, steam baths, and saunas. The exercise rooms were so designed that the walls separating them can be removed in the future if that is the desire of the membership. A fitness director was hired for the first time to provide

The campout on the grounds, 2002.

Centennial Chairman Scott Fisher with grandson Andrew Cofield at the campout.

personal exercise programs for members. Classes in aerobics, yoga, tai chi, and cardio kickboxing were started. The Club purchased a defibrillator and trained staff members in its use for cardiac emergencies.

Members had to be reminded that the new health club was a no smoking area.

The club's tree logo was adopted, and a tree survey was done, making recommendations for maintaining one of the Club's greatest assets, its twenty-five hundred trees. Monthly dues rose to $330 for regular members, still lower than at comparable clubs. Security cards for the front entrance gates were issued. A new guardhouse and new pool locker rooms were constructed. The former Buntyn Restaurant was torn down to enlarge the east parking lot and provide a new golf club drop area. All this constituted the largest construction project since the building of the new clubhouse in 1956.

A New Member party was re-introduced, having lapsed in the 1980s. A cocktail party to recognize past board members was held, and will be held at five year intervals. The Fourth of July saw swimming races, pony rides for children, a picnic buffet, and fireworks.

Entertainments ranged from a Basketball, Beef, and Beer evening in the Tap Room for the NCAA Tournament Final to an Evening in Paris, featuring Galantine de Volaille en Gelee et Saumon a l'Oseille, Consomme aux Petits Legumes, Carre d'Agneau Roti aux Primeurs, Salade de Chevre Chaud, and Tarte Tatin, for sixty-five dollars a person. Dinner in the Kitchen was a great success, as members enjoyed watching the chefs at work. The Front Porch Crawfish/Seafood party, held in May 2001, was such a success that it was repeated in the following year.

The celebration of Jay McDonald's one hundredth birthday, December 4, 2001. McDonald with Billy Webster at right.

Collie Krausnick, Lee Powell, and Charlie Lowrance boiled crawfish on the porch while The Sneakers, a band whose members include club members Joel Hobson and Wise Jones, played.

New Year's Eve featured a five-course gourmet wine dinner, music by the Memphis Soulettes, and a cigar and martini bar, with television for those wanting to catch the college bowl games. Cocktails by the Pool and Dinner

The Easter Bunny, 2003.

In October 2002, the Country Club hosted a dinner in honor of the late Pat Abbott, long time golf pro, upon his induction into the Tennessee Golf Hall of Fame. His family members attended, and memorabilia of his career was displayed. The 2002 Memorial Golf Tournament honored Don Drinkard. In 2003, two women from the Memphis Country Club, Marguerite Gaut and Margaret Gunther Lee, were inducted into the Tennessee Golf Hall of Fame.

A new award was instituted to give recognition to outstanding service from an employee in 2002. The first winner was twenty-year employee of the business office, Sandy Spencer. A Memorial Tree Fund was established to give members an opportunity to honor an individual's memory by contributing to tree planting.

Technology was called into service to aid golfers. New video with two cameras in the hitting room, golf swing analysis software, and the ability to use technology outside on the

Dances with Jim Johnson's Orchestra were other activities.

The family campout was another success that became an annual affair. A bonfire and cookout area was set out in the trees between the 8th and 11th fairways, and families pitched tents around it. Sack races, three legged races, wiffle ball, flag football, a glow stick search, and a hayride made sure that everyone had a good time. Other family activities included Santa's Workshop, Haunted Hayrides, and Thanksgiving to Go.

On December 4, 2001, Jay McDonald was honored on his one hundredth birthday as the Club's oldest member. He had been inducted into the Washington and Lee Athletic Hall of Fame for lettering in four sports all four years of college. He still plays bridge regularly at the Memphis Country Club.

Santa Claus with Mac, Meredith, and Natalie Magness, 2003.

The staff, 2004.

practice tee via laptop and camera gave golfers new views of their game.

Stillman "Stilly" McFadden became president in 2002. He graduated from the University of Virginia, and earned an MBA at Vanderbilt. He is president of McFadden Communications LLC, owner of S. C. Toof and Company. He has served as president of the Children's Museum.

His great-uncles, Jack and Billy McFadden, were members of the Memphis Country Club, and his father, Barclay McFadden, joined when he moved to Memphis after World War II to work in the family cotton business.

McFadden's term began with the usual events, the debutante ball and the carnival party. In May, the Memphis Country Club was named a Platinum Club of America by the Club Leaders Forum, putting it among the top one percent of America's five thousand private clubs in terms of perceived excellence. The Fourth Annual Memorial Tournament honored DeWitt "Tiger" Shy. The family campouts were so successful that two were held, one on May 3, 2003, and one on October 4.

In 2003, McFadden wrote:

things really started hopping, some planned, and others not. On the morning of July 22nd a fierce summer storm hit the city of Memphis unlike anything experienced in recent memory. Winds of over ninety miles per hour ripped through the city and the club property was not spared.

Into the Twenty-first Century

The opening of the new Red Room cocktail lounge, August 2003: Wallace and Olivia Bruce, Howard and Loring Byers, Jane and John Dulin, and Beverly and Glynn Alexander (with portrait of Bobby Jones in the background).

Many large trees were lost, mainly on the golf course, and portions of number eight green were damaged as a result. The club lost power for twelve days and most, if not all operations were suspended as the club and entire community cleaned up the aftermath. In less than four days after the storm, the course and outdoor tennis courts were opened for limited use, but it still represented the longest single closure of the club since the burning of the clubhouse in 1910.

In 2003, a special membership meeting was called to vote upon the expulsion of a member for unbecoming conduct. It was the only such expulsion in the club's history.

The Father-Son Tournament: Bobby Weaver, Bobby Hudson, Hal Boyd Jr., and Hal Boyd III.

The freak storm of July 22, 2003, damaged the golf course.

❧

The highlight of the year was the reopening of the remodeled Red Room. Memphis architect Reb Haizlip, working with Montgomery Martin Contractors, took the old Red Room down to the wall studs and then created a new dining room and cocktail lounge. To commemorate the grand reopening, a party was held in late August with an estimated four hundred members attending.

Things at the club settled down after the end of summer. Another successful Men's Member-Guest golf tournament was hosted in mid-September and the club hosted the Tennessee Golf Association Men's Mid Amateur during the first week of October. The best 144 amateur players from across the state played a three day tournament at the MCC course.

The winner, Danny Green of Jackson, spoke eloquently of his love for the Donald Ross-designed course, and the way golf has changed since he won his first State Amateur title in 1993, also at the MCC: "It's too bad there's not more of 'em around like the Memphis Country Club."

One member of the club made it to the tournament, Robert "Bobby" Weaver. Bobby's grandson, Bobby Hudson, carries on the family tradition by being the youngest member of the

Parties in the new millennium: Lele and Bobby Weaver and Lida and Walter Bross.

MCC to win the club championship. His grandfather began taking him to the golf course to putt and chip when he was seven. Soon young Bobby was pestering his grandfather, who won the club championship in 1970, to take him to practice every day. He won the club championship himself in 2002 at age fifteen, and repeated his victory again in 2003 and 2004.

Also in 2004, ten-year-old Scott Cofield, grandson of Centennial Chairman Scott Fisher, shot a hole in one, 123 yards from the Number 4 tee. He was the youngest person ever to make a hole in one at the Memphis Country Club. Later that year the Member-Guest Tournament team of Bill Mueller and Jack Trumpore became the first team to ever win the tournament three times.

Lindsey and Liz Farnsworth with Gala Elliott.

The former presidents plan for the centennial:
(Back row)—W. Neely Mallory (1978–1980); Billy Webster (1976–1978);
and Joseph Orgill III (1981–1983).
(Front row)—Thomas H. Hutton (1970–1972); Lewis K. McKee (1961–1963); and
Albert M. Austin III (1965–1966).

*While the former presidents plan for the centennial,
President Stilly McFadden thanks centennial chairman Scott Fisher for his hard work.*

The 2004–2005 president of the Memphis Country Club is James McCown Smith. A Memphis native, he graduated from the University of Alabama and the University of Memphis Law School. He has practiced law with the firm of Smith and Smith since 1976, and has been a member of the club since 1985. He will preside over the centennial festivities at the club.

The Weaver-Hudson and the Fisher-Cofield golf dynasties typify the spirit of the Memphis Country Club. For one hundred years, families have been the backbone of the club. Originally located away from the city, the club is now at its center. Many things have changed. But the traditions and spirit of the country club remain the same. The golf course is still its pride; its purpose is still that stated by its founders: "for social enjoyment, and not for profit." Families are still the heart of the club.

As the Memphis Country Club enters the twenty-first century, it remains at the center of competition and camaraderie; fun and fellowship; sports; and social life.

Recent presidents plan for the centennial:
(Back row)—Jackson W. Moore (1990–1992); Hallam Boyd (1986–1988);
and Cary Whitehead (2000–2002).
(Front row)—Peter Pettit (1998–2000); Lewis K. McKee Jr. (1988–1990);
Stillman McFadden (2002–2004); and Reid Sanders (1996–1998).

Appendix A

Officers of the Memphis Country Club

1905–1906
President	P. P. Van Vleet
Vice President	S. T. Carnes
Treasurer	E. B. McHenry
Secretary	Percy Galbreath

1906–1908
President	S. T. Carnes
First Vice President	P. P. Williams
Second Vice President	William P. Metcalf
Treasurer	E. B. McHenry
Secretary	E. C. Cochran

1908–1909
President	S. T. Carnes
First Vice President	P. P. Williams
Second Vice President	William P. Metcalf
Treasurer	N. C. Jones
Secretary	Homer K. Jones

1909–1910
President	S. T. Carnes
First Vice President	J. A. Evans
Second Vice President	I. McD. Massey
Treasurer	C. H. Raine
Secretary	Homer K. Jones

1910–1913
President	S. T. Carnes
First Vice President	F. G. Jones
Second Vice President	J. W. Martin
Treasurer	N. C. Perkins
Secretary	Homer K. Jones
Assistant Secretary	E. C. Ellison

1913–1916
President	S. T. Carnes
First Vice President	F. G. Jones
Second Vice President	J. A. Evans
Treasurer	N. C. Perkins
Secretary	Homer K. Jones
Assistant Secretary	E. C. Ellison

1916–1919
President	M. J. Condon
First Vice President	F. G. Jones
Second Vice President	C. K. Smith
Treasurer	Josiah L. Hutton
Secretary	Homer K. Jones
Assistant Secretary	E. C. Ellison

1919–1920
President	T. J. Turley
First Vice President	W. P. Battle
Second Vice President	Fred B. Jones
Treasurer	Noland Fontaine
Secretary	Homer K. Jones
Assistant Secretary	E. C. Ellison

1920–1921
President	T. J. Turley
First Vice President	W. P. Battle
Second Vice President	Fred B. Jones
Treasurer	Noland Fontaine

Secretary	Homer K. Jones
Assistant Secretary	J. S. C. Churchill

1921–1922
President	T. J. Turley
First Vice President	W. P. Battle
Second Vice President	B. A. Bogy
Treasurer	S. E. Ragland
Secretary	J. F. Dickinson
Assistant Secretary	J. S. C. Churchill

1922–1923
President	T. J. Turley
First Vice President	B. A. Bogy
Second Vice President	T. A. Goodwin
Treasurer	S. E. Ragland
Secretary	J. F. Dickinson
Assistant Secretary and Manager	J. S. C. Churchill

1923–1924
President	T. J. Turley
First Vice President	T. A. Goodwin
Second Vice President	W. W. Simmons
Treasurer	S. E. Ragland
Secretary	J. F. Dickinson
Assistant Secretary	R. L. Steadman
Manager	J. S. C. Churchill

1924–1925
President	T. J. Turley
First Vice President	W. W. Simmons
Second Vice President	Charles O. Pfeil
Treasurer	S. E. Ragland
Secretary	J. E. Harwood
Assistant Secretary	R. L. Steadman
Manager	J. S. C. Churchill

1925–1926
President	T. J. Turley
First Vice President	W. W. Simmons
Second Vice President	W. J. Britton
Treasurer	S. E. Ragland
Secretary	J. E. Harwood
Assistant Secretary	R. L. Steadman
Manager	J. E. Beck

1926–1927
President	J. P. Norfleet
First Vice President	Dr. Percy H. Wood
Second Vice President	W. L. McKee
Treasurer	S. Preston Fortune
Secretary	James E. Stark
Assistant Secretary	R. L. Steadman
Manager	J. E. Buck

1927–1928
President	J. P. Norfleet
First Vice President	Dr. Percy H. Wood
Second Vice President	W. L. McKee
Treasurer	S. Preston Fortune
Secretary	James E. Stark
Assistant Secretary	R. V. Wiley
Manager	Allie Stark Patteson

1928–1929
President	Dr. Richmond McKinney
First Vice President	Dr. Percy H. Wood
Second Vice President	L. P. Eustis
Secretary-Treasurer	L. Y. Williamson
Assistant Secretary	R. V. Wiley
Manager	Allie Stark Patteson

1929–1931
President	Dr. Richmond McKinney
First Vice President	W. L. McKee
Second Vice President	H. P. Jordan
Secretary-Treasurer	L. Y. Williamson
Assistant Secretary	R. V. Wiley
Attorney	Walter P. Armstrong
Manager	Allie Stark Patteson

1931–1932
President	Dr. Richmond McKinney
First Vice President	W. L. McKee
Second Vice President	Leroy Cooper
Secretary-Treasurer	S. W. Farnsworth
Assistant Secretary	R. V. Wiley
Manager	Allie Stark Patteson

1932–1933
President	Dr. Richmond McKinney
First Vice President	Sidney W. Farnsworth
Second Vice President	Henry H. Haizlip
Secretary-Treasurer	Neely Grant
Assistant Treasurer	Robert V. Wiley
Manager	Allie Stark Patteson

1933–1934
President	Dr. Richmond McKinney
First Vice President	Henry H. Haizlip
Second Vice President	Malcolm G. Barboro
Secretary-Treasurer	Neely Grant
Assistant Treasurer	Robert V. Wiley
Attorney	Earl King
Manager	Allie Stark Patteson

1934–1935
President	Dr. Richmond McKinney
First Vice President	H. Martin Dunscomb
Second Vice President	Gladden H. Spigener
Secretary-Treasurer	McEwen Ransom
Assistant Secretary	Robert. V. Wiley
Attorney	Earl King
Manager	Allie Stark Patteson

1935–1936
President	Dr. Richmond McKinney
First Vice President	Richard H. Bodine
Second Vice President	J. Pervis Milnor
Secretary-Treasurer	R. Vance Norfleet
Assistant Secretary	Robert V. Wiley
Attorney	Edward P. Russell
Manager	Allie Stark Patteson

1936–1937
President	Dr. Richmond McKinney
First Vice President	J. Pervis Milnor
Second Vice President	Brown Burch
Secretary-Treasurer	R. Vance Norfleet
Assistant Secretary	Robert V. Wiley
Attorney	Edward P. Russell
Manager	Allie Stark Patteson

1937–1938
President	Dr. Richmond McKinney
First Vice President	Sidney W. Farnsworth
Second Vice President	Frank G. Barton
Secretary-Treasurer	R. Vance Norfleet
Assistant Secretary	Robert V. Wiley
Attorney	Edward P. Russell
Manager	Allie Stark Patteson

1938–1939
President	Dr. Richmond McKinney
First Vice President	Thomas C. Adams
Second Vice President	Winston F. Cheairs
Secretary-Treasurer	Charles M. Kortrecht
Assistant Secretary	Robert V. Wiley
Attorney	Earl King
Manager	Allie Stark Patteson

1939–1940
President	Dr. Richmond McKinney
First Vice President	Everett R. Cook
Second Vice President	Winston F. Cheairs
Secretary-Treasurer	Charles M. Kortrecht
Assistant Secretary	Robert V. Wiley
Attorney	Earl King
Manager	Allie Stark Patteson

1940–1941
President	Dr. Richmond McKinney
First Vice President	Everett R. Cook
Second Vice President	Earl King
Secretary-Treasurer	Richard Harwood
Assistant Secretary	Richard V. Wiley
Manager	Allie Stark Patteson

1941–1942
President	W. Lytle McKee
First Vice President	Everett R. Cook
Secretary-Treasurer	Malcolm G. Barboro
Assistant Secretary	Robert V. Wiley
Attorney	Edward P. Russell
Manager	Allie Stark Patteson

1942–1943
President	McKay Van Vleet
First Vice President	Edward P. Russell
Second Vice President	George Treadwell
Secretary-Treasurer	Malcolm G. Barboro
Assistant Secretary	Robert V. Wiley
Manager	Allie Stark Patteson

1943–1944
President	George Treadwell
First Vice President	Edward P. Russell
Second Vice President	Frank C. Pidgeon
Secretary-Treasurer	W. Groom Leftwich
Assistant Secretary	Robert V. Wiley
Manager	Allie Stark Patteson

1944–1945
President	George Treadwell
First Vice President	Edward P. Russell
Second Vice President	James E. Stark
Secretary-Treasurer	Norfleet Turner
Assistant Secretary	Robert V. Wiley
Manager	Allie Stark Patteson

1945–1946
President	George Treadwell
First Vice President	James E. Stark
Second Vice President	Dunbar Abston
Secretary-Treasurer	Norfleet Turner
Assistant Secretary	Robert V. Wiley
Attorney	Edward P. Russell
Manager	Oscar B. Bell

1946–1947
President	Edward P. Russell
First Vice President	W. Groom Leftwich
Second Vice President	Charles W. Loomis
Second Vice President	Julian B. Bondurant
Secretary-Treasurer	Vance J. Alexander
Assistant Secretary	Robert V. Wiley
Attorney	Millsaps Fitzhugh
Manager	W. F. Buttrey

1947–1948
President	Edward P. Russell
First Vice President	W. Groom Leftwich
Second Vice President	Julian B. Bondurant
Secretary-Treasurer	Norfleet Turner
Assistant Secretary	Robert V. Wiley
Attorney	Millsaps Fitzhugh
Manager	Carl L. Bannas

1948–1949
President	W. Groom Leftwich
First Vice President	J. Bayard Boyle
Second Vice President	Hugh Francis
Secretary-Treasurer	A. Van Pritchartt
Assistant Secretary	Robert V. Wiley
Attorney	Alfred B. Pittman
Manager	Carl L. Bannas

1949–1950
President	W. Groom Leftwich
First Vice President	Hugh Francis
Second Vice President	James E. Harwood Jr.
Secretary-Treasurer	Emmet Joyner
Assistant Secretary	Robert V. Wiley
Attorney	Alfred B. Pittman
Manager	Charles W. Wynn

1950–1951
President	James E. Harwood
First Vice President	A. Van Pritchartt
Second Vice President	L. Palmer Brown III
Secretary-Treasurer	Herbert P. Jordan

Assistant Secretary   Robert V. Wiley
Attorney   Edward L. Lawler Jr.
Manager   Mary B. Campbell

1951–1952
President   James E. Harwood
First Vice President   A. Van Pritchartt
Second Vice President   L. Palmer Brown Jr.
Secretary-Treasurer   Martin J. Condon III
Assistant Secretary   Mary B. Campbell
Attorney   Thomas C. Farnsworth

1952–1953
President   James E. Stark
First Vice President   Martin J. Condon III
Second Vice President.   Dunbar Abston
Secretary-Treasurer   Maury Wade
Assistant Secretary   Robert V. Wiley
Attorney   Thomas C. Farnsworth
Manager   Mary B. Campbell

1953–1954
President   James E. Stark
First Vice President   Charles C. Cathey
Second Vice President   Thomas C. Farnsworth
Secretary-Treasurer   J. Neely Grant
Assistant Secretary   Robert V. Wiley
Manager   Mary B. Campbell

1954–1955
President   Martin J. Condon III
First Vice President   Charles C. Cathey
Second Vice President   C. D. Smith
Secretary-Treasurer   Chauncey W. Butler Jr.
Assistant Secretary   Robert V. Wiley
Manager   Mary B. Campbell

1955–1956
President   Martin J. Condon III
First Vice President   Alfred B. Pittman
Second Vice President   S. Richard Leatherman
Secretary-Treasurer   William A. Connaughton
Assistant Secretary   Robert V. Wiley
Attorneys   Edward P. Russell *and* Thomas R. Price
Manager   Anthony T. Speechley

1956–1957
President   Martin J. Condon III
First Vice President   Lewis K. McKee
Second Vice President   S. Richard Leatherman
Secretary-Treasurer   Tim Treadwell III
Assistant Secretary   Robert V. Wiley
Attorney   Dunlap Cannon Jr.
Manager   Anthony T. Speechley

1957–1958
President   James D. Robinson
First Vice President   Lewis K. McKee
Second Vice President   J. Bayard Boyle
Secretary-Treasurer   Henry L. Taylor
Attorney   Dunlap Cannon
Manager   Anthony T. Speechley

1958–1959
President   James D. Robinson
First Vice President   J. Bayard Boyle
Second Vice President   Henry L. Taylor
Secretary-Treasurer   Eugene J. Pidgeon
Attorney   Dunlap Cannon Jr.
Manager   Anthony J. Speechley

1959–1960
President   James D. Robinson
First Vice President   A. Van Pritchartt
Second Vice President   Eugene J. Pidgeon
Secretary-Treasurer   E. B. LeMaster
Attorney   Dunlap Cannon Jr.
Manager   Anthony J. Speechley

1960–1961
President   James D. Robinson
First Vice President   E. B. LeMaster

Second Vice President	Dunlap Cannon Jr.		**1966–1967**	
Secretary-Treasurer	Samuel S. Rembert Jr.	*President*	Albert M. Austin III
Manager	Anthony T. Speechley	*First Vice President*	Neely Mallory Jr.
		Second Vice President	J. A. Crisler III
		Secretary-Treasurer	Frank Donelson Jr.
		Attorney	James M. Manire
		Manager	Eugene Hollo

1961–1962
President	Lewis K. McKee
First Vice President	Samuel S. Rembert Jr.
Second Vice President	T. J. White
Secretary-Treasurer	W. E. Buxton
Attorney	Larry Creson
Manager	A. J. Edmondson

1967–1968
President	Dr. Bland W. Cannon
First Vice President	Robert D. McCallum
Second Vice President	Jack Petree
Secretary-Treasurer	Frank Donelson Jr.
Attorney	James M. Manire
Managers	George Burton *and* Eugene Hollo

1962–1963
President	Lewis K. McKee
First Vice President	Samuel S. Rembert Jr.
Second Vice President	Hugh Sprunt
Secretary-Treasurer	Henry Wetter
Attorney	Larry Creson
Manager	Mrs. Ada Davidson

1963–1964
President	Samuel S. Rembert Jr.
First Vice President	T. J. White
Second Vice President	Larry Creson
Secretary-Treasurer	John R. Pepper
Manager	Mrs. Ada Davidson

1968–1969
President	Dr. Bland W. Cannon
First Vice President	Robert D. McCallum
Second Vice President	Dunbar Abston Jr.
Secretary-Treasurer	Frank M. Crump Jr.
Attorney	Dan D. Canale
Manager	George Burton

1969–1970
President	Dr. Bland W. Cannon
First Vice President	Thomas H. Hutton
Second Vice President	Frank M. Crump Jr.
Secretary-Treasurer	S. R. Leatherman Jr.
Attorney	Dan Canale
Manager	Charles M. Coffield

1964–1965
President	Samuel S. Rembert Jr.
First Vice President	Albert M. Austin III
Second Vice President	John D. Canale
Secretary-Treasurer	Thomas H. Hutton
Manager	Mrs. Ada Davidson

1965–1966
President	Albert M. Austin III
First Vice President	Thomas H. Hutton
Second Vice President	Neely Mallory Jr.
Secretary-Treasurer	Ben Adams
Manager	Eugene Hollo

1970–1971
President	Thomas H. Hutton
First Vice President	M. M. Gordon
Second Vice President	Donald Drinkard
Secretary-Treasurer	M. Eugene Hill Jr.
Attorney	Charles R. Sherman
Manager	Charles M. Coffield

1971–1972
President — Thomas H. Hutton
First Vice President — M. M. Gordon
Second Vice President — Donald Drinkard
Treasurer — Charles R. Sherman
Secretary — M. Eugene Hill Jr.
Attorney — Jack Petree
Manager — Charles M. Coffield

1972–1973
President — E. C. Krausnick
First Vice President — Jack Petree
Second Vice President — W. D. Galbreath
Treasurer — Allen B. Morgan Jr.
Secretary — Henry W. Jones Jr.
Attorney — Charles R. Sherman
Manager — Charles M. Coffield

1973–1974
President — E. C. Krausnick
First Vice President — W. Neely Mallory
Second Vice President — Hugh Francis
Treasurer — Allen B. Morgan Jr.
Secretary — Henry W. Jones Jr.
Attorney — Dale Woodall
Manager — Charles M. Coffield

1974–1975
President — Giles A. Coors Jr.
First Vice President — W. Neely Mallory
Second Vice President — William B. Dunavant Jr.
Treasurer — Allen B. Morgan Jr.
Secretary — James H. Wetter
Attorney — Dale Woodall
Manager — Charles M. Coffield

1975–1976
President — Giles A. Coors Jr.
First Vice President — W. Neely Mallory
Second Vice President — James H. Wetter
Treasurer — Frederick C. Schaeffer
Secretary — William A. Webster
Attorney — Dale R. Woodall
Manager — Anthony T. Speechley

1976–1977
President — William A. Webster
First Vice President — Richard H. Allen Jr.
Second Vice President — Frederick C. Schaeffer
Treasurer — James H. Wetter
Secretary — Dr. Owen B. Tabor
Attorney — Phil Canale Jr.
Manager — Anthony T. Speechley

1977–1978
President — William A. Webster
First Vice President — Richard A. Allen Jr.
Second Vice President — Robert G. Snowden
Treasurer — E. B. LeMaster
Secretary — Michael McDonnell
Attorney — Phil Canale
Manager — Anthony T. Speechley

1978–1979
President — W. Neely Mallory
First Vice President — Robert G. Snowden
Second Vice President — Dr. Richard B. Raines
Secretary-Treasurer — J. A. Crisler III
Attorney — Thomas R. Price
Manager — Lewis Frank

1979–1980
President — W. Neely Mallory
First Vice President — Dr. Richard B. Raines
Second Vice President — Donald Drinkard
Secretary-Treasurer — J. A. Crisler III
Attorney — Thomas R. Price
Manager — Lewis Frank

1980–1981
President — John Hull Dobbs
First Vice President — Donald Drinkard
Second Vice President — A. J. Hays Jr.

Secretary-Treasurer	Joseph Orgill Jr.
Attorney	J. W. McDonnell Jr.
Manager	Lewis Frank

1981–1982
President	John Hull Dobbs
First Vice President	Michael McDonnell
Second Vice President	Davant Latham
Secretary-Treasurer	Frederick Schaeffer
Attorney	J. W. McDonnell Jr.
Manager	Lewis Frank

1982–1983
President	Joseph Orgill III
First Vice President	Michael McDonnell
Second Vice President	Davant Latham
Secretary-Treasurer	Frederick Schaeffer
Attorney	J. W. McDonnell
Manager	Lewis Frank

1983–1984
President	Joseph Orgill III
First Vice President	R. Grattan Brown Jr.
Second Vice President	Allen Morgan
Secretary-Treasurer	Dr. Owen B. Tabor
Attorney	J. W. Moore
Manager	Lewis Frank

1984–1985
President	Michael McDonnell
First Vice President	Thomas M. Garrott
Second Vice President	Frank M. Crump III
Secretary-Treasurer	Samuel S. Rembert III
Manager	Lewis Frank

1985–1986
President	Michael McDonnell
First Vice President	Dr. Allen Hughes
Second Vice President	J. Hallam Boyd Jr.
Secretary-Treasurer	Frank M. Crump III
Attorney	Fred Ridolphi Jr.
Manager	Lewis Frank

1986–1987
President	J. Hallam Boyd Jr.
First Vice President	Dr. Peter Quinn
Second Vice President	Lewis K. McKee Jr.
Secretary	John C. Dobbs
Treasurer	C. Barham Ray
Attorney	Fred Ridolphi Jr.
Manager	Lewis Frank

1987–1988
President	J. Hallam Boyd Jr.
First Vice President	Lewis K. McKee Jr.
Second Vice President	James C. Rainer
Secretary-Treasurer	C. Barham Ray
Attorney	Fred Ridolphi Jr.
Manager	Lewis Frank

1988–1989
President	Lewis K. "Mac" McKee Jr.
First Vice President	Jackson W. Moore
Second Vice President	Edward B. LeMaster Jr.
Treasurer	C. Barham Ray
Secretary	John S. Collier
Attorney	Wm. Lytle Nichol IV
Manager	Lewis Frank

1989–1990
President	Lewis K. "Mac" McKee Jr.
First Vice President	William Carrington Jones
Second Vice President	John S. Collier
Treasurer	Jackson W. Moore
Attorney	Wm. Lytle Nichol IV
Manager	Lewis Frank

1990–1991
President	Jackson W. Moore
First Vice President	Clyde L. Patton Jr.
Second Vice President	William Carrington Jones

Treasurer	C. Barham Ray
Secretary	James W. McDonnell Jr.
Attorney	Wm. Lytle Nichol IV
Manager	Lewis Frank

1991–1992
President	Jackson W. Moore
First Vice President	Peter R. Pettit
Second Vice President	James W. McDonnell Jr.
Treasurer	C. Barham Ray
Secretary	Frederick C. Schaeffer
Attorney	Wm. Lytle Nichol IV
Manager	Lewis Frank

1992–1993
President	Frederick C. Schaeffer
First Vice President	James W. McDonnell Jr.
Second Vice President	Willis H. Willey III
Treasurer	Thomas C. Adams Jr.
Secretary	James H. Barton
Attorney	Wm. Lytle Nichol IV
Manager	Lewis Frank

1993–1994
President	Frederick C. Schaeffer
First Vice President	Thomas C. Adams Jr.
Second Vice President	Willis H. Willey III
Treasurer	Dr. James C. Varner
Secretary	W. Neely Mallory III
Attorney	Wm. Lytle Nichol IV
Manager	Lewis Frank

1994–1995
President	Thomas C. Adams Jr.
First Vice President	Dr. James C. Varner
Second Vice President	Roy C. Bell Jr.
Treasurer	Charles R. Brindell Jr.
Secretary	Dr. Haywood Henderson
Attorney	Wm. Lytle Nichol IV
Manager	Lewis Frank

1995–1996
President	Thomas C. Adams Jr.
First Vice President/ Treasurer	Charles R. Brindell Jr.
Second Vice President	Dr. Haywood Henderson
Secretary	W. Reid Sanders
Attorney	W. Lytle Nichol IV
Manager	Lewis Frank

1996–1997
President	W. Reid Sanders
First Vice President	Peter R. Pettit
Second Vice President	William G. Mueller IV
Secretary/Treasurer	W. Cary Whitehead III
Attorney	W. Lytle Nichol IV
Manager	Lewis Frank

1997–1998
President	W. Reid Sanders
First Vice President	Peter R. Pettit
Second Vice President/ Treasurer	W. Cary Whitehead III
Secretary	J. William Pierce Jr.
Attorney	Oscar C. Carr III
Manager	Lewis Frank

1998–1999
President	Peter R. Pettit
First Vice President	W. Cary Whitehead III
Second Vice President	Donald C. McClure Jr.
Treasurer	James J. Keras Jr.
Secretary	Bruce B. Hopkins
Attorney	Oscar C. Carr III
Manager	Lewis Frank

1999–2000
President	Peter R. Pettit
First Vice President	J. Stillman McFadden
Second Vice President	James M. Smith
Treasurer	Glenn W. Cofield
Secretary	Michael H. Thompson
Attorney	Oscar C. Carr III
Manager	Michael Babb

2000–2001

President	W. Cary Whitehead III
First Vice President	J. Stillman McFadden
Second Vice President	James M. Smith
Treasurer	Glenn W. Cofield
Secretary	Michael H. Thompson
Attorney	Oscar C. Carr III
Manager	Michael Babb

2001–2002

President	W. Cary Whitehead III
First Vice President	Thomas C. Farnsworth III
Second Vice President	Marshall A. Clark
Treasurer	Glenn W. Cofield
Secretary	J. Beasley Wellford
Attorney	Oscar C. Carr III
Manager	Michael Babb

2002–2003

President	J. Stillman McFadden
First Vice President	Thomas C. Farnsworth III
Second Vice President	J. Hallam Boyd III
Treasurer	Joseph M. Morrison
Secretary	William G. Mueller IV
Attorney	Oscar C. Carr III
Manager	Michael Babb

2003–2004

President	J. Stillman McFadden
First Vice President	Charles F. Smith Jr.
Second Vice President	Elmer W. Stout
Treasurer	Joseph M. Morrison
Secretary	E. Carl Krausnick Jr.
Attorney	James M. Smith
Manager	Michael Babb

2004–2005

President	James M. Smith
First Vice President	Samuel A. Gassaway
Second Vice President	William G. Mueller
Treasurer	George M. Griesbeck
Secretary	Frank M. Crump III
Attorney	Oscar C. Carr III
Manager	Michael Babb

Appendix B

Golf Tournament Winners

MCC Men's Golf Championship

Year	Winner/*Runner-Up*
1929	Frank Dyer/*L. A. Montedonico Jr.*
1930	Percy Parker Jr./*Leroy Taylor*
1931	Edward F. Falls/*Leroy Taylor*
1932	Edward F. Falls/*J. Hunter Phillips*
1933	Edward F. Falls/*Millard C. Jones*
1934	Leroy Taylor/*Lawrence Eustis*
1935	Edward F. Falls/*C. Wesley Goyer*
1936	Edward F. Falls/*R. Beverley Ray*
1937	George Treadwell/*Charles D. Richardson*
1938	George Treadwell/*T. J. White*
1939	T. J. White/*W. F. Andrews*
1940	T. J. White/*W. F. Andrews*
1941	T. J. White/*Wendell Spragins*
1942	George Treadwell/*T. J. White*
1943	George Treadwell/*Capt. J. A. Welch*
1944	Dr. George A. Coors/*Leroy Taylor*
1945	T. J. White/*J. Alcorn Russell*
1946	Hugh Francis/*T. J. White*
1947	Emmet E. Joyner/*Hugh Francis*
1948	Dr. George A. Coors/*Hugh Francis*
1949	Dr. George A. Coors/*T. J. White*
1950	J. T. Saunders/*Dr. George A. Coors*
1951	E. K. Allis/*Eugene J. Pidgeon*
1952	Dr. George A. Coors/*S. R. Lee Jr.*
1953	T. J. White/*John Sheahan*
1954	George Treadwell/*T. J. White*
1955	W. J. Denton/*Dr. George A. Coors*
1956	W. J. Denton/*Dr. George A. Coors*
1957	W. J. Denton/*L. P. Miles Jr.*
1958	Dr. George A. Coors/*John Sheahan*
1959	Dr. George A. Coors/*Henry L. Taylor*
1960	Dr. George A. Coors/*J. Tunkie Saunders*
1961	John J. Pepin Jr./*Maney Heckle*
1962	Dr. George A. Coors/*J. Tunkie Saunders*
1963	John J. Wellford Jr./*Dr. George A. Coors*
1964	John Sheahan/*John J. Pepin Jr.*
1965	John Sheahan/*Dr. George A. Coors*
1966	C. Barham Ray/*J. Ripley Greer*
1967	C. Barham Ray/*John J. Pepin Jr.*
1968	John Nickey/*C. Barham Ray*
1969	John Nickey/*Dr. George A. Coors*
1970	Robert Weaver/*Eugene J. Pidgeon*
1971	Roy A. Moore/*John J. Pepin Jr.*
1972	John Nickey/*Robert Weaver*
1973	Lee Cheairs/*Kenneth Clark III*
1974	Kirk Bailey/*Lee Cheairs*
1975	Lee Cheairs/*Dan Canale*
1976	Kirk Bailey/*Lee Cheairs*
1977	Lee Cheairs/*Roy A. Moore*
1978	Jim Haygood III/*Lee Nichols*
1979	Lee Cheairs/*Jim Haygood III*
1980	Lee Cheairs/*Barham Ray*
1981	Kirk P. Bailey/*Roy Moore Jr.*
1982	Roy A. Moore/*Tom Divine*
1983	Roy A. Moore/*Walter T. Bross*
1984	Kirk Bailey/*Roy A. Moore*
1985	Walter T. Bross/*Robert Weaver*
1986	Kirk Bailey/*Barham Ray*
1987	Kirk Bailey/*Charles Slatery*
1988	Kirk Bailey/*Whit Beall*
1989	Kirk Bailey/*Robert Weaver*
1990	Frank Gusmus/*Kirk Bailey*
1991	Charles Slatery/*Whit Beall*

Year	Member/Guest		Year	Member/Guest
1992	Kirk Bailey/*Bobby Weaver*		1999	Charles Slatery/*Kirk Bailey*
1993	Kirk Bailey/*Sellers Shy*		2000	Kirk Bailey/*Robert Weaver*
1994	Kirk Bailey/*Sellers Shy*		2001	Brice Bailey/*Kirk Bailey*
1995	Bill Mueller/*Kirk Bailey*		2002	Bobby Hudson/*Bill Mueller*
1996	Kirk Bailey/*Charles Slatery*		2003	Bobby Hudson/*Hal Boyd III*
1997	Kirk Bailey/*James Varner*		2004	Bobby Hudson/*Charles Slattery*
1998	Roy A. Moore/*Kirk Bailey*			

MCC Member-Guest Golf Tournament

Year	Member/Guest		Year	Member/Guest
1963	Daniel D. Canale/*Joe Davis*		1984	Dr. William Andrews/*Dr. William Andrews Jr.*
1964	Henry L. Taylor/*Mack P. Brothers*		1985	Tom Adams Sr./*Eddie Hoopes*
1965	J. Ripley Greer/*Dudley Casey*		1986	Jan Gwin/*Allen Mott*
1966	J. K. Willey/*Don Walker*		1987	Robert Gardner Jr./*Bert Johnston*
1967	Thomas R. Price/*Daniel Oehmiq*		1988	Sam Varner/*Gayden Drew*
1968	W. Neely Mallory Jr./*Robert Stovall*		1989	Marshall Clark/*Alex Moore*
1969	Dr. Fontaine Moore Jr./*Dr. Andrew Dale*		1990	John Dillon/*Lou Wittenberg*
1970	Dr. George Coors/*Jack Lupton*		1991	Marshall Clark/*Norm Chapman*
1971	Dunlap Cannon/*Jack Minton*		1992	Bill Mueller/*Jack Trumpere*
1972	Phil Canale/*John Smallpage*		1993	Richard Hollis/*David Krouse*
1973	Donald Drinkard/*I. T. Oesterle*		1994	Bob E. Mallory/*Paul Pollack*
1974	Roy Moore/*William Leonard*		1995	Tommy Farnsworth III/*Sam Wodetzki*
1975	Dr. Bland Cannon/*Dr. Haddon Peck*		1996	Duke Clement/*Jay Babb*
1976	Scott Fisher/*William Cutler*		1997	Calvin Ozier/*Sid Cash*
1977	Mike McDonnell/*Andrew Baur*		1998	Chip Dickinson/*Raymond Regard*
1978	James K. Hoyt/*Hank Broyles*		1999	Wellford Tabor/*Sam Farnham*
1979	DeWitt M. Shy/*Wm. B. Hamilton*		2000	Robert Weaver/*Dr. Charles Ames*
1980	Ronald M. Byrnes/*Steve Stevens*		2001	Michael B. Turley/*John L. Turley*
1981	Trow Gillespie Jr./*Willis M. Ball III*		2002	Bill Mueller/*Jack Trumpere*
1982	Dwight Drinkard/*Dr. Charles Hubbard*		2003	Michael B. Turley/*John L. Turley*
1983	Scott Fisher/*William Cutler*		2004	Bill Mueller/*Jack Trumpore*

Middlecoff Four Ball

Year	Winners/*Runners-Up*
1975	Edgar Bailey and George Treadwell/ *Dr. Randy Turner and Dan Canale*
1976	Reggie Barnes and Edgar Bailey/ *Robert Gardner Jr. and Dr. Randy Turner*
1977	Dr. Frank Adams and Reggie Barnes/ *E. B. LeMaster Jr. and Robert Gardner Jr.*
1978	Fred Schaeffer and Ronald Byrnes/ *Dr. Owen B. Tabor and George S. Kirk II*
1979	Claude Crawford and Jack Hays/ *John Doggett and Charles D. Richardson*
1980	Edgar Bailey and Whit Beall/ *Dr. Randy Turner and Oscar C. Carr III*
1981	W. Neely Mallory and George E. Cates/ *Joseph Orgill III and James Harwood III*
1982	Joseph Orgill III and Girard P. Brownlow III/ *W. Neely Mallory and Mike Kiser*
1983	Jac Crisler and Scott Fisher/ *Tom Divine and Robert L. Weaver*
1984	Robert L. Weaver and Dr. George A. Coors/ *Scott Fisher and Russell Wood*
1985	Jim Haygood III and Reggie Barnes/ *Roy A. Moore and Robert Gardner Jr.*
1986	Henry Cannon and Dwight Drinkard/ *Charles R. Brindell Jr. and John Petree*
1987	Steve Morrow and Robert L. Weaver/ *Charles Slatery and John Russell*
1988	Albert M. Austin and Edgar Bailey/ *James W. McDonnell Jr. and Dr. Randy Turner*
1989	Kirk Bailey and Beasley Wellford/ *Robert Tayloe and Bill Mueller*
1990	Ronald M. Byrnes and James L. Barksdale/ *George Kirk and Walter Bross*
1991	Reggie Barnes and Albert M. Austin/ *Robert Gardner Jr. and James W. McDonnell Jr.*
1992	Will Pierce and Kirk Bailey/ *Harvey Kay and Robert Tayloe*
1993	Greg Wright and Hal Boyd III/ *Sellers Shy and Bob E. Mallory*
1994	Marshall Clark and Jim Varner/ *Neely Mallory III and Sam Varner*
1995	Dr. Tom Morris and Greg Morten/ *Dr. Owen B. Tabor and Alan Pritchard*
1996	Charles Slatery and Will Pierce/ *Steve Morrow and Harvey Kay*
1997	Jim Witherington and Walter Bross/ *Jim Keras and Dr. George Coors*
1998	Reggie Barnes and Bob E. Mallory/ *Robert Gardner Jr. and Hal Boyd III*
1999	Pepper Allen and Bob E. Mallory/ *Fred Ridolphi Jr. and Hal Boyd III*
2000	Mike McDonnell and Charles Slatery/ *Dudley Bridgeforth and Steve Morrow*
2001	Bob E. Mallory and Tommy Farnsworth III/ *Hal Boyd III and Bo Braswell*
2002	John Dicken and Reggie Barnes/ *Bill Mueller and Robert Gardner Jr.*
2003	Dr. Ned Laughlin Jr. and Robert Tayloe/ *Ned Laughlin III and Jay Tayloe*
2004	Dow McVean and Coleman Connell/ *Keith Barton and Beasley Wellford*

Marguerite Gaut Senior Women's Invitational

Year	Winner	Year	Winner
1961	Mrs. Dell Guthrie Henson	1976	Mrs. C. D. Graves
1962	Mrs. Dell Guthrie Henson	1977	Mrs. Edward J. Lawler
1963	Mrs. Dell Guthrie Henson	1978	Mrs. Dell Guthrie Henson
1964	Mrs. Dell Guthrie Henson	1979	Mrs. Bert Weaver
1965	Mrs. C. D. Graves	1980	Mrs. Dudley Beal
1966	Mrs. John L. Taylor	1981	Ms. Colleen Beck
1967	Mrs. H. J. Baker	1982	Mrs. Dudley Beal
1968	Mrs. H. J. Baker	1983	Mrs. Frank Phillips
1969	Mrs. S. R. Lee Jr.	1984	Mrs. Dudley Beal
1970	Mrs. S. R. Lee Jr.	1985	Mrs. Thomas G. Tackett Jr.
1971	Mrs. H. J. Baker	1986	Mrs. Thomas G. Tackett Jr.
1972	Mrs. Ben E. Glasgow	1987	Mrs. Thomas G. Tackett Jr.
1973	Mrs. Ben E. Glasgow	1988	Mrs. Edward C. Duke
1974	Mrs. Ronald E. Johnston	1989	Mrs. Thomas G. Tackett Jr.
1975	Mrs. C. D. Graves	1990	Mrs. Thomas G. Tackett Jr.

MCC Memorial Tournament Honorees

Year	Name	Year	Name
2000	Fred C. Schaeffer Sr.	2003	DeWitt Shy
2001	Tom Adams	2004	James Haygood
2002	Don Drinkard		

Women's Southern Golf Association Twelfth Annual Tournament

Team Trophy Won by Memphis Country Club,
River Crest Country Club,
Fort Worth Texas, 1923
Mrs. Dave Gaut
Mrs. L. W. Magruder
Mrs. Kenneth Duffield

MCC Women's Nine-Hole Championship

Year	Winner
1976	Mrs. Hugh R. Cunningham
1977	Mrs. George G. Early
1978	Mrs. George G. Early
1979	Mrs. Henry L. Taylor
1980	Mrs. Henry L. Taylor
1981	Mrs. Hugh R. Cunningham
1982	Mrs. James R. Haygood Jr.
1983	Mrs. D. Dwight Drinkard
1984	Mrs. Hugh R. Cunningham
1987	Mrs. Burton H. Milnor
1988	Mrs. Paul Gillespie
1989	Mrs. Edward J. Lawler
1990	Mrs. Henry L. Taylor
1991	Mrs. Kenneth F. Clark Jr.
1992	Mrs. Walter G. Wunderlich
1993	Mrs. Hubert K. Turley
1994	Mrs. Walter G. Wunderlich
1995	Mrs. Walter G. Wunderlich
1996	Mrs. Dolores C. Dobbs
1997	Mrs. Ygondine Creasy
1998	Mrs. Hubert K. Turley

Marguerite Gaut Short Game Trophy

Year	Winner
1997	Mrs. Ann Cicala
1998	Mrs. Dolores Dobbs
1999	Mrs. Ann Marie Dobbs
2000	Mrs. Carrie Semmes
2001	Mrs. Ann Cicala
2002	Mrs. Carrie Semmes
2003	Mrs. Liz Farnsworth
2004	Mrs. Marilyn Wiener

William F. Bowld Trophy

Year	Winner
1958	Mrs. Hugh Wynne
1959	Mrs. James Richard Welsh
1960	Mrs. Robert P. Cooke
1961	Mrs. Paul T. Gillespie
1962	Mrs. Wm. Calvert Chaney
1963	Mrs. J. A. Crisler III
1964	Mrs. James Saunders
1965	Mrs. DeWitt M. Shy
1966	Mrs. William H. Glasgow Jr.
1967	Mrs. J. R. Hyde Jr.
1968	Miss Mollie McCord
1969	Mrs. Fred W. James
1970	Mrs. Edwin D. Bozeman III
1971	Mrs. Russel Wilkinson
1972	Mrs. Max A. Holden
1973	Mrs. W. Frank Aycock Jr.
1974	Mrs. Russel L. Wiener
1975	Mrs. Edward J. Lawler
1976	Miss Margaret Warren
1977	Mrs. Bethel T. Hunt Jr.
1978	Mrs. John Salmon
1979	Mrs. Mary G. Phillips
1980	Mrs. Kay Reed
1981	Mrs. Virgie Ballou
1982	Mrs. E. Cary Middlecoff
1983	Mrs. John Young
1984	Mrs. Louis C. Jehl
1985	Mrs. Edward W. Walthal Jr.
1986	Mrs. Edward C. Duke
1987	Mrs. Ella Dudley
1988	Mrs. Edmond Cicala
1989	Mrs. Betty Pepin Gerber
1990	Mrs. Marjorie Withers
1996	Mrs. Blair MacDonald

Sue Hightower Hyde Handicap Tournament—Nine Hole

Year	Winner
1982	Mrs. George G. Early
1983	Mrs. Allen Cox Jr.
1984	Mrs. William P. Maury
1985	Mrs. J. R. Haygood
1986	Mrs. J. Malcolm Aste
1987	Mrs. Rebecca W. Maury
1988	Mrs. Paul Gillespie
1991	Mrs. Richard Harwood
1992	Mrs. Henry Jones Jr.
1993	Mrs. William F. Murrah
1994	Mrs. Nancy Cook
1995	Mrs. Chipsy Butler
1996	Mrs. Clare MacDonald

Sue Hightower Hyde Handicap Tournament—Eighteen Hole

Year	Winner
1980	Mrs. John L. Salmon
1981	Mrs. J. R. Haygood Jr.
1982	Mrs. John L. Salmon
1983	Mrs. William E. Gerber
1984	Mrs. Louis C. Jehl
1985	Mrs. Edward C. Duke
1986	Mrs. William P. Maury III
1987	Mrs. J. Malcolm Aste
1988	Mrs. Edward C. Duke
1989	Mrs. John L. Salmon
1990	Mrs. J. A. Crisler III
1991	Mrs. Betty Pepin Gerber
1992	Mrs. Chauncey W. Butler III
1993	Mrs. Selden Empson
1994	Mrs. Chauncey W. Butler III
1995	Mrs. Betty Malmo
1996	Mrs. Betty Malmo
1997	Mrs. Ann Cicala
1998	Mrs. Ellen R. Clark
1999	Mrs. Ygondine Creasy
2000	Mrs. Liz Farnsworth
2001	Mrs. Liz Farnsworth
2002	Mrs. Marilyn Wiener
2003	Mrs. Barton Lynch
2004	Mrs. Marilyn Wiener

MCC Women's Championship Cup

Year	Winner
1914	Mrs. F. G. Jones
1962	Mrs. Shelley Lee
1963	Mrs. Shelley Lee
1964	Mrs. Shelley Lee
1965	Mrs. Shelley Lee
1966	Mrs. Edward J. Lawler
1967	Mrs. Shelley Lee
1968	Mrs. Edward J. Lawler
1970	Mrs. Jack Brock
1971	Mrs. Jack Brock
1972	Mrs. Jack Brock
1973	Mrs. Edward J. Lawler
1974	Mrs. Edward J. Lawler
1975	Mrs. Russel Wiener
1976	Mrs. Edward J. Lawler
1977	Mrs. Edward J. Lawler
1978	Mrs. Edward J. Lawler
1979	Mrs. Edward J. Lawler
1980	Miss Martha Joy Wiener
1981	Mrs. Edward C. Duke
1982	Miss Martha Joy Wiener
1983	Miss Beth Walthal
1984	Miss Beth Walthal
1985	Mrs. Martha W. Horton
1986	Mrs. Edward C. Duke
1987	Miss Beth Walthal
1988	Mrs. Edward C. Duke
1989	Mrs. Jack Brock
1990	Mrs. J. A. Crisler III
1991	Mrs. Michael Lynch
1992	Mrs. Edward C. Duke
1993	Mrs. Susan Lynch
1994	Mrs. Edward C. Duke
1995	Mrs. Susan Lynch
1996	Mrs. Katie Hutton
1997	Mrs. Katie Hutton
1998	Mrs. Katie Hutton
1999	Mrs. Katie Hutton
2000	Mrs. Carrie Semmes
2001	Mrs. Katie Hutton
2002	Mrs. Katie Hutton
2003	Mrs. Katie Hutton
2004	Mrs. Katie Hutton

Memphis City Championship

Memphis Country Club
First Flight Winner October 1932
Harriet Van Vleet

Van Vleet Memorial Trophy

P. P. Van Vleet
Born 1849, Died 1915
Presented to the Memphis Country Club by the family of him whose name and fame is here commemorated.
The First President of this Club:
"Resolved that The Memphis Country Club in accepting this trophy, make thereon permanent record of its thanks to the donors, its acceptance of the memorial and the recognition of the splendid qualities of the deceased gentleman, the absence of whose familiar form from our links will ever be a source of profoundest sorrow. Adopted, November 25, 1915."

Year	Winner/*Runner-Up*	Year	Winner/*Runner-Up*
1916	B. B. Harris	1977	S. R. Leatherman Jr./*J. W. McDonnell Jr.*
1939	Richard H. Bodine	1978	Dwight Drinkard/*Mason Hawkins*
1954	R. G. Morrow Jr./*John Tully*	1979	Glynn Alexander/*E. B. LeMaster Jr.*
1957	Dr. Marcus J. Stewart/ *Dr. Bland W. Cannon*	1980	Roy A. Moore/*Reginald Barnes*
1958	Charles Cathey/*Larry Creson*	1981	John H. Doggett Jr./*Robert Gardner Jr.*
1959	O. H. Miller Jr./*Dr. H. K. Turley*	1982	Robert Gardner Jr./*Jackson W. Moore*
1960	Jay T. Saunders/*Henry L. Taylor*	1983	Kirk P. Bailey/*Frederick C. Schaeffer*
1961	W. M. Fay/*W. F. Fay*	1984	Reginald Barnes/*Roy A. Moore*
1962	E. B. LeMaster/*L. Hall Jones*	1985	Robert L. Weaver/*Scott Fisher*
1963	J. R. Greer/*Dunlap Cannon Jr.*	1986	Kirk P. Bailey/*Frederick C. Schaeffer*
1964	R. G. Gardner Jr./*Ben Crawford*	1987	Kirk P. Bailey/*Frederick C. Schaeffer*
1965	Henry Taylor/*Dan Canale*	1990	Harvey Kay III/*Will Pierce Jr.*
1966	John H. Dobbs/*George T. Nickey*	1991	Coleman Connell/*Dudley Park*
1967	E. B. LeMaster/*W. E. Cheairs Jr.*	1992	Robert Gardner Jr./*Jack Moore*
1968	James R. Haygood III/ *Claude C. Crawford*	1993	Ronnie Byrnes/*Walter Bross*
1969	Dr. George A. Coors/ *Dr. Cary Middlecoff*	1994	Beasley Wellford/*Stuart Collier*
1970	Dr. R. A. Miller/*L. P. Miles Jr.*	1995	Kent Wunderlich/*Phillip Wunderlich*
1971	Roy Moore Jr./*Hugh Allan Jr.*	1996	Kirk P. Bailey/*Frederick C. Schaeffer*
1973	George Treadwell/*Henry L. Taylor*	1997	Hal Boyd III/*Bob E. Mallory*
1974	Dr. Hubert K. Turley/ *Dr. Peter J. Quinn*	1998	Keith Barton/*Duke Clement*
1975	Dr. Robert G. Allen/*Dr. Marcus Stewart*	1999	Ned Laughlin Jr./*Ned Laughlin III*
1976	John P. Sheahan/*Burton Milnor*	2000	Beasley Wellford/*Jim Varner*
		2001	Jack Roberts/*Robert Tayloe*
		2002	Lee Marshall/*Wiley Robinson*
		2003	George Kirk/*Dudley Bridgeforth*
		2004	Tommy Farnsworth III/*Michael Reddoch*

Father-Son Handicap Trophy

Year	Winner—Father/Son
1954	J. W. McDonnell/*J. W. McDonnell Jr.*
1956	J. W. McDonnell/*J. W. McDonnell Jr.*
1958	R. Maynard Holt/*R. Maynard Holt Jr.*
1959	J. K. Dobbs Jr./*J. C. Dobbs*
1960	R. Beverly Ray/*C. Barham Ray*
1961	R. Beverly Ray/*C. Barham Ray*
1962	J. J. Pepin/*J. J. Pepin Jr.*
1963	R. Beverly Ray/*Robert Ray*
1964	A. B. Nickey/*John Nickey*
1965	J. R. Haygood Jr./*J. R. Haygood III*
1966	R. Beverly Ray/*C. Barham Ray*
1967	R. Beverly Ray/*C. Barham Ray*
1968	J. R. Haygood Jr./*J. R. Haygood III*
1969	R. Beverly Ray/*Robert Ray*
1970	J. A. Crisler III/*Stewart Crisler*
1971	R. Beverly Ray/*C. Barham Ray*
1972	A. B. Nickey/*John Nickey*
1973	R. Beverly Ray/*C. Barham Ray*
1974	J. R. Haygood Jr./*J. R. Haygood III*
1975	J. A. Crisler III/*Stewart Crisler*
1976	J. G. Owen Jr./*J. G. Owen III*
1977	S. R. Leatherman Jr./*S. R. Leatherman III*
1978	Dr. Sam Raines/*Bill Mueller*
1979	E. B. LeMaster Jr./*E. B. LeMaster III*
1980	Edgar H. Bailey/*Kirk P. Bailey*
1981	Neely Mallory/*Bob E. Mallory*
1982	Bobby Weaver/*Robert Weaver*
1983	Tommy Oates/*Thomas Oates*
1984	Thomas C. Adams/*Thomas C. Adams Jr.*
1985	John P. Dulin/*John P. Dulin Jr.*
1986	John P. Dulin/*John P. Dulin Jr.*
1987	J. W. Brakebill/*W. Ray Brakebill*
1988	Thomas C. Adams/*Thomas C. Adams Jr.*
1989	Robert Tayloe/*Rob Tayloe*
1990	Albert E. Laughlin/*John M. Laughlin*
1991	Albert E. Laughlin/*John M. Laughlin*
1992	Lewis McKee/*Lewis McKee Jr.*
1993	Michael Kiser/*Michael Kiser Jr.*
1994	Kent Wunderlich/*Gary Wunderlich*
1995	Kent Wunderlich/*Gary Wunderlich*
1996	Robert Tayloe/*Jay Tayloe*
1998	Glynn Alexander/*Glynn Alexander Jr.*
2000	Duke Clement/*Bowers Clement*
2001	Allen Morgan/*Worth Morgan*
2002	Jim Smith/*McCown Smith*
2003	Bailey Wiener/*Don Wiener*
2004	Bobby Weaver/*Robert Weaver*

Burns Barry Co. Golf Trophy for Ladies

Mrs. Alice Collier
Miss Margaret Taylor
Miss Edyth Mallory
Miss Edyth Mallory

Mrs. F. G. Jones
Mrs. Julia Carnes
Miss Estelle Lamb
Miss Edyth Mallory

Memphis Country Club—Second Annual Tournament

September 11–14, 1907
DeSoto Cup Runner-Up
Won by R. G. Morrow

Appendix B

Emmet E. Joyner Memorial Cup

1912–1962
"He was a Gentle Man whose Friends were Legion"

Year	Winners	Year	Winners
1963	Dr. George Coors	1967	John D. Canale
	Dunlap Cannon Jr.		John Phillips III
	C. L. Piplar		John T. Stout
	A. G. Patteson		Robert Gardner
1964	Roy A. Moore	1968	W. Neely Mallory
	Dr. Malcolm Aste		Dr. J. Malcolm Aste
	Dwight Drinkard		George Perry
	Reid Sanders		R. Grattan Brown Sr.
1965	Alex Wellford	1969	Hugh Allan Jr.
	Al Austin III		R. D. Harwood
	Max Holden		L. Hall Jones
	Floyd Swift		Jim Barton
1966	George Coors		
	L. Y. Kerr		
	Vance Alexander Jr.		
	H. G. Bartlett		

Appendix C

Tennis Tournament Winners

MCC Ladies Tennis Championship—Singles

Year	Winner/*Runner-Up*
1961	Mrs. Walter L. (Maggie) Smith Jr./ *Miss Ann Driver*
1962	Miss Ann Driver/ *Mrs. Robertson (Anna) Morrow Jr.*
1963	Miss Ann Driver/ *Mrs. Robertson (Anna) Morrow Jr.*
1964	Mrs. Phil (Dottie) Pidgeon/ *Mrs. Thomas C. (Mary Jo) Kimbrough*
1965	Mrs. John (Lee) Davis Jr./ *Miss Madelyn Richardson*
1966	Miss Lucia Turnbill/ *Mrs. Robertson (Anna) Morrow Jr.*
1967	Mrs. John (Lee) Davis Jr./ *Miss Lucia Turnbill*
1968	Mrs. Thomas C. (Mary Jo) Kimbrough/ *Mrs. Robertson (Anna) Morrow Jr.*
1969	Mrs. Thomas C. (Mary Jo) Kimbrough/ *Mrs. C. B. (Libby) Dudley Jr.*
1970	Mrs. Thomas C. (Mary Jo) Kimbrough/ *Mrs. Joseph (Madelyn) Brock*
1971	Mrs. Thomas C. (Mary Jo) Kimbrough/ *Mrs. C. B. (Libby) Dudley Jr.*
1972	Mrs. William Carrington (Peggy) Jones/ *Miss Amie Todd*
1973	Mrs. William Carrington (Peggy) Jones/ *Mrs. Hugh (Marie Louise) Allen Jr.*
1974	Miss Amie Todd/ *Mrs. William Carrington (Peggy) Jones*
1975	Mrs. William Carrington (Peggy) Jones/ *Miss Amie Todd*
1976	Mrs. C. B. (Libby) Dudley Jr./ *Mrs. Thomas M. (Allison) Garrott III*
1977	Mrs. Thomas M. (Allison) Garrott III/ *Mrs. William Carrington (Peggy) Jones*
1978	Mrs. Thomas M. (Allison) Garrott III/ *Mrs. William Carrington (Peggy) Jones*
1979	Mrs. Wallace (Nora) Witmer Jr./ *Mrs. Thomas M. (Allison) Garrott III*
1980	Mrs. Thomas M. (Allison) Garrott III/ *Mrs. Wallace (Nora) Witmer Jr.*
1981	Miss Amie Todd/ *Mrs. Thomas M. (Allison) Garrott III*
1982	Mrs. Henry (Christy) Cannon/ *Mrs. Thomas M. (Allison) Garrott III*
1983	Miss Alicia Harwood/ *Mrs. Charles F. (Nancy) Smith Jr.*
1984	Mrs. Charles F. (Nancy) Smith Jr./ *Miss Alicia Harwood*
1985	Mrs. Dudley (Laine) Park/ *Mrs. Charles F. (Nancy) Smith Jr.*
1986	Mrs. Charles F. (Nancy) Smith Jr./ *Mrs. James M. (Lela) Smith*
1987	Mrs. Cooper Y. (Melissa) Robinson/ *Mrs. DeWitt M. (Sally) Shy*
1988	Miss Allison Clark/ *Mrs. David (Selden) Popwell*
1989	Mrs. Charles F. (Elizabeth) Smith Jr./ *Mrs. Charles (Meg) Gerber*
1990	Mrs. Charles F. (Elizabeth) Smith Jr./ *Mrs. Duke (Janet) Clement*
1991	Mrs. Charles F. (Elizabeth) Smith Jr./ *Mrs. Duke (Janet) Clement*
1992	Mrs. Duke (Janet) Clement/ *Mrs. Charles (Meg) Gerber*

Year	Winner / Runner-up
1994	Mrs. Thomas (Mary Ann) Lee/ *Mrs. James (Margaret) McGahey*
1995	Mrs. Duke (Janet) Clement/ *Mrs. Charles (Meg) Gerber*
1996	Mrs. Richard (Jeanne) Hollis/ *Mrs. William (Becky) Maury*
1997	Mrs. Brett (Megan) Grinder/ *Miss Margaret Gibson*
1998	Mrs. Charles (Meg) Gerber/ *Mrs. Duke (Janet) Clement*
1999	Mrs. Richard (Jeanne) Hollis/ *Mrs. Albert (Cathy) Carruthers*
2000	Mrs. Anthony (Ygondine) Creasy/ *Runner-up information not available*
2001	Mrs. Joseph (Brandon) Morrison/ *Mrs. John H. (Lisa) Grayson*
2002	Miss Virginia Dickinson/ *Mrs. John H. (Lisa) Grayson*
2003	Mrs. Cameron (Taylor) Taylor/ *Mrs. Thomas (Jane) Byrnes*
2004	Hayly Humphreys/ *Mrs. Thomas (Jane) Byrnes*

MCC Ladies Tennis Championship—Doubles

Year	Winners/*Runners-Up*
1962	Miss Ann Driver and Mrs. Walter L. (Maggie) Smith Jr./ *Mrs. Robertson (Anna) Morrow Jr. and Mrs. C. B. (Libby) Dudley Jr.*
1964	Mrs. Henry (Lee) Wetter Jr. and Mrs. John (Lee) Davis Jr./ *Mrs. Frank M. (Jean) Norfleet and Mrs. John C. (Betsy) Weaver*
1965	Mrs. John (Lee) Davis Jr. and Mrs. Henry (Lee) Wetter Jr./ *Mrs. Frank M. (Jean) Norfleet and Mrs. Phil (Dottie) Pidgeon*
1966	Mrs. John (Lee) Davis Jr. and Mrs. Robertson (Anna) Morrow Jr./ *Mrs. Henry (Lee) Wetter Jr. and Mrs. Dunbar (Pete) Abston Jr.*
1967	Mrs. John (Lee) Davis Jr. and Mrs. Dunbar (Pete) Abston Jr./ *Miss Lucia Turnbill and Mrs. B. Snowden (Daphne) Boyle*
1968	Mrs. Robertson (Anna) Morrow Jr. and Mrs. Thomas C. (Mary Jo) Kimbrough/ *Mrs. Phil (Dottie) Pidgeon and Mrs. B. Lee (Susan) Mallory III*
1969	Mrs. B. Lee (Susan) Mallory III and Mrs. Daniel (Marie) Copp/ *Mrs. Thomas C. (Mary Jo) Kimbrough and Mrs. Robertson (Anna) Morrow Jr.*
1970	Mrs. B. Lee (Susan) Mallory III and Mrs. Thomas (Mary Jo) Kimbrough/ *Mrs. Robertson (Anna) Morrow and Mrs. Dunbar (Pete) Abston Jr.*
1971	Mrs. Thomas C. (Mary Jo) Kimbrough and Mrs. Robertson (Anna) Morrow Jr./ *Mrs. C. B. (Libby) Dudley Jr. and Mrs. Joseph (Madelyn) Brock*
1972	Mrs. Joseph (Madelyn) Brock and Mrs. Phil (Dottie) Pidgeon/ *Mrs. Robertson (Anna) Morrow Jr. and Mrs. Daniel (Marie) Copp*
1973	Mrs. C. B. (Libby) Dudley Jr. and Mrs. Roy (Jan) Bell Jr./ *Mrs. Robertson (Anna) Morrow Jr. and Mrs. Ewing (Jane) Carruthers*
1974	Mrs. B. Lee (Susan) Mallory III and Mrs. Michael (Bickie) McDonnell/ *Mrs. William Carrington (Peggy) Jones and Mrs. Malcolm (Nancy) Aste*
1975	Mrs. Ewing (Jane) Carruthers and Mrs. C. B. (Libby) Dudley Jr./ *Mrs. Roy (Jan) Bell Jr. and Mrs. William Carrington (Peggy) Jones*
1976	Mrs. C. B. (Libby) Dudley Jr. and Mrs. Roy (Jan) Bell Jr./ *Mrs. William Carrington (Peggy) Jones and Mrs. Ewing (Jane) Carruthers*

1977	Mrs. C. B. (Libby) Dudley Jr. and Mrs. Roy (Jan) Bell Jr./ *Mrs. William Carrington (Peggy) Jones and Mrs. Ewing (Jane) Carruthers*
1978	Mrs. C. B. (Libby) Dudley Jr. and Mrs. Roy (Jan) Bell Jr./ *Mrs. William Carrington (Peggy) Jones and Mrs. Ewing (Jane) Carruthers*
1979	Mrs. C. B. (Libby) Dudley Jr. and Mrs. Roy (Jan) Bell Jr./ *Mrs. William Carrington (Peggy) Jones and Mrs. Ewing (Jane) Carruthers*
1980	Mrs. C. B. (Libby) Dudley Jr. and Mrs. Roy (Jan) Bell Jr./ *Mrs. William Carrington (Peggy) Jones and Mrs. Ewing (Jane) Carruthers*
1981	Miss Amie Todd and Mrs. Roy (Jan) Bell Jr./ *Mrs. Paul C. (Elizabeth Todd) Palmer and Mrs. Ewing (Jane) Carruthers*
1982	Mrs. William Carrington (Peggy) Jones and Mrs. Ewing (Jane) Carruthers/ *Mrs. C. B. (Libby) Dudley Jr. and Mrs. Wallace (Nora) Witmer Jr.*
1983	Mrs. Alex (Karen) Wellford Jr. and Mrs. Roy (Jan) Bell Jr./ *Mrs. Wallace (Nora) Witmer Jr. and Mrs. Ewing (Jane) Carruthers*
1984	Mrs. William Carrington (Peggy) Jones and Mrs. Dudley (Laine) Park/ *Mrs. Charles F. (Nancy) Smith Jr. and Mrs. Bailey (Marilyn) Wiener*
1985	Mrs. William Carrington (Peggy) Jones and Mrs. Wallace (Nora) Witmer Jr./ *Mrs. Charles F. (Nancy) Smith Jr. and Mrs. Alex (Karen) Wellford Jr.*
1986	Mrs. Ewing (Jane) Carruthers and Mrs. Charles F. (Nancy) Smith Jr./ *Mrs. Roy (Jan) Bell Jr. and Mrs. William Carrington (Peggy) Jones*
1987	Mrs. Nancy Welch Smith and Mrs. Roy (Jan) Bell Jr./ *Mrs. William Carrington (Peggy) Jones and Mrs. Ewing (Jane) Carruthers*
1988	Mrs. Nancy Welch Smith and Mrs. Roy (Jan) Bell Jr./ *Mrs. William Carrington (Peggy) Jones and Mrs. Ewing (Jane) Carruthers*
1989	Mrs. Charles F. (Elizabeth) Smith Jr. and Mrs. Charles (Meg) Gerber/ *Mrs. John G. (Lisa) Morten and Mrs. Dudley (Laine) Park*
1990	Mrs. Charles F. (Elizabeth) Smith Jr. and Mrs. Charles (Meg) Gerber/ *Mrs. John G. (Lisa) Morten and Mrs. Dudley (Laine) Park*
1991	Mrs. Charles F. (Elizabeth) Smith Jr. and Mrs. Dudley (Laine) Park/ *Mrs. John G. (Lisa) Morten and Mrs. Duke (Janet) Clement*
1992	Mrs. Dudley (Laine) Park and Mrs. Roy (Jan) Bell Jr./ *Mrs. Charles (Meg) Gerber and Mrs. Ewing (Jane) Carruthers*
1993	Mrs. Charles F. (Elizabeth) Smith Jr. and Mrs. John G. (Lisa) Morten/ *Mrs. Thomas (Carolyn) Morris and Mrs. Jack (Judy) Powell*
1994	Mrs. Thomas (Carolyn) Morris and Mrs. Charles (Meg) Gerber/ *Mrs. Jack (Judy) Powell and Mrs. Thomas (Mary Ann) Lee*
1995	Mrs. Thomas (Carolyn) Morris and Mrs. Duke (Janet) Clement/ *Mrs. Charles (Meg) Gerber and Mrs. Dudley (Laine) Park*
1996	Mrs. Thomas (Carolyn) Morris and Mrs. William (Becky) Maury/ *Mrs. Charles (Meg) Gerber and Mrs. Arthur (Michelle) Fulmer*
1997	Mrs. Thomas (Carolyn) Morris and Mrs. Anthony (Ygondine) Creasy/ *Mrs. Charles (Meg) Gerber and Mrs. Gary (Jennifer) Wunderlich*
1998	Mrs. Thomas (Carolyn) Morris and Mrs. Duke (Janet) Clement/ *Mrs. Charles (Meg) Gerber and Miss Austin Varner*

Year	Winner/Runner-Up
1999	Mrs. Anthony (Ygondine) Creasy and Mrs. Richard (Jeanne) Hollis/ *Mrs. Henry (Mena) Morgan and Mrs. William (Becky) Maury*
2000	Mrs. William (Becky) Maury and Mrs. Richard (Jeanne) Hollis/ *Runner-up information not available*
2001	Mrs. John D. (Leslie) Dunavant and Mrs. Richard (Jeanne) Hollis/ *Mrs. David (Selden) Popwell and Mrs. William (Becky) Maury*
2002	Mrs. John H. (Lisa) Grayson and Mrs. Alex (Karen) Wellford Jr./ *Mrs. David (Selden) Popwell and Mrs. Edward (Wendy) Ansbro*
2003	Mrs. Bruce (Melody) Taylor and Mrs. Thomas (Carolyn) Morris/ *Mrs. Cameron (Taylor) Taylor and Mrs. Charles (Meg) Gerber*
2004	Taylor Taylor and Melody Taylor/ *Lisa Grayson and Kate Gould*

MCC Men's Tennis Championship

Year	Winner/Runner-Up
1960	Daniel D. Canale/*Alex W. Wellford*
1961	Alex W. Wellford/*Alex W. Wellford Jr.*
1962	C. D. Smith III/*Alex W. Wellford Jr.*
1963	C. D. Smith III/*Alex W. Wellford Jr.*
1964	C. D. Smith III/*Alex W. Wellford*
1965	C. D. Smith III/*Robert McCallum Jr.*
1966	C. D. Smith III/*Robert McCallum Jr.*
1967	Alex W. Wellford Jr./*Alex W. Wellford*
1968	Robert McCallum Jr./*Alex W. Wellford*
1969	Alex Wellford/*George Dunklin*
1970	Alex Wellford/*George Dunklin*
1971	George Dunklin/*W. B. Dunavant Jr.*
1972	W. B. Dunavant Jr./*Donald C. McClure Jr.*
1973	W. B. Dunavant Jr./*Dr. T. J. White Jr.*
1974	W. B. Dunavant Jr./ *Donald C. McClure Jr.*
1975	G. Carroll Todd Jr./*W. B. Dunavant Jr.*
1976	G. Carroll Todd Jr./*W. B. Dunavant Jr.*
1977	Don McClure Jr./*W. B. Dunavant Jr.*
1978	W. B. Dunavant Jr./*Allen Morgan Jr.*
1979	W. B. Dunavant Jr./*Harry W. Wellford*
1980	Donald C. McClure Jr./ *Dr. Thomas J. White III*
1981	Donald C. McClure Jr./*Charles F. Smith Jr.*
1982	Sam H. Varner/*Donald C. McClure Jr.*
1983	Donald C. McClure Jr./*Richard H. Allen Jr.*
1984	G. Carroll Todd Jr./*Donald C. McClure Jr.*
1985	G. Carroll Todd Jr./*G. P. Brownlow III*
1986	G. Carroll Todd Jr./*Sam H. Varner*
1987	G. Carroll Todd Jr./*Sam H. Varner*
1988	Donald C. McClure Jr./*Sam H. Varner*
1989	G. Carroll Todd Jr./ *Donald C. McClure Jr.*
1990	John Thomas Morris/ *Donald C. McClure Jr.*
1991	G. Carroll Todd Jr./*Donald C. McClure Jr.*
1992	Donald C. McClure Jr./ *G. Carroll Todd Jr.*
1993	G. Carroll Todd Jr./*Warren G. Milnor*
1994	Donald C. McClure Jr./*George C. Pettey*
1995	George C. Pettey/*Warren G. Milnor*
1996	David L. Bowlin Jr./*George C. Pettey*
1997	Charles Gerber/*Warren G. Milnor*
1998	Warren G. Milnor/*Charles C. Gerber*
1999	Paul McClure Jr./*Charles C. Gerber*
2000	Paul McClure Jr./*Charles C. Gerber*
2001	Charles Gerber/*Warren G. Milnor*
2002	Warren G. Milnor/*Charles C. Gerber*
2003	Warren G. Milnor/*Josh Lackie*
2004	Warren G. Milnor/*Charles C. Gerber*

MCC Men's Doubles Tennis Championship

Year	Winners/*Runners-Up*
1970	W. B. Dunavant Jr. and Frank H. Marshall/ *Giles A. Coors Jr. and Norman H. Blake*
1971	W. B. Dunavant Jr. and Allen Morgan Jr./ *Giles A. Coors Jr. and Donald C. McClure Jr.*
1972	W. B. Dunavant Jr. and Allen Morgan Jr./ *Giles A. Coors Jr. and Donald C. McClure Jr.*
1973	Allen Morgan Jr. and W. B. Dunavant Jr./ *Donald C. McClure Jr. and Giles A. Coors Jr.*
1974	W. B. Dunavant Jr. and Allen Morgan Jr./ *Giles A. Coors Jr. and Donald C. McClure Jr.*
1975	W. B. Dunavant Jr. and C. Barham Ray/ *Harry W. Wellford and G. Carroll Todd Jr.*
1976	G. Carroll Todd Jr. and Giles A. Coors Jr./ *W. B. Dunavant Jr. and Harry W. Wellford*
1977	Giles A. Coors Jr. and W. B. Dunavant Jr./ *Harry W. Wellford and Lewis K. McKee*
1978	W. B. Dunavant Jr. and G. Carroll Todd Jr./ *George Dunklin Jr. and C. Barham Ray*
1979	W. B. Dunavant Jr. and Tom J. White III/ *George Dunklin Jr. and Allen Morgan Jr.*
1980	G. P. Brownlow III and Giles A. Coors Jr./ *Charles F. Smith Jr. and Richard H. Allen Jr.*
1981	G. P. Brownlow III and Sidney A. Stewart Jr./ *Charles F. Smith Jr. and Edward B. Morrow Jr.*
1982	G. P. Brownlow III and Sidney A. Stewart Jr./ *Charles F. Smith Jr. and Edward B. Morrow Jr.*
1983	G. P. Brownlow III and Sidney A. Stewart Jr./ *Charles F. Smith Jr. and Edward B. Morrow Jr.*
1984	G. Carroll Todd Jr. and Sidney A. Stewart Jr./ *Donald C. McClure Jr. and Edward B. Morrow Jr.*
1985	G. P. Brownlow III and Tom Morris/ *Charles F. Smith Jr. and John Morris*
1986	G. Carroll Todd Jr. and G. P. Brownlow III/ *Donald C. McClure Jr. and Charles F. Smith Jr.*
1987	G. Carroll Todd Jr. and G. P. Brownlow III/ *Donald C. McClure Jr. and Charles F. Smith Jr.*
1988	Donald C. McClure Jr. and G. P. Brownlow III/ *G. Carroll Todd Jr. and Charles F. Smith Jr.*
1989	G. Carroll Todd Jr. and G. P. Brownlow III/ *Donald C. McClure Jr. and Charles F. Smith Jr.*
1990	John Morris and G. P. Brownlow III/ *Mike Mills and Charles F. Smith Jr.*
1991	G. Carroll Todd Jr. and G. P. Brownlow III/ *Donald C. McClure Jr. and Charles F. Smith Jr.*
1992	Donald C. McClure Jr. and G. P. Brownlow III/ *G. Carroll Todd Jr. and Charles F. Smith Jr.*
1993	G. P. Brownlow III and G. Carroll Todd Jr./ *Tyne Brownlow and Donald C. McClure Jr.*

Year	Winners/Runners-Up	Year	Winners/Runners-Up
1994	Mike Mills and G. P. Brownlow III/ *John Thomas Morris and Tyne Brownlow*	2000	Girard P. Brownlow and Peter Monaghan Jr./ *Paul McClure Jr. and G. Demetri Patikas*
1995	Warren G. Milnor and G. P. Brownlow III/ *G. Carroll Todd Jr. and George C. Pettey*	2001	Girard P. Brownlow and Hubert Turley/ *Warren G. Milnor and C. F. Varner*
1996	David L. Bowlin Jr. and Charles C. Gerber/ *George C. Pettey and James B. Wellford*	2002	Girard P. Brownlow and G. Carroll Todd Jr./ *Warren G. Milnor and Charles C. Gerber*
1997	Charles C. Gerber and Charles F. Smith Jr./ *Warren G. Milnor and Lewis Smith*	2003	Girard P. Brownlow and G. Carroll Todd Jr./ *Warren G. Milnor and Josh Lackie*
1998	Warren G. Milnor and Donald C. McClure Jr./ *Charles C. Gerber and Paul K. McClure Jr.*	2004	Warren Milnor and Charles Gerber/ *Girard P. Brownlow and G. Carroll Todd Jr.*
1999	Charles F. Smith Jr. and G. P. Brownlow III/ *Lewis Smith and Alex Wellford Jr.*		

MCC Mixed Doubles Club Tennis Champions

Year	Winners/Runners-Up	Year	Winners/Runners-Up
1981	Peggy Jones and William Carrington Jones/ *Marie Louise Allen and Allen Morgan Jr.*	1993	Janet Clement and Carroll Todd Jr./ *Carolyn Morris and Girard Brownlow*
1982	Peggy Jones and William Carrington Jones/ *Nancy Erb and Guy Erb*	1994	Janet Clement and Carroll Todd Jr./ *Elizabeth Smith and Donald C. McClure Jr.*
1983	Alicia Harwood and Girard P. Brownlow III/ *Nancy Smith and Charles F. Smith Jr.*	1995	Janet Clement and Carroll Todd Jr./ *Karen Wellford and Alex Wellford Jr.*
1984	Nancy Smith and Charles F. Smith Jr./ *Alicia Harwood and Allen Morgan Jr.*	1997	Janet Clement and Carroll Todd Jr./ *Megan Grinder and Warren Milnor*
1985	Carolyn Morris and Thomas Morris / *Karen Wellford and Alex Wellford Jr.*	2000	Karen Wellford and Alex Wellford Jr./ *Megan Grinder and Van Raby*
1991	Janet Clement and Carroll Todd Jr./ *Elizabeth Smith and Charles F. Smith Jr.*	2001	Karen Wellford and Alex Wellford Jr./ *Lisa Grayson and John H. Grayson*
1992	Elizabeth Smith and Charles F. Smith Jr./ *Ellie Tayloe and Robert Tayloe*	2002	Meg Gerber and Charles Gerber/ *Carolyn Morris and Warren Milnor*
		2003	Taylor Taylor and Hubert Turley III/ *Meg Gerber and Charles Gerber*

MCC Indoor Club Tennis Championship

Year	Singles/*Doubles*
1992	G. Carroll Todd Jr./ *Bob E. Mallory and Robert D. Gooch III*
1993	G. Carroll Todd Jr./ *Ferrell Varner and Sam Varner*
1994	Biggs Powell/ *Biggs Powell and Lee Powell*
1995	Biggs Powell/ *G. Carroll Todd Jr. and Alex Wellford Jr.*
1996	Charles C. Gerber/ *Charles C. Gerber and Lewis F. Smith*
1997	Lewis F. Smith/ *Charles C. Gerber and Warren G. Milnor*
1998	Jay Curtis/ *Warren G. Milnor and Burton Milnor*
1999	Charles C. Gerber/ *Paul McClure Jr. and Girard P. Brownlow III*
2000	Charles C. Gerber/ *Paul McClure Jr. and Girard P. Brownlow III*
2002	Warren G. Milnor/ *Hubert Turley and Ferrell Varner*
2003	Josh Lackie/ *Charles C. Gerber and Warren G. Milnor*
2004	Warren Milnor/ *Martin Pryor and Clyde Patton*

MCC MUGS Tennis Championship

Year	Singles/*Doubles*
1993	John Bondurant/ *Billy Reed and Cary Whitehead III*
1994	B. Lee Mallory/ *Bruce Hopkins and James Wetter*
1995	John Maxwell/ *Clyde Patton Jr. and James Witherington Jr.*
1996	Kent Wunderlich/ *Bruce Hopkins and Carroll Todd Sr.*
1997	John Maxwell/ *Bruce Hopkins and Martin Shea*
1998	Peter Monaghan/ *Peter Monaghan and G. Demetri Patikas*
1999	Terry Canale/ *Bruce C. Taylor and James Witherington Jr.*
2000	Hal D. Crenshaw/ *Clyde Patton Jr. and John Bondurant*
2001	Hubert Turley/ *Hubert Turley and Marty Pryor*
2002	Robert I. Smith/ *Hubert Turley and Joe Morrison*
2003	Martin Pryor/ *Clyde Patton and Robert I. Smith*
2004	Bob Smith/ *Martin Pryor and Joe Morrison*

Leila Chaney Trophy—Low Net

Year	Winner	Year	Winner
1978	Lou Keltner	1985	Ruth Simmons
1979	Colleen Beck	1986	Peg Salmon
1980	Sara Green	1987	Betty Pepin Gerber
1981	Jan Singer	1988	Doris Kelly
1982	Lonnie Baker	1989	Brenda Porter
1983	Lou Keltner	1990	Brenda Porter
1984	Louise Montgomery		

Appendix D

Gin Rummy Tournament Winners

MCC Gin Rummy Partners Championship

Year	Winners/Runners-Up
1989	Scott Fisher and M. E. Hill/ *DeWitt Shy and John Marshall*
1991	Trow Gillespie and Claude Crawford/ *Allen Morgan and Will Luck*
1992	Bill Geralds and Malcolm Wood/ *John Sheahan and Russell Wood*
1993	Tom Price and Malcolm Wood/ *Tim Treadwell and Russell Wood*
1994	Reggie Barnes and John Adamson/ *Bobby Weaver and Carl Langschmidt*
1995	John Bondurant and Claude Crawford/ *Charles Cannon and Mike McDonnell*
1996	John Marshall and Will Luck/ *Jack Wilson and Max Ostner*
1997	John Bondurant and John Petree/ *Charles Cannon and Jack Roberts*
1998	John Marshall and John Bondurant/ *Jack Wilson and Charles Cannon*
1999	John Petree and Glen Cofield/ *Jack Roberts and Scott Fisher*
2000	Walter Bross and Trow Gillespie/ *Ferrell Varner and Allen Morgan*
2001	Elmer Stout and Trow Gillespie/ *Robert Tayloe and Allen Morgan*
2002	Elmer Stout and Claude Crawford/ *Robert Tayloe and Mike McDonnell*
2003	Trow Gillespie and John Adamson/ *Allen Morgan and Malcolm Wood*
2004	Trow Gillespie and Allen Morgan/ *John Bondurant and Charles Cannon*

MCC Gin Rummy Championship

Year	Winner/Runner-Up
1966	H. F. Sinclair/*Dan Canale*
1967	H. P. Curd/*W. W. Deupree Jr.*
1968	H. P. Curd/*J. Walter McDonnell*
1969	Jack Petree/*Worthington Brown*
1970	Jack Petree/*G. B. Wilson III*
1971	G. B. Wilson III/*John T. Stout*
1972	Allen Morgan Jr./*M. E. Hill Jr.*
1973	DeWitt Shy/*Walter L. Smith*
1974	John C. Marshall/*Reid Sanders*
1975	James D. Collier Jr./*Will Luck*

Bibliography

Thanks to the many members and friends who shared their memories, photographs, and scrapbooks, and also to the staff of the Memphis and Shelby County Room at the Memphis/Shelby County Public Library.

Bond, Beverly G., and Janann Sherman. *Memphis in Black and White*. Charleston, S.C.: Arcadia Press, 2003.
Carruth, Gorton. *The Encyclopedia of American Facts and Dates*. New York: Harper & Row, 1987.
Conway, Ruby. *Tales of Tennessee*. Port Colborne, Ontario: R. Conway, 1994.
Coppock, Paul. *Memphis Sketches*. Memphis, Tenn.: Friends of Memphis and Shelby County Libraries, 1976.
———. *Mid-South*. vol. 4. Privately printed, 1994.
Fay, Michael J. *Golf: As It Was Meant to Be Played*. New York: Universe Publishing, 2000.
Gibson, Nevin. *The Encyclopedia of Golf*. New York: A. S. Barnes and Company, 1964.
———. *A Pictorial History of Golf*. New York: A. S. Barnes and Company, 1968.
Halle, Arthur. "History of the Memphis Cotton Carnival." West Tennessee Historical Society Papers, 1952.
Hammond, Tom. *Showdown in Memphis, An Epic Tale of the Forties*. Dallas: Retrospective Productions, n.d.
Harkins, John E. *Metropolis of the American Nile*. Woodland Hills, Calif.: Windsor Publications, 1982.
Konik, Michael. "The Years with Ross." *Sky* (March 2001).
Lanier, Robert A. *Memphis in the Twenties*. Memphis, Tenn.: Zenda Press, 1979.
Magness, Perre. *Good Abode*. Memphis, Tenn.: Junior League of Memphis, 1983.
———. *In the Shadow of the Elms: Elmwood Cemetery 2002*. Memphis, Tenn.: Elmwood Cemetery, 2001.
———. *Past Times*. Memphis, Tenn.: Parkway Press, 1994.
Mayo, James M. *The American Country Club*. New Brunswick, N. J.: Rutgers University Press, 1998.
McIlwaine, Shields. *Memphis Down in Dixie*. New York: E. P. Dutton and Company, 1948.
Miller, William D. *Memphis During the Progressive Era: 1900–1917*. Memphis, Tenn.: Memphis State University Press, 1957.
Pearce, Gene. *The History of Tennessee Golf: 1894–2001*. Franklin, Tenn.: Hillsboro Press, 2002.
Ross, Donald J. *Golf Has Never Failed Me: The Lost Commentaries of Legendary Golf Architect Donald J. Ross*. Chelsea, Mich.: Sleeping Bear Press, 1996.
Sigafoos, Robert A. *Cotton Row to Beale Street*. Memphis, Tenn.: Memphis State University Press, 1979.
Social Register of Memphis, 1925.
Tilley, Bette B. with Pat Faudree and Bettie Shenk. 1979. *A Visit to Buntyn*. Memphis, Tenn.: Metropolitan Inter-Faith Association (MIFA).
Tucker, David M. *Memphis Since Crump*. Knoxville, Tenn.: The University of Tennessee Press, 1980.
Vedder, O. F. *History of the City of Memphis*. vol. 2. Syracuse, N.Y.: D. Mason, 1888.
Wills, Ridley, II. *Belle Meade Country Club, The First Hundred Years*. Franklin, Tenn.: Hillsboro Press, 2001.
Young, J. P. *Standard History of Memphis, Tennessee*. Knoxville, Tenn.: H. W. Crew & Co, 1912.

Scrapbooks of Marguerite Piazza Bergtholdt, Ellen Ramsay Clark, Eleanor Abernathy Crawford, Cathie Kirk, Patrick DeMere, Betsy Earp, Lida Willey Kimbrough, Richard and Carroll Leatherman, Ruth Morrison, Dorothy Anderson Pennepacker, Scottie Rembert, Walter Scott, Sally Shy, Gordon Stark, Laurence Mitchell Streuli, Sandra Warlick, Warfield Williams, Logan Young, and others.

Index

Abbott, Charlotte, 106
Abbott, Pat, 106, 131, 140, 150, 165, 194, **105**, **142**, **149**
Abernathy, Eleanor, 90–91, **71**, **91–92**
Abernathy, Helen (Mrs. Shields), 73, 90
Abernathy, Shields, 90
Able, Mrs. Paul, 112
Abston, Dunbar, 102, 182
Abt, Mike, 82
Ackroyd, Walter, 82
Adams, Cooper, Sr., 182
Adams, Tempe, **146**
Adams, Thomas C., Jr., 185–86, **184**
Adams, Tom, Sr., 191
Adamson, John, 132
Agee, Wortham, 55
Agee, Mrs. Wortham, 90
Alexander, Beverly, **196**
Alexander, Glynn, **196**
Allan, Hugh "Blackie," 131, 174
Allen, Diana, 142
Allen, Estelle Lamb, **43**
Allen, Frank, **30**
Allen, Minnie Lee, 140
Allen, Pep, 119
Allen, Pepper, **180**
Allen, Richard, 117, 142
American Golfer, 38, 54
Anthony, Jean, **106**
Archer, Ward, Sr., 182
Armstrong, Walter, Jr., 92
Armstrong, Mrs. Walter, 92
Aste, Malcolm "Nasty," 117, **153**
Aste, Nancy, 100
Atkinson, Mrs. William R., 103
Austin, Albert M., III, 138–39, 141, 150, **149**, **161**, **199**
Austin, Connie, 122
Austin, Ginger, **161**
Austin, John, 132, **133**
Austin, Joy, 140
Austin, Richard, 132, **133**
Awsumb, George, 19
Aycock, Mrs. Frank, Jr., **143**
Babb, Michael, vii, 189, **183**
Ballenger, Peter, 132
Bamberger, Mr. and Mrs., 10

Bands/Orchestras. *See* Orchestras/Bands
Barboro, Julia, 73
Barboro, Lucy, 73
Barboro, Mrs. Malcolm, 71, 75, **70**
Barnes, Reggie, **183**
Barrasso, Tony, 186
Barry, Edward F., 123
Barth, Sarah, 94
Bartlett, Mary Lee, **146**
Barton, Ann, **185**
Barton, Frank, 102
Bass, Margaret Ivy, 93
Beasley, Mrs. A. C. Treadwell, 103
Beasley, Ruth "Wootie," 100
Beck, Clyde, **118**
Beck, Jimmy, 131
Bell, Jan, 142, 160
Bell, Roy, 142, 182
Bennett, Ed, 132
Billings, C. K. G., 30
Bingley, George, 25
Binswanger Milton, **84**
Binswanger, Lenore, **84**
Blake, Norman, Jr., 182
Blakely, Clarence, 96
Blasingame, Dr., 114
Board of Directors, ix, 50–51, 57, 64, 79, 142, 186
Bodine, Dick, 132, **121**
Bodine, Mary Budd, **121**
Bondurant, John, 100, 182
Bondurant, Julian, 102
Boone, Inez, 140
Boone, James, 131
Boone, Pat, 83
Boulden, J. Eugene, 59
Bowen, Armour, 100
Bowling, Casey, 182
Boyd, Hal, III, **196**
Boyd, James Hallam, Jr., 171, **85**, **196**, **201**
Doyle, Daphne, **85**
Bridgforth, Donna Kay, **185**
Britton, Billy, 182
Britton, William Johnstone, 77, **77**
Brooks, Berry, 135
Brooks, Mrs. Berry, 103
Brooks, Letty, 92
Bross, Lida, **198**

Bross, Walter, **198**
Brown, Bill, 49, 55
Brown, Ida (Mrs. Toof), 71, **121**
Brown, Palmer, 142, 171, 182, **84**
Brown, Sally, 142
Brown, Toof, 153, 182, **85**, **121**
Bruce, Olivia, **196**
Bruce, Wallace, **196**
Buckingham, Nash, 38, 60
Budge, Don, 102
Bueller, Bill, 198
Buntyn, Ann Eliza, 6
Buntyn, Geraldus Oscar, 5–6
Buntyn House, 6–8, 17
Buntyn Station, xii, 3, 5–7, 9, 15, 75, 122
Burch, Elsie, 100
Burnett, Phil, 182
Butler, Bill, 100, 182
Butler, Heathy, **76**
Buxton, Billy, 124, **134**
Buxton, Mary, **134**
Byers, Howard, **187**, **196**
Byers, Loring, **187**, **196**
Cabin in the Cotton, 82
Caldwell, A. S., 3
Campbell, Bessie (Mrs. Willis), 73, 90
Canale, Dan, 115, 138, **155**, **159**
Canale, John D., 142, **134**
Canale, Martha, 140, **155**
Canale, Peggy, 142, **134**
Canale, Phil "Godfather" or "General," 117–18, **116**
Cannon, Bland W., 139, 141–42, 182, **141**, **161**, **169**
Cannon, Dunlap "Sky King," 114–15, 125, **124**, **159**
Cannon, Henry, 139
Cannon, Louise (Mrs. Bland), **141**, **161**
Carnes, Samuel Tate "S. T.," xii, 5, 13, 15, 17, 25, 30, **18**
Carnival Memphis, 87. *See also* Cotton Carnival
Carruthers, Ewing, Jr., 142, 182
Carruthers, Jane, 142
Carson, Beth, 186
Cartwright, Newton E., 96
Cathey, Suzette, 100

Cawthon, John, 132
Central Avenue, 32, 39
Cheairs, Dodie, 100
Cheairs, Lee, 157, **156**
Cheairs, Winston, 102
Churchill, Mr., 57
Clark, Allison, **157**
Clark, Ellen (daughter), 85, **157**
Clark, Ellen Ramsay, vii, 122, 157, 163. *See also* Ramsay, Ellen
Clark, Ken, **157**
Clark, Ken, III, **157**
Clark, Marshall, **157**
Clark, Ramsay, **157**
Clarke, George, 132
Clarke, Louise, 94
Cobb, Charles, 132
Cobb, Martha Jane, 168, **167**
Cobb, Ruth Marie, 140
Cochran, E. C., 13
Cocktail Lounge, 110, **110**
Cofield, Andrew, **192**
Cofield, Scott, 198
Colbert, Elinor, **112**
Collier, John, 132
Commercial Appeal, 4, 8–9, 11–12, 14–15, 21, 25, 30–31, 52, 60–61, 64, 71, 84, 116, 127, 178, **126**
Condon, Billy, 78
Condon, Marguerite Piazza, 132
Condon, Martin J., 25, 32, 48–49, **48**
Condon, Martin J., III, 48, 100, 110, 119, 140, **119**
Cook, Everett, 82, 102, **85**
Cook, Nancy (Mrs. Edward W.), 123, 127, 135, **126**, **134**
Cooke, Mrs. Robert, Jr., **143**
Coolidge, Bill, 182
Cooper, Leroy, 24
Coors, George, vii, 112, 125, **123**, **142**
Coors, Gertrude, **121**
Coors, Giles, **118**, **121**
Coors, Giles A., Jr., 102, 150, 182, **112**, **150**
Coors, Jeanne, 99
Coors, Jeanne (daughter), **99**
Coors, Sophie Woodson (Mrs. Giles), 135, 150

233

Copp, Belton, 92
Coppock, Paul, 11
Corrigan, Estelle (Mrs. John J.),
    127, 168, **126, 167**
Cotton Carnival, 64, 69, 71, 75,
    82–83, 87, 94 107, 150, 155,
    166, **141**
Cotton Makers Jubilee. *See* Cotton
    Carnival
Crawford, Claude, 84, 157, **180**
Crawford, Eleanor Abernathy
    (Mrs. P. Thurman). *See*
    Abernathy, Eleanor
Crawford, Helen, **140**
Crawford, P. Thurman, **92**
Crawford, Pat, **140**
Crawford, Susan, **185**
Crenshaw, Hal, 182
Crisler, Jac, 132, **133**
Crosby, Bing, 96–98, **97**
Crump, Betty, 100
Crump, Blanche, 71, **72**
Crump, Diana, vii
Crump, Edward Hull, 11, 54
Crump, Frank M., 32, 71
Crump, Mrs. Frank M., 71
Crump, Marie Louise, 100
Crump, Sally, 100
Crump, Sara, 71, **72**. *See also*
    Humphreys, Sara
Cunningham, Betty, 157
Cunningham, Hugh, 182
Cunningham, J. C., 25
Curruthers, Jane, 160
Dalstrom, Jean, 100
Darnell, Herbert, 100
Darnell, Rowland, 60
Daughdrill, Jim, 132, 142, 182
Daughdrill, Libby, 142
Davis, Jefferson, Jr., 7
Davis, Mrs. Joe, 103
Davis, Nancy, 175
Debutante Ball, 137, 166, **103, 147**
Demere, Patrick, vii
Denton, Mrs. Clyde, 90
Denton, Bill Joe, **76**
Deupree, Frances, **112**
Dewey, Craft, 132
Dewey, Louise, **121**
Dicken, John, **183**
Dillard, Mayrene, **112**
Dimpson, David, 182
Dixon, Agnes, **146**
Dixon, Beth, 96
Dobbs, Jimmy, 112
Dobbs, John Hull, 164, **164**
Dockery, Frances, 60
Dockery, Joe Rice, 59
Doggrell, Frank, **140**
Doggrell, Martha, **140**
Donelson, Nancy, 92, 94

Dorgan, Milton, 15
Dorsey, Tommy, 83
Drew, George I., 22
Drew, Mrs. George I., 22
Drinkard, Don, 194
Drinkard, Dwight, 157
Drop In Tennis, 182, 184
Ducklo, Babs, **185**
Dudley, Ed, 96
Dudley, Libby, 100, 160
Dulin, Jane, **187, 196**
Dulin, John, **187, 196**
Dunavant, Billy, 102, 157
Dunklin, George, Jr., 157
Dunlap Street, 31
Dunscomb, Mary Martin, 84
Dunscomb, Mrs. Rayburn, 60
Early, Dorritte, **185**
Early, Mrs. George, **156**
Edrington, Bethel, **155**
Edrington, John Price "Jack" or "J. P.,"
    5, 12, 14, 25, 29–30, 32, 53, **14, 30**
Eichling, Athenais, 73, **70**
Elebash, Shearon, 139
Elliott, Gala, **198**
Ellis, Suzanne, 100
Ellison, E. C., 15
Emerson, Nat, 24
Erb, Guy, 182
Erb, Nancy, **186**
Evans, Chick, 15, 53
Evening of Champions, 157, **156**
Fakes, Roger, vii, 153
Fallis, Bob, 132
Fargason, John, **106**
Fargason, Nell, **106**
Farnsworth, Elizabeth, 92
Farnsworth, Lindsey, **198**
Farnsworth, Liz, **198**
Faunce, John, 102
Firestone Company, **23**
Fisher, Daisy, **84**
Fisher, Eddie, 83
Fisher, Lucille Terrell Knowlton, 15
Fisher, Thomas Scott, vii, ix, 132,
    167, 198, **183, 192, 200**
Fitzhugh, Guston, 54, 57
Fitzhugh, Millsaps, 102
Flippin, John R., 95
Folk, Humphrey, Sr. "Folkie" or
    "the Hawk," 117, **116**
Fondren, Jake, 96
Fontaine, Jennie, 7
Fontaine, Noland, 7
Foulis, James, Jr., 7
Fox, Cress, 92
Francis, Hugh, Jr., **105**
Francis, Hugh, Sr., 44
Frank, Lew, 156, 167, 189
Fraser, Malcolm, 169
Freer, Norman B., 70

Frozen Tomato Salad, 65, 77
Frye, Bea, 165–6, 184
Fuller, Ada Norfleet, 100
Fulmer, Arthur, Jr., 182
Gailor, Frank, 82
Galbreath, Percy, 3, 5, 13, 32
Galloway, Hope, 92
Galloway, Mimi, 94
Galloway, Robert, 100
Gardner, C. H., 14
Gardner, F. D., 25
Gardner, Joe, 71
Garrott, Allison, 160
Garson, Greer, 83
Gaut, David C., 49
Gaut, Marguerite, 49–50, 78, 105,
    194, **49–50**
Geralds, Bill, 153
Gerber, Bill, 132, 182, **133**
Gerber, Mrs. Charles, 103
Gibbs, Dr. R. B., 103
Gibson, Nevin, 45
Gillespie, Dottie (Mrs. Paul), 122,
    167, **131, 139, 143**. *See also*
    Pennepacker, Dottie
Gillespie, Gaye, 85
Gillespie, Paul "Old Blue" or "Blue
    Boy," 112, 117, **140**
Gillespie, Trow, vii, 184, **183**
Golf Digest, 114, 178
Golfer's Garland, The—1793, 45
Gooch, Robert, Jr., 100
Gooch, Robert, IV, **190**
Goodbar, Mrs. B. J., 11
Goodrich, Henry, **169**
Goodwyn, Tom, 32
Goodwyn Street, 6, 74, 127
Gordon, Jack, 132, **133**
Graves, Paul, **140**
Graves, Virginia, **140**
Great River Carnival, 87. *See also*
    Cotton Carnival
Green, Danny, 197
Greer, J. Ripley "Rip" or "Ripper,"
    114–15, 125, 160, **124, 159**
Greer Gang, 114–15, 160, **159**
Greer Street, 39, 58
Gregg, Frances, 94
Grout, Frank, 82
Gualdual, Ralf, 96
Gunther, Margaret. *See* Lee,
    Margaret Gunther
Gwin, Carla, vii
Gwin, Jan, vii
Hackworth, Otto, 15
Haizlip, Reb, 197
Hall, Parker, 78
Halle, A. Arthur, 82
Halliday, W. P., 13, 30, 32
Hamner, James "Jimmy," 44, 113,
    148, 155

Hand, Edie, 142
Hand, Ralph, 142, 182
Handy, W. C., 11
Harding, Mrs. Richard, 71, 73, **70**
Harrington, Susie M., 9
Harris, Susan, **112**
Harrison, Ben, 117
Harwood, James E., Jr., 48, 110,
    113, 140, **161**
Harwood, James E., III "Jim," 132,
    182
Harwood, Kate, 100
Harwood, Katherine, **161**
Harwood, Richard, 78, **153**
Hayes, Addison, 7
Hayes, Peggy, 7
Haygood, Jim, 157
Hayles, Mrs. Hugh S., 61
Hays, Jack, 157
Health Club, 56, 139, 148, 179, **189**
Heckle, Ferd, 112
Heiskell, Adeline, 100
Heiskell, John, 117
Heiskell, Judge, 13
Heiskell, L. L., 25
Henderson, Haywood, 184, **183**
Henry, Jack, 78
Henry, E. William, 97
Heyer, Ruth, **43**
Hill, Gene "Clean Gene," 117, 182
Hill, Mary, 7
Hill, Napoleon, 7
Hilton, Jack, **155**
Hilton, Lucy, **155**
Hines, Mary Mac, 92
History of Tennessee Golf, The, 7,
    12, 96, 106, 114
Hoare, W. B., 30
Hobson, Joel, 182, 193
Hodges, J. H., 54
Hodges, Mrs. J. H., 54
Hogan, Ben, 131–32
Holiday Ball, 148, **146**
Hood, W. A., 25
Hooker, Charlotte Stout, 74
Hope, Bob, 96–97, **97**
Hopkins, Bruce, 182, 184
Howard, Jessie, **146**
Hoyt, Grace, 90
Hubbard, Edwin, 179
Hudson, Bobby, 197–98, **196**
Hudson and Saleeby, 186
Hughes, Allen, 160, 182
Humphreys, George, 71
Humphreys, Sara (Mrs. George),
    150–52, 157, **112, 132**. *See also*
    Crump, Sara
Hutchison, Mary, 90
Hutton, Thomas H., Sr., 132,
    147–48, **199**
Irby, Joe, 115

James, Fred, 132, **133**
Jemison, Frank, 142
Jemison, Peggy, 142
Jennings, Herbert, 82
Johnson, Carroll, 182
Johnson, Fletcher **169**
Johnson, Harry Price "H. P.," 1–2, 5
Johnson, William Cumming "W. C.," 1–3, 5
Johnston, Tom, 182
Jones, Bill Carrington, 182
Jones, Mrs. Carrington, 103
Jones, Charles, 7
Jones, Mrs. Charles, 7
Jones, Frank Graham "F. G.," 22, 25, 30–31, 182
Jones, Henry, 132, **133**
Jones, Homer K., 22, 127
Jones, Jack, 182
Jones, Joyce, 143
Jones, Nina (Mrs. Frank Graham "F. G."), 22, 25, 31
Jones, Peggy (Mrs. William Carrington), 160, **156**
Jones, Robert Tyre "Bobby," 51–53, **52**, **196**
Jones, Walk, III, 152
Jones, Walk C., Jr., 121
Jones, Wise, 193
Josephine Circle, the, 135
Joyner, Emmet, 71
Joyner, Mrs. Emmet, Jr., **132**
Kavanaugh, Marion Russell, 90
Keesee, Buddy, **140**
Keesee, Emily, **140**
Keesee, Tommy, 174
Kehoe, Cullen, 131
Kehoe, Jane, 131
Kellogg, Betty Jane, 94
Kenney, John, 132
Kenney, Kevin, 132
Kerr, John L. "J. L.," 12–13, **30**
King, Earl, 99, 102
Kirk, Cathie, vii
Kirk, George, **183**
Kittle, Carla, **146**
Kittle, Charles, 131, **105**
Klyce, Brig, 182
Klyce, Esther, 140
Koehler, Casper, 148
Konik, Michael, 33
Kovacs, Frank, 102
Kraft, John, 100
Krausnick, Collie, 193
Krausnick, E. Carl Jr. "Buddy," 142, 148–49, **148**
Krausnick, Margaret, 142
Kupfer, Adolph, 7
Kupfer, Flora, 7
LaFoy, John, 43, 173
Lake, Laura, 94

Lamb, Laurence, 1–3, 5
Lamb, Walter, **43**
Lanson, Snookie, 75
Latham, Davant, 182, **166**
Latham, Natalie (Mrs. Davant), **166**
Latham, Mrs. Swayne, Jr., **132**
Latham, Mrs. Swayne, Sr., 90
Latham, Swayne, Sr., 102
Laughton, Charles, 83
Lawler, Ed, 117
Lawler, Liz (Mrs. Edward J.), 122, 157, **139**, **156**
Leadsinger, Billy, **153**
Lear, Ben, 93
Leatherman, Carroll, 160, **160**
Leatherman, Richard, Sr., vii, 115, 123, 132, 150, 160, **149**, **160**
Leatherman, S. R., 167
Leatherman, Mrs. S. R., 167
Leatherman, Mrs. William, 122
Lee, Bayless, 73
Lee, Gypsy Rose, 83
Lee, Jimmy, 73
Lee, Margaret Gunther (Mrs. Shelby), 105, 194, **143**
Lee, Mrs. Rees, 73
Leftwich, Bill, 102
Leftwich, William Groom, Jr., 107, 140, **107**
LeMaster, Camille, **187**
LeMaster, Eb, **187**
Lewis, Phil, 182
Lewis, Ted, **153**
Lingle, Rodney, 42, 44, 155
Littler, Gene, 131
Loeb, Bob, **86**
Lombardo, Guy, 83
Lowrance, Charlie, 193
Lowrance, Josephine, 100, 131
Lucky Swingers, The, 140
Lurton, H. H., 12–13
Mafia, 116–19, **116**
Magness, Mac, **194**
Magness, Meredith, **194**
Magness, Natalie, **190**, **194**
Magness, Perre, ix
Magsig, Patty, 184
Main Lounge, 110
Mallory, Albert H. "A. H.," 12, 61, **36**
Mallory, B. Lee, 100, 182
Mallory, Elizabeth Willins, 61, **61**
Mallory, J. H., 13
Mallory, Laura Willins (Mrs. Albert H.), 61
Mallory, W. D., 25, 32
Mallory, W. Neely, Jr., vii, 154–55, 157, 161, 182, **199**
Malmo, John, 132
Malone, Alice, 157
Malone, Allen, 100

Manassas Street, 31
Manire, Jim "the Nose," 117–19
Mann, Cameron, 92
Mann, Jeff, 132
Marshall, Bunts, 100
Marshall, Cecil, **186**
Marshall, John, 132
Martin, Andrew Jackson Donelson, 7
Martin, John Donelson, 7
Martin, Mary Alice, **140**
Martin, Pate, **140**
Martin, Rosa Buntyn, 7
Mathis, W. D., Jr., 135
Maury, Bill, 132, 182
Maury, W. Poston, 3, 32, **30**
Maxwell, John, 182
McCadden, Betty, **103**
McCallum, Bickie, 100
McCaughan, J. J., **121**
McCloy, Randy, **180**
McCoy, Harry, Jr., 135
McDonald, Blair, 132
McDonald, Jay, 194, **193**
McDonnell, Jim, 157
McDonnell, Mrs. J. W., Jr., 127, **126**
McDonnell, Michael, 168, **168**, **180**
McFadden, Barclay, 195
McFadden, Billy, 195
McFadden, Jack, 195
McFadden, Stillman "Stilly," ix, 195, 200–201
McGeorge, Hal "McJock," 117–18
McHenry, E. B., 5
McIlwaine, Sheilds, 56
McKee, Heloise, **134**
McKee, Lewis K. Jr. "Mac," 172, 201
McKee, Lewis K., Sr., vii, 102, 115, 135–6, 140, 172, **134**, **199**
McKee, W. Lytle, 90, 102, 172–73, **90**
McKinney, Richmond, 43, 68–71, 73–74, 78–79, 82, 90, **68**
McPhillips, Reed, 106
Memphi Midwinter Ball, 83, **140**
Memphis Appeal, 7
Memphis Area Women's Golf Association, 156
Memphis Commercial Appeal, ix, xii, 2
Memphis Cotillion, 174, **170-1**
Memphis Driving Park, 1, 30, **30**
Memphis Golf Club, 31
Merrin, Mrs. Clifford, 127, **126**
Metcalf, Robert M., 127
Metcalf, Mrs. William Park, **8**
Mewborn, G. W., 55
Middlecoff, Cary, 113–14, 122, 149, 184, **113**, **142**
Midland Avenue, 19, 39, 58
Miles, Jim, 117
Miles, Lovick, Jr., 71

Miles, Mr., 57
Miles, Ted, 100
Miller, Peggy, **146**
Milnor, Bill, 132
Milnor, John Pervis, Jr., 93
Milnor, Pervis, 102
Milnor, Mrs. Pervis, 71, 73, **70**
Milton, Frank Clark "F. C.," 1–2, 5
Milton, R. C., 3
Minor, Lucian, 132
Montedonico, L. A., Jr., 58
Montedonico, Mrs. J. V., 143
Mooney, C. P. J., 54
Moore, Jackson W., Sr., 178, **178**, **183**, **201**
Moore, Virginia Adair, **76**
Morgan, Allen, Jr, 157, **180**, **183**
Morgan, Allen, Sr., 100, 102, 182
Morgan, Bill, 182
Morgan, Elise, 100
Morris, Tom, **180**
Morrison, Joe, 182
Morrow, Ed, 182
Morrow, R. G., 13, 32, **12**
Morrow, Steve, **183**
Morse, Byron, 142
Mueller, Bill, 157
Muller, Dexter, **77**
Nashville Banner, 50
Nelson, Byron, 96, 114
Nenon, Chris, 165
Nenon, David, 165
Newland, Harrod C. "H. C.," 1, 3, 5, 13
Norfleet, Elise Vance (Mrs. Jesse Peders), 64
Norfleet, Frank, 102, 112
Norfleet, Jesse Peders "J. P.," 64, 127, **64**
O'Leary, F. J., 68
Oates, Mrs. William E., 111
"Ode to MCC"—Christmas 1982, 175
"Old Forest, The," 22, 65
Oliver, George C., 13–14, **14**
Omlie, Vernon, 102
Orchestras/Bands
  Berl Olswanger, 139, 141, 160–61
  David Humphreys, 179
  Flash Back, 167
  Handy's Band, 11
  Jim Johnson, 153, 173, 194
  Ray Stidham, 87
  Reba and the Portables, 173
  River City Six, 165
  Russ David, 137
  Sneakers, The, 193
  T. O. Earnhardt, 167
  Tony Barrasso, 168
Orgill, Adele, 73, 111, **111**

Orgill, Edmund, **111**
Orgill, Mrs. Edmund, 111
Orgill, Irene (Mrs. Joseph, III), 140
Orgill, Joseph, Jr., **111**
Orgill, Mrs. Joseph, Jr., 111
Orgill, Mrs. Joseph, Sr., 112
Orgill, Joseph, III, 166, 168, **199**
Orgill, Mrs. Kenneth, 111
Paine, Rowlett, 55
Pat Abbott Future Champions Fund, 106
Patrick, Dave, 25
Patterson, Malcolm, 54
Patterson, Mrs. Page, 90
Patteson, Allie Starke (Mrs. James), 64–65, 82, 104
Patteson, Elaine, 64, 82
Patteson, James, 64
Patton, Clyde, 182
Pegler, Westbrook, 83
Pennepacker, Dottie, vii, 142. *See also* Gillespie, Dottie
Pennepacker, Wallace, 152
Perry, Fred, 102
Petree, Katherine, **146**
Pettey, Beverly, **140**
Pettey, John, **140**
Pettit, Peter R., 188, **188**, **201**
Pfeil, Charles Oscar "Charlie" or "C. O.," 18–19, 51, 53, 58, 60
Phillips, John, III, 152, 179
Phillips, Josephine, 179
Phillips, S. H., 13, 54
Phillips, Mrs. S. H., 54
Pictorial Encyclopedia of Golf, 45
Pidgeon, Bobby, 131
Pidgeon, Eugene, 117
Pidgeon, Mrs. Eugene, **139**
Pidgeon, J. Everett, 83
Pidgeon, Phil "Neander," 117
Pidgeon, Mrs. Phil, **132**
Pidgeon, Renny (Mrs. Bobby), 130–31
Pierotti, Jane, **185**
Pittman, Gig, 157
Polk, Sylvanus, 100, 182
Potts, A. B., 100
Potts, Ramsey, 100
Potts, Ramsey, Jr., 100
Powell, Lee, 193
Presley, Elvis, 83
Press Scimitar, ix, 68, 70–71, 84, 111, 123, 131, 134, 165, **122**
Prest, Barbara, **187**
Prest, Bill, **187**
Price, Tommy "Sweetmeat," 102, 112, 117–18, 182, 189, **116**
Pritchartt, Van, Jr., 102, 182
Pritchartt, Van, Sr., 102
Pryor, Ainslie, 95
Pryor, Marty, 182

Purcell, Bill, 182
Pyeatt, Wayne, 182
Quackenboss, Bab, 142
Quackenboss, Tom, 142
Quinn, Peter, 132
Ragland, Samuel Evan, 3, 8, 14–15, 39
Raine, Gilbert, 32
Rainer, Jim, 131
Rainer, Jim, III, 182
Rainer, Lawrence, 130–31
Raines, Sam, 157
Ramsay, Ellen, **103**, 106. *See also* Clark, Ellen Ramsay
Ray, Barham, 157
Red Room, 70, 73, 77, 84, 95, 104, 107, 120, 122, 125, 130, 136, 139, 142, 151–53, 180–82, 186–87, 197, **196**
Reese, Mrs. Hubert, 71, **70**
Rembert, Samuel S., Jr., 84, 137, 140, **134**, **139**, **161**
Rembert, Scottie (Mrs. Sam), 123, **134**, **161**
Reynolds, Mrs. Eugene, 90
Rhea, Herbert, 182
Rhea, J. W. S., **36**
Rhea, Steve, 182
Rice, Frank, 54
Richardson, Madeline, 100
Riddick, Edward G., 60
Riddick, Mrs. Edward G., 60
Ridolphi, Fred, **180**
Riggs, Bobby, 102
River Room Lounge, 179, 181
Roberson, Lake, 78
Roberts, Bill "Billy Boy," 117, 142, **116**
Roberts, Katie (Mrs. William L.), 142, **131**
Robertson, Mrs. Caffey, 71, 73, **70**
Robertson, Mary Ann, 73
Robertson, Minor, 73
Robinson, Cooper, 142
Robinson, James D., 120, 124–25, 130, 140, **123–24**, **153**
Robinson, Mrs. James D., **123**
Robinson, Nina (Mrs. W. W.), 73, 90
Robinson, Sue, 142
Rodgers, Warfield, 64–65
Roosevelt, Franklin D., 83
Ross, Donald, 19, 25, 33, 35, 37–38, 43, 165, 173, 197, **34**
Rowe, Landis, 55
Royal Eyes, 90
Ruffin, Bob, 151
Runyon, I., **76**
Rush, Tim, 165
Russell, Amelia, **103**
Russell, Betty, 142
Russell, Carroll, **103**

Russell, Charlie, 142
Russell, Edward P., 78, 103, 140, **104**
Russell, Jane, 123
Russell, "Skinny," 114
Sabin, Wayne, 102
Salmon, John, 132, **133**
Samelson, Mrs. Lester, **131**
Sanders, Edward Harvey, 187
Sanders, H. M., 24
Sanders, W. Reid, 187, **201**
Saturday Morning Dogs, 132, **133**
Saunders, Charlotte, **146**
Saunders, Clarence, 32, 56–57
Saunders, Dr., 12
Saunders, J. T. "Tunkie," 92, 104, 114–15, 119
Saxon, Clara, 100
Saxon, Malcolm, 100
Scape, Mattie Howard, 107
Schadt, Mrs. Harry, 71
Schaeffer, Frederick C., Sr., 179–80, 191, **179–80**
Schmeisser, Mrs. Harry, 103
Scott, Elgin, 141
Scott, Walter, 132, **133**
Selden, C. C., 22
Selden, Mrs. C. C., 22
Shannon, Jim, 182
Shea, John "the Ear," 117
Shea, Martin "Cousin No No," 117, 182, **116**
Sheahan, John, 131
Sheehan, Mike, 179
Sherwood, Willis Clyde "W. C." or "Sherry," 13–15, 25, 32, 96, 105
Shy, DeWitt "Tiger," 117, 183–84, 195, **183**
Simmons, Mrs. W. W., 90
Sims, Enid, 60
Sims, Mrs. Thetus, 60
Sinclair, Hugh, 138, **84**
Sinclair, Jean, **84**
Sinfonetta Ball, 132
Skinner, Bunnie, 7
Skinner, J. W., 7
Smith, Alex, 15
Smith, Bobby Day, 102, 182
Smith, C. D., 100
Smith, Craig, 189
Smith, Dottie, 100. *See also* Pidgeon, Mrs. Phil
Smith, Eleanor, 51
Smith, Harriet Huger (Mrs. McKay Van Vleet), 94
Smith, Hugh, 153, 187
Smith, James McCown "Jimmy," 200, **183**
Smith, James Rogers, 51
Smith, Mrs. James Rogers, 51
Smith, Maggie, 100

Smith, Peggy, 100. *See also* Latham, Mrs. Swayne, Jr.
Smith, Ron, 186
Smith, Stan, 188
Smith, Walter Lane, 102
Smithwick, Catherine, **186**
Snack Bar, 136
Snead, Sam, 96, 114
Snow, Stanley, 182
Snowden, Bobby, 94, 142, 182
Snowden, Flo, 142
Southern Avenue, 15, 58, 127
Spencer, Sandy, 194
Sprunt, Barbara, 123
Sprunt, Hugh "Cotton Man" or "Ghost," 117
Stanton, Carl, **140**
Stanton, Mary, **140**
Stark, James Edward, 112–13, 140, **161**
Stark, San, **161**
Stevens, John A., 165, 182
Steward, Sid, 182
Stokes, Anne, **186**
Stout, Charles B. "Charlie," 74, 76–77
Stout, Elizabeth (Mrs. John T.), 142
Stout, Helen, 73
Stout, John A., 77
Stout, John T., 102, 132, 142
Stout, Warda (Mrs. Charles B.), 74
Stratton, Flora, **84**
Stratton, George, **84**
Stratton, Leslie, 95
Stratton, Mrs. Leslie, 95
Sturdivant, Jan, 151
Sturdivant, Mike P., **151**
Sturdivant, Ygondine, **151**
Svenssen, Johan, 191
Symphony Ball, 132, **131**
Tabor, Owen, 153, **180**
Tabor, Sherman, **190**
Tap Room, 10, 58, 73, 119, 122, 125, 167, 172, 180, 182, 186, 193
Tate, Christine, 123, 135
Tate, Evelyn, **43**
Tate, Robert F. "R. F.," 12–13, 123
Tate Lane, 141
Tate Room Tattler, 138
Tate Room, 123, 134
Tayloe, George Green, 64
Tayloe, Mrs. George Green, 64
Tayloe, Margaret, 64
Tayloe, Robert, **180**
Tayloe, Virginia, 64
Taylor, Audrey, 100
Taylor, Bruce, 182, **181**
Taylor, Henry "Sweetie Pie," 114–15
Taylor, Mrs. H. Duncan, 122
Taylor, Peter, 22, 65
Taylor, W. L., 100

Tennessee Golf Hall of Fame, 50, 105–6, 194
Tennessee Sports Hall of Fame, 50, 114
Terrell, Samuel Durr, 15
Terry, Ray, **105**
Thomas, Danny, 123
Thompson, Blanche, 151
Thompson, Chas. W., 57
Thompson, Ellen, 142
Thompson, Larry "Pops" or "Greyhound," 117, 142, **116**
Thompson, Martin, 182
Thrasher, Marguerite. *See* Gaut, Marguerite
Tilden, Bill, 69, 102
Todd, Carroll, Jr., 157, 182
Todd, Carroll, Sr., 182
Tournaments
  Golf
    Buntyn Trophy, 78
    Championship of the United States Golf Association, 107
    City of Memphis, 58
    City Pro-Am, **105**
    Father-Son, **196**
    FedEx St. Jude Classic, 132. *See also* Tournaments, Golf, Memphis Open
    International Four Ball, 149–50, **149**
    Joyner Memorial Scramble, 157
    Ladies Member-Guest, 167
    Marguerite Gaut Senior Women's Golf Invitational, 50
    Masters, 106
    MCC Ryder Cup Invitational, 181
    Member-Guest, 137, 153, 160, 167, 169, 198, **139, 142, 155, 173**
    Memorial, 194–95
    Memphis Country Club Memorial, 191
    Memphis Open, 131. *See also* Tournaments, Golf, FedEx St. Jude Classic
    Men's Member-Guest, 197
    Middlecoff Four Ball, 157
    National Open, 35
    PGA, 106
    Pro-Am, 131
    Senior, 95
    Senior Member-Guest, 173, **169**
    State Amateur, 95, 105
    State of Tennessee Championship, 58
    Tennessee Golf Association Men's Mid Amateur, 197
    Tennessee Open, 106, 125, **124**
  United States Women's Golf Championship, 78
  U.S. Amateur, 95
  USGA Championship, **39–40**
  USGA Senior Amateur Championship, 113
  USGA Women's Amateur, 156
  U.S. Senior Amateur, 95
  U.S. Women's Amateur, 95
  Van Vleet, 157, 180
  Western Amateur Best Ball Championship, 122
  Western Amateur Golf Championship, 51, 69
  Western Open, 25
  Women's City, **143**
  Women's Invitational, 69
  Women's Invitational for the Marguerite Gaut Trophy, 78
  Women's Southern, 49
  Women's Southern Amateur, 50
  Women's Southern Championship, 105
  Women's State Amateur, 105
  Women's United States Golf Association Tournament (USWGA), 50
  Women's Western Amateur, 50
  Tennis
    Anna Morrow Memorial, 165
    Memphis Country Club Invitation, 69
    Senior Tennis Invitational, 173
    Southern Open Professional, 102
Treadwell, George "Gorgeous George," 95–96, 107, 114–16, 98–99, 140, 160, **94, 159, 161**
Treadwell, Mary, **134**
Treadwell, Tim "Bug Eye" or "T. L.," 32, 95, 112, 117, **116**
Treadwell, Wister (Mrs. George), **161**
Trophies
  Broken Racket, 184, **181**
  Buntyn Cup, 12, 184
  Club Team Competition, 56
  Club Team Match Cup, 13
  Consolation Cup, 13
  DeSoto Cup, 13, **12**
  Gaut Short Game, **114**
  James D. Robinson, **42**
  Leftwich, 107
  Marguerite Gaut Senior Women Invitational, **138**
  Marker (Goblet), **24**
  MCC Memorial Tournament, **173**
  Memphis Gold Cup, 31
  Paris, 98
  Ryder Cup, 185
Southern Golf Association Tournament, **25**
Tennessee State Amateur, 48
Thursday Choice Score, 74
Van Vleet Memorial, **82**
Wiener Golf Improvement, **152**
Trumpore, Jack, 198
Tuesday Study Club, 73, 103, 166
Turley, Aggie, 140
Turley, Dee, **146**
Turley, Hubert, III, 182
Turley, Mrs. T. J., 60
Turley, Thomas Battle, 53
Turley, Thomas Jefferson (grandfather), 53
Turley, Thomas Jefferson, 53, 57, **54**
Turner, Carroll, **121**
Turner, Marguerite, **121**
USGA, 95, 187
Van Horn, Welby, 102
Van Vleet, McKay, 94, 127, **93**
Van Vleet, Peter Percy "P. P.," 3–5, 7, **5**
Varner, Ferrell, **180**
Varner, Jim, **180**
Varner, Sarah Ann, 151
Vasse, Lionel, 111–12, **111**
Vines, Elsworth, 96
Voltz, Del, **112**
Wade, Linda, 131
Wade, Scrammy, 131
Walker, Barbara, 99
Walthal, Ed, 132, **133**
Walton, Sue, **112**
Ward, Jimmy, 53
Ward, W. W., 12–13
Warriner, H. L., 13
Weaver, Betsy, 130
Weaver, Chappy, 130
Weaver, D. S., 32, 58, **36**
Weaver, Dudley, 100
Weaver, Lele, **198**
Weaver, Mary Ann, 100
Weaver, Robert "Bobby," 197, **183, 196, 198**
Webster, Marie, **155**
Webster, Peggy, **76**
Webster, William A. "Billy," vii, 117, 150, 152, **76, 149, 155, 169, 193, 199**
Welch, Jim "the Giant," 117
Wellford, Alex Sr. "Bear," 114–15, 182, **159**
Wellford, Alex, Jr., 100
Wellford, Alex, III, 182
Wellford, Harry, 69, 157, **156**
Wellford, Peggy, 100
Welsh, Nancy (Mrs. James R.), vii, 127, 135, **126**
West, Waddy, Jr., 92
Western Golf Association, 70
Wetter, Henry, 117
Wetter, Jimmy, 102, 182
Whalen, Joe, 99
White, Buck, 96
White, G. C., 7
White, Thomas, 102, 132, 182
White, Thomas J., 95–96, **154, 156**
White, Tom, 100
Whitehead, W. Cary, III, vii, ix, 182, 189, **201**
Whitman, Tom, **187**
Whittle, Caroline, **185**
Wiener, Bailey, 132
Wiener, Jean Anne, **185**
Wiener, Lee, 182
Wilbourn, Frank, 102
Willey, Lida, 84
Willey, Norma (Mrs. Howard), 135, **134**
Willey, Willis, 132
Williams, F. P., 3
Williams, J. J., xii
Williams, Jason D., 173
Williams, John Sneed, 127
Williams, Jon D., 174
Williams, Philips P. "P. P.," 1–2, 5
Williams, Ray, **153**
Williamson, Flora, 94
Williamson, S. M., 25, 32, 59
Wilroy, Sidney, 182
Wilson, Dorothy, 142, **166**
Wilson, Elizabeth, **86**
Wilson, Kemmons, Sr., 142, 171, 178, 182, **166**
Witherington, Jim, Jr., 182
Witmer, Wallace, Jr., 182
Wolfe, Mrs. John Quincy, 103
Wolff, Clarence, 53
Women's Southern Golf Association, 25, 50
Women's Tennessee Golf Association, 49
Women's Western Golf Association, 50
Wood, Percy H., 60, **118**
Wood, Mrs. Percy, 60
Wood, Russell "Woodie," 92, 117, **116**
Woodson, Sophie, 100, **112**
Woolverton, F. T., 15
World Golf Hall of Fame, 114
Wunderlich, Kent, 182
Wynne, Hugh, 32
Wynne, Jane, 151
Yandell, Billy, 182
Yandell, Will, 182
Young, J. P., 22
Yuletide Revelers, 65, 93
Zaharias, Babe Didrickson, 49
Zanone, Phil, 182

ABOUT THE AUTHOR

Perre MacFarland Magness grew up in Columbia, Tennessee, and was educated at Madeira School and Vassar College. Since moving to Memphis in 1965, she has been president of the Junior League of Memphis, president of the Volunteer Center of Memphis, chairman of the board of the Memphis Arts Council, and has served on the Board of Trustees of LeMoyne-Owen College and the Board of Visitors of the University of Memphis.

She is the author of *Good Abode: An Architectural History of Memphis and Shelby County*; *Past Times: Stories of Early Memphis*; *The History of Idlewild Presbyterian Church*; and *In the Shadow of the Elms: Elmwood Cemetery 2002*. For sixteen years, she wrote "Past Times," a weekly local history column in the *Commercial Appeal*.

In researching this book, she discovered that her grandfather, Josiah Lawson Hutton, was treasurer of the Memphis Country Club from 1916 to 1919.

ABOUT THE PHOTOGRAPHER

Murray Riss took the cover images, photos of the golf course, and many other pictures for this book.

He was educated at City College of New York, Cooper Union School of Art, and the Rhode Island School of Design. His work has been shown in many museums, and he is currently a professional photographer for magazines, advertising agencies, and corporations, with clients locally, nationally, and internationally.

This is the fourth book on which Perre and Murray have collaborated.

Blue Tees	397	417	536	154	412	432	191	400	313	3252
Red Tees	383	369	501	141	361	417	174	373	290	3009
White Tees	375	353	495	128	355	382	155	365	280	2888
Par	4	4	5	3	4	4	3	4	4	35
Handicap	8	10	2	18	12	4	16	6	14	
Hole	1	2	3	4	5	6	7	8	9	OUT
Yellow Tees	328	304	433	118	286	390	147	309	272	2587
Par	4	4	5	3	4	5	3	4	4	36
Handicap	6	10	2	18	12	4	16	8	14	

BLUE 72.3/130 **WHITE** 69.6/122
RED 70.7/126 **YELLOW** 72.3/123

Blue Tees	227	515	386	409	372	448	168	432	380	3337	6589
Red Tees	211	473	362	386	363	428	154	412	358	3147	6156
White Tees	201	460	350	376	317	420	150	404	344	3022	5910
Par	3	5	4	4	4	4	3	4	4	35	70
Handicap	11	7	9	5	15	1	17	3	13		
Hole	10	11	12	13	14	15	16	17	18	IN	TOT
Yellow Tees	139	436	306	313	297	417	131	395	327	2761	5348
Par	3	5	4	4	4	5	3	5	4	37	73
Handicap	13	1	9	7	15	3	17	5	11